ARCHITECTURES OF INEQUALITY

Feminist Perspectives on Work and Organization

Series Editors: **Emma Bell**, The Open University and **Sheena Vachhani**, University of Bristol

This interdisciplinary series publishes books that explore a range of issues around feminism, feminist theory and philosophy, and intersectional and decolonial feminist approaches applied to various contexts of formal and informal work and organization. Books offer a critical approach to organizations as sites of ethical and political feminist practice.

Scan the code below to discover new and forthcoming titles in the series, or visit:

bristoluniversitypress.co.uk/
feminist-perspectives-on-work-and-organization

ARCHITECTURES OF INEQUALITY

Gender Pay Inequity and Britain's Finance Sector

Rachel Verdin

BRISTOL
UNIVERSITY
PRESS

First published in Great Britain in 2024 by

Bristol University Press
University of Bristol
1–9 Old Park Hill
Bristol
BS2 8BB
UK
t: +44 (0)117 374 6645
e: bup-info@bristol.ac.uk

Details of international sales and distribution partners are available at bristoluniversitypress.co.uk

British Library Cataloguing in Publication Data
A catalogue record for this book is available from the British Library

ISBN 978-1-5292-4508-0 paperback
ISBN 978-1-5292-4111-2 ePub
ISBN 978-1-5292-4112-9 OA PDF

Cover design: Liam Roberts Design
Front cover image: Unsplash/Siegfried Poepperl
Bristol University Press uses environmentally responsible print partners.
Printed and bound in Great Britain by CPI Group (UK) Ltd, Croydon, CR0 4YY

FSC
www.fsc.org
MIX
Paper | Supporting
responsible forestry
FSC® C013604

Contents

List of Figures and Tables

Figures

Tables

List of Abbreviations

AFC	Agenda for Change
ASHE	Annual Survey of Hours and Earnings
ATM	Automated Teller Machine
Big four banks	refers to HSBC, Barclays, Lloyds and RBS/ NatWest (the group was renamed in 2020 from RBS to NatWest)
CAC	Central Arbitration Committee
CBI	Confederation of Business and Industry
EA02	Employment Act 2002
EAT	Employment Appeal Tribunal
ECA72	European Communities Act 1972
ECJ	European Court of Justice
EEC	European Economic Community
EHRC	Equality and Human Rights Commission
EIA	Equality Impact Assessments
EOC	Equal Opportunities Commission
EqA2010	Equality Act 2010
EqPA70	Equal Pay Act 1970
EqVA83	Equal Value Amendment 1983
ERA99	Employment Relations Act 1999
ET	Employment Tribunal
EU	European Union
GDP	Gross Domestic Product
GED	Gender Equality Duty
GM	Gender Mainstreaming
GPG	Gender Pay Gap
GPRR	Gender Pay Reporting Regulations
ICB	Independent Commission on Banking
IMF	International Monetary Fund
HR	Human Resources
HRM	Human Resource Management
ML	Maternity Leave
NHS	National Health Service

OMC	Open Method of Communication
ONS	Office for National Statistics
PRP	Performance-Related Pay
PSED	Public Sector Equality Duty
PTWR00	Part-Time Workers Regulations 2000
RRA65	Race Relations Act 1965
SDA75	Sex Discrimination Act 1975
SDA86	Sex Discrimination Act 1986
SIC	Standard Industrial Classification
SMP	Statutory Maternity Pay
SPL	Shared Parental Leave
SSA	Single Status Agreement
STEM	Science, Technology, Engineering and Mathematics
ToR57	Treaty of Rome 1957
TUC	Trades Union Congress
WiFC	Women in Finance Charter

Acknowledgements

I would like to extend thanks to those without whom this book would not have been possible. Firstly, to the University of Sussex Business School, for generously funding my PhD, upon which this book is based. The subsequent development of this research into a monograph has been funded during my time as a post doc researcher. This work was supported by the UK Economic and Social Research Council [grant number ES/S012532/1] as part of the Digital Futures at Work Research Centre (Digit), which is gratefully acknowledged.

I am massively grateful for all the other academic support I have received from across the university. Particular thanks to Jacqueline O'Reilly for her expert advice and enthusiasm. Huge thanks are due to my family for their encouragement and unwavering support. I would like to express my sincere gratitude to my research participants for sharing their stories and insights. Your words helped me understand your experience of a decades old problem and gave depth and meaning to the research.

I am incredibly grateful to the reviewers for their comments and suggestions. Finally, a warm thanks to the editorial team at BUP.

Laying the Architectural Foundations

Introducing the research

When the Gender Pay Reporting Regulations (GPRR) were introduced in 2017, firms in the finance sector knew the data was not going to look good. There was a sense of panic, and rightly so: on average firms reported gender pay gaps (GPGs) of around 30% and bonus gaps twice that size (Treasury Committee, 2023a: 14). Some six years on the dust has settled but little has changed. 'Sexism in the city' remains rife as the dial on gender pay inequity within the finance sector has barely moved (Treasury Committee, 2023a). This book takes a holistic approach to examine the problem and what is stopping it.

The introduction of the GPRR in 2017 marked a step change in the UK's approach to GPGs. The furore surrounding the subsequent publication of company reports prompted a resurgence of attention and focus on the problem. The fear of negative reputational impacts prompted by a bad report sharpened organizational focus on the equality, diversity and inclusion agenda. This increased transparency surrounding pay was intended to drive change. However, this has been dampened by current and pressing threats to the UK's equality framework, such as the COVID-19 pandemic, Brexit and associated economic impacts, alongside the changing world of work through the process of digitalization (Verdin and O'Reilly, 2020; Verdin and O'Reilly, 2021). The UK's socio-economic situation is changing, but what does this mean for gender pay inequity?

The overall GPG in the UK stands at 14.9% for all employees, and remains markedly higher within the finance sector (White, 2022). This complex, significant and persistent problem has defied legislative attempts to eradicate it. This mixed methodological study synthesizes the different explanatory perspectives on the topic and presents a new conceptualization with which to examine the trajectory of the gap. In this book I have constructed the 'Architectures of Inequality' model to help explain the intransigence of GPGs and demonstrate the insufficiency of current legal and policy initiatives.

The architectures methodology is utilized to examine the GPG, why it is unfair for women, economically irrational and yet stubbornly persistent. Despite the continual extension of approaches to combat gender pay inequity, the model shows how inequalities still breathe through the building. At a macro institutional level, Britain's progressively broadened legal arrangements are traced, spotlighting the role of a variety of actors in this change process. At the meso organizational level, gender pay reporting data are scrutinized. Particular attention is paid to the finance sector where GPGs are largest. The changing shape of women's career paths is mapped alongside an examination of how the sector has developed over time. Finally, at the micro level, qualitative interviews with trade union organizers and women working for a range of finance organizations reveal their experiences of working in and around large pay inequities. As Professor Goldin is awarded the Nobel economics prize for her work on understanding gender gaps, this book provides a timely and ever necessary opportunity to take stock of progress and the barriers to change.

To begin this novel multilevel examination, this chapter first introduces the topic, why it matters and why progress has been so slow and stalled. The competing explanatory approaches used to explain gender pay inequity are described. In recognition of this complex theoretical landscape, and to situate the research, a real-life setting is required. My rationale for selecting the finance sector is presented and the methodology adopted described. Prompted by the introduction of the GPRR, the research questions addressed in this volume are then specified. To conceptualize the research design, the architectures of inequality model is introduced. Finally, chapter-by-chapter summaries outline the blueprint from which the architectures model is constructed and through which this research proceeds.

What is the gender pay gap and why does it matter?

The GPG is the percentage difference between the average hourly earnings of men and women and distinct from equal pay. Figure 1.1 shows the trajectory of the GPG over the last 50 years, revealing the progress that has occurred and where decline has plateaued. These periods of stasis and change are examined alongside legislative development in Chapters 2 and 3.

The ONS headline statistics in the UK calculate using the Annual Survey of Hours and Earnings (ASHE) data and typically report the median figure.

Figure 1.1: GPG % for full time employees 1971–2022

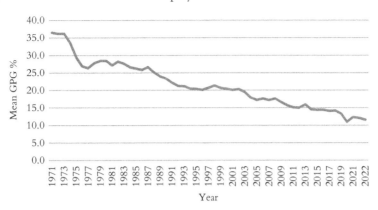

Notes: The graph shows New Earnings Survey GB data for 1971–97 and ASHE UK data for 1997–2022 (all employee data is only available from 1997). The data are not entirely consistent as survey methodologies changed in 2004, 2006 and 2011.

Source: ONS data from the New Earnings Survey and ASHE gender gap timeseries, licensed under the Open Government License v.3.0.

In 2022 this was 14.9% for all workers, 8.3% for full-time workers and −2.8% for part-time workers (White, 2022). The negative part-time GPG reflects the prominence of women in part-time work.

The GPG at the top of the earnings distribution is typically larger and the proportional rate of closure is slower (Francis-Devine, 2020). While the Office for National Statistics (ONS) recognizes that occupation, sector, region, size of workplace and tenure are central explanatory features, they find two thirds of the GPG is unaccounted for by these factors (Ardanaz-Badia and Rawlings, 2018; Colebrook et al, 2018; Tetlow, 2018). Gender pay inequities grow over the life course impacted by different working patterns, career breaks, family structure and levels of education. To tackle this complex problem, it is vital to understand the factors driving gender pay inequities. The GPRR were introduced to help shine a spotlight on inequities and, in so doing, bring much needed transparency to the problem. Ultimately the regulations were intended to narrow differences in pay between men and women.

This research examines the development of Britain's GPG alongside the development of equality law and equal pay, revealing the murky relationship between the two. Equal pay concerns the legal requirement to pay women and men doing the same, broadly similar, or equivalent work the same amount. However, despite the GPRR, a lack of transparency and the culture of silence surrounding pay makes the enforcement of this legislative entitlement problematic. When asked how to encourage more women into male-dominated workplaces, Dr Imafidon, CEO of Stemettes, a charity working to improve diversity in STEM, proposes "pay people equally" (BBC Sounds, 2023). While her rallying cry seems obvious, she acknowledges, "it's so simple and yet so difficult". A lack of linked employer data on the GPG makes assessment of within firm inequities hard to assess (Penner et al, 2023). Discriminatory behaviour, pervasive cultural stereotypes, and the low value ascribed to women's work can help to explain the more unobservable components of the GPG.

Moral obligations aside, failing to ensure fair pay can be staggeringly expensive. Eye-watering amounts, such as the £1.2 billion settlement in the *Abdulla v Birmingham City Council* (2012) equal pay case, demonstrate the need to get this right for both organizations and their employees (Deakin et al, 2015). Improved approaches to transparency to observe, understand and counteract the problem are vital. Compounding the need for change there is evidence of growing momentum towards group litigation beyond the public sector. Projected liabilities of £8 billion for the ongoing retail equal value claims in the UK (Butler, 2018), and the $215 million payout by Goldman Sachs in the US, demonstrate this development in the private sector (Franklin and Miller, 2023). Conversely, enabling women to fully participate in the workforce could add much needed productivity gains. McKinsey (2016) estimated the UK's gross domestic product (GDP) could benefit to the tune of £150 billion by 2025. However, the fresh equal pay claims against Birmingham City Council demonstrate that addressing gendered inequities in the workplace remains a pandora's box (BBC, 2022). Similarly, the BBC Director General's claim that "only" having eight open equal pay cases at the organization is an "achievement" underlines the extent of the problem (Clarke, 2023).

The moral, legal and financial stakes around equal pay are high. Understanding the effect and limitations of legislation and organizational approaches to address the pay gap remain extremely relevant, despite over 50 years of legislation to resolve the issue. This book examines the multiple causes and consequences of gender pay inequity and seeks to identify the most promising pathways to address it. The equilibrium of gender pay inequity is continually redrawn. However, assessment of why and how institutional and organizational progress to achieve pay equity are so slow and stalled exposes recurring themes that counteract progress (see Figure 1.1). Woven into the very fabric of gender pay inequities are foundational barriers: deeply embedded historic inequities shrouded by a systemic lack of transparency and preference for free market governance (Dickens, 2007; Conley and Torbus, 2019; Pfefer, 2020). This work establishes the need to redesign approaches to gender pay inequity beyond the perfunctory transparency of the GPRR, to tackle these pervasive cultures that undermine progress at the macro, meso and micro levels.

Theoretical explanations for the gender pay gap

The wide academic and critical reflection on the GPG indicates the embedded and multifaceted nature of resistance to addressing the evolving problems associated with closing this gap. At both a conceptual and theoretical level, there remains considerable interdisciplinary controversy concerning the causes of and remedies to reduce the GPG. Legal scholars, organizational theorists, economists and sociologists have identified competing explanatory factors to account for its persistence. The extensive and contested explanations of gender pay inequality are reviewed by Rubery and Grimshaw (2015), who thematize these perspectives as institutional, organizational, economic and sociological. These perspectives are fundamentally interrelated, as recognized in the employment systems literature in the relationships between regulation (macro level), firms (meso level) and workers (micro level) (Rubery, 2003; O'Reilly, 2006; Gallie, 2007b; Rubery and Hebson, 2018). An overview of these perspectives is now provided.

Macro-level institutional examination

Institutional perspectives on the GPG encompass elements such as the legislative framework that seeks to address gender pay inequity. The research charts the development of equality law and examines its utility as a vehicle for change. There is extensive academic critique considering how and why legislation and policy have failed in their apparent objectives (England, 2010; Hepple, 2011; Rubery and Grimshaw, 2015). Taking a feminist socio-legal approach enables analysis of the law in context (Watkins and Burton, 2013). A descriptive analysis of legal rules, alongside a more empirical socio-legal methodology, provides a means to understand the law's theoretical and practical limitations. This highlights the multitude of factors that impact on the law's trajectory, from the courts' application of the law to the wider social and political movements of the time. In turn they help elaborate why the GPG so stubbornly persists.

Understanding the evolution of gender equality since the introduction of the Equal Pay Act 1970 (EqPA70) requires a contextual analysis of the catalysts that have helped drive or hinder legal change (Dickens, 2007). Elements such as political will and the seemingly ever-present laissez faire deference to the need of business have impacted and shaped the legal approach to inequality. The law in this way is an inherently social and political phenomenon. While legal rules may appear to have the potential to create level playing fields, the adoption of a feminist methodological approach evidences how the accessibility, application and interpretation of the law remains gendered.

Law is interpreted and regulated on multiple levels. Despite constantly changing, norms such as the 'reasonable man' test reflect 'laws [ongoing] complicity with masculine culture' (Davies, 2008: 295). The Feminist Judgement Project highlighted the utility of feminist theory through practically applying feminist jurisprudence to rejudge existing cases (Hunter et al, 2010). It is used here to help evaluate and determine the effectiveness of legislation to address the GPG. While that does not suggest that law can resolve the problem of the GPG, identifying the barriers to this endeavour remains critical (O'Leary, 1992).

Meso-level organizational examination

Meso-level enquiries are addressed in Chapter 4, incorporating analysis of how hard and soft law requirements are interpreted, applied and developed in the workplace. Gender pay inequity is a built environment and so is best understood in a real-world setting. Analysis requires consideration of institutional approaches within organizations, given the inevitable interaction between the two spheres. Legislative requirements are interpreted to varying degrees through existing structures and deference to case law within the courts and tribunals. Equally, there is no formulaic and rigorous approach to the application of new workplace policies and initiatives. Organizations have a key role in determining broad requirements and initiating them in a workable way. Organizational perspectives recognize the growth of Human Resource Management (HRM), the effect of norms and values within the workplace, and the impact of key actors, both as drivers and barriers to change.

The sector of employment is widely recognized as a key variable in understanding GPGs (Ardanaz-Badia and Rawlings, 2018; Colebrook et al, 2018). Evaluation of the GPRR and the first six years of reported data is given within a case study setting. Organizational strategies to alleviate pay gaps are examined, via assessment of reports accompanying the data.

This draws on both institutional and organizational perspectives providing a quantitative analysis of the GPRR data and accompanying narratives. Under the scrutiny of the Equality and Human Rights Commission (EHRC), organizations have demonstrated compliance with the Regulations (Adams et al, 2018). The way that organizations have approached pay reporting is instructive both in terms of monitoring pay gaps, but also with reference to transparency.

Organizational policies, processes and norms filter and interpret institutional regulations. They can both drive and impede legislative initiatives, contributing to the resilience of gender pay inequities at the workplace. Dobbin et al's (1993) compelling analyses highlighted the central role of human resource experts in the US, where they drove the agenda and developed solutions to inequality. He traces the interaction between policy and law, and how to achieve change, citing a shift from the language of moral imperative to that of financial necessity for organizations, which is central to this research (Healy et al, 2011; Oswick and Noon, 2014). Corporate governance and accountability, industry-wide standards, and the risk of reputational damage provides organizational incentive to drive change (Browne, 2004; Klarsfeld et al, 2012).

However, the stubborn persistence of the GPG demonstrates that diversity management is not a panacea for this intractable problem (Treasury Committee, 2023b). This highlights the need to analyse other factors, such as normative values and behaviours within the workplace, which may limit the effectiveness of policies and contextualize the way this occurs.

In accordance with the feminist lens applied to the socio-legal perspective, a feminist conceptualization of inequality and gender in organizations is also useful. Much like the law, the workplace is not a gender-neutral arena. There is a gendered interplay between how policies are constructed, their accessibility and, ultimately, their impact. Applying a feminist approach to the institutional theory of organizations is therefore relevant and illustrative of the deeper foundations of gender inequality that policies to close the GPG need to address (Mackay et al, 2009). Central to this analysis is Acker's work (1989: 213; 2006, 2009), describing how organizations produce and reproduce inequalities and the workplace hierarchies that enable this to happen. The daily activities that take place, such as pay practices, recruitment, promotion and task assignment are central to the construction and maintenance of inequalities. Acker describes the regimes that enable this to happen, such as organizational class hierarchies, which position white men as the natural leaders at the top, and the role of the unencumbered good worker, that embodies typically male characteristics and abilities. Efforts to address GPGs clash against these pervasive structures and assumptions.

Resistance to countering inequities operates in different ways within different organizational settings. Penner et al's (2023) employer-linked analysis of the GPG confirms that inequalities and differences within jobs and the processes that sort people into jobs remain central factors accounting for ongoing inequities. The finance sector case study provides a situated analysis of how the levers and resistance to change occur, and the lived experience of this for employees (Ruddin, 2006). Similarity within organizational fields has been evidenced by the overarching trends displayed in the gender pay reporting data. DiMaggio and Powell (1983) have suggested that various factors impact upon organizations to encourage similarity. This can be evidenced by the need to comply with legal requirements, operate within professional standards or keep up with the innovations of others to enhance organizational legitimacy.

Micro-level economic and sociological examination

The final micro level of this inquiry affords an opportunity to understand the qualitative experiences of working women. Women's perceptions of pay policy, the shaping of their career paths, and initiatives designed to support the drive for equality give further depth to this analysis. This includes the relevance of economic and sociological explanations for gender pay inequities alongside the lived experience and impact of legislative and organizational requirements (Perry, 2011).

Economic perspectives have sought to explain how pay is distributed, encompassing and developing the foundational work of Becker (1985). His classic work on human capital theory attributed inequalities in pay to women's reduced investments in education and work: women were paid less given their less productive skill sets, because of reduced educational investment and reduced labour market participation. Labour market investments and expectations are attributed to the rational choices women make and the different caring and household labour responsibilities they have. Polachek (2004) suggested that the declining GPG confirmed the economic approach, as reductions correlated with work expectations between the sexes becoming more similar.

As women's educational and labour market position has changed, this theory has developed and the conventional explanatory factors have been amended (Blau and Kahn, 2017). For instance, while there have been significant increases in women's labour force participation and experience in the workplace (Harkness, 1996), it has been suggested that only full-time work can prevent human capital 'rusting', and thus can still legitimately explain the pay gap (Rubery and Grimshaw, 2015: 327). As the goalposts surrounding inequality have shifted economic theories have developed to account for the persistent GPG (Goldin, 2021). In 2019 women's participation in higher education in the UK was 12.5% higher than men's, and growing at a faster rate (DfE, 2019a). Given women's educational attainment has surpassed that of men (O'Reilly et al, 2015), economic explanations have refocused on factors such as the subject studied (Machin and Puhani, 2003; Chevalier, 2007). The substantially lower proportion of women studying Science, Technology, Engineering and Mathematics (STEM) subjects and, correspondingly, their underrepresentation in STEM jobs is now a more relevant explanation (Sorgner et al, 2017; Quiros et al, 2018). Given the anticipated impacts of automation and the changing world of work, the consequences of these choices of investment are concerning for the pay gap (Brussevich et al, 2018; European Commission, 2019). These trends may have a strong effect in maintaining pay differentials moving forward.

Sociological explanations have implicitly informed and contributed to the institutional, organizational and economic perspectives already discussed.

The duality of requirements on women, in terms of their unpaid labour, was discussed by Hochschild (2003). Her seminal text described the 'Second Shift' women face at home and the impacts that this has. While the improved awareness and understanding of equality and diversity, visible in legal developments and women's increased workforce participation, has been accompanied by an increase in egalitarian attitudes, she contended that the gender revolution has been stalled. More recently, England (2010) concurs, finding the revolution is still stalled and the dual burden persists. Societal expectations around childcare are still very much persistent and geared towards typical gender positions (England, 2010; Miller, 2012).

Societal norms and values, related to women's identities in both the public and private sphere, can and do impact career choices and pay outcomes (Bensidoun and Trancart, 2018). Individual ambition and skills, inevitably informed by these identities, operate alongside bias in recruitment practices and the preferences shown by employers. These factors are all central to understanding occupational gaps (Reskin and Maroto, 2011).

The micro-level qualitative assessment evaluates legislative change and workplace policy, highlighting how resistance functions at the firm level. Gendered identities can create a double bind for women in the workplace (Acker, 2012). Stereotypically masculine character traits, such as self-promotion and the capacity to negotiate, may be viewed positively for men but engender negative associations when carried out by women (Babcock and Laschever, 2003; Pham et al, 2018). The multidimensional way that gender identity is constructed and valued illustrates Rubery and Grimshaw's (2015) shifting goalposts theory, which builds on the work of Acker (1989; Rubery, 2018a). Women's achievements are subject to continually changing targets that legitimize the persistence of gaps.

The interplay within and between these explanatory approaches is illustrative of the complexity embodied by gender pay inequities and denotes the need for a real-world setting to observe the linkage and understand how initiatives have impacted (Aharoni, 2011).

The finance sector

The finance sector is central to the British economy, providing significant levels of employment and contributions to GDP. The industry employs 1.08 million British workers accounting for 3% of British jobs (Hutton, 2022). In 2021, the sector contributed £30.7 billion in tax receipts, a value of £173.6 billion to the UK economy, providing 8.3% of our total economic output (Hutton, 2022: 5 and 13). The overall gender ratio of employment is balanced: in the UK the workforce is 51% female (Metcalf and Rolfe, 2009: 12). However, a sectoral evaluation of both ASHE and GPRR data evidences that jobs and career paths have historically been, and remain, highly gendered (Healy et al, 2018). The sector has some of Britain's largest pay gaps (BEISa, 2018; Treasury Committee, 2023a). Analysis of GPRR data by PwC (2022: 1) finds that for financial services the mean GPG for all workers is 26.6%, with gaps ranging between 17% and 32% (compared to 12.1% in all sectors).

The terminology used to describe the industry is important given the marked occupational segregation within the sector. The finance sector is used here as an umbrella term to cover the range of services provided by banking and finance institutions. This research incorporates insights from those working both in retail and commercial banking (typically associated with lower revenue-generating roles such as deposits, lending, personal account management) and those engaged in investment and corporate banking occupations at the top end of the finance pay spectrum (typically associated with asset management, hedge funds, trading). McDowell (1998) described the separate geographical and gendered spheres within which these occupations exist, a distinction that is painfully slow to change. To illustrate, the lack of movement on GPGs in corporate and investment banking since the GPRR were introduced has been described as 'appalling'. Experts suggest that 26% of firms in the investment and savings industry will never reach gender parity (Treasury Committee, 2023a: 3).

The 2007–08 financial crisis starkly illustrated the need for more diverse governance (Sealy et al, 2008: 44; Treasury Committee, 2010: 3). The EHRC inquiry into unequal pay and sex discrimination within financial services, prompted by the crisis, encouraged reform to address the 'marked and persistent sex discrimination that permeates the industry' (EHRC, 2009: 5). The EHRC quantified the overall GPG in the sector in 2009 at 55% for full-time workers, double the national average at the time (EHRC 2009: 5; Atkinson, 2011: 243).

The reasons for the stark inequities in finance are numerous and complex. To illustrate, despite women's involvement and experience in the industry, they typically do not occupy the most senior roles. The GPRR data demonstrates that their scant presence in the highest paying parts of the sector and their prominence in lower pay grades remains ubiquitous (see Chapter 4). To illustrate, Table 1.1 shows the shockingly large pay and bonus gaps within Britain's 'big four' banks and the equivalent percentage of women in each 25% pay banding. The big four banks provide a range of both banking and financial services, undertaken both at branch and head office level.

The GPRR finance sector data also varies by organization type as different types of banking and finance occupations operate in separate organizational entities. Evaluation of the workplace affords an opportunity to disentangle organizational processes and norms, and the various causative aspects of gender pay inequity that occur within them. A combination of key actors – such as the role of government and institutional arrangements, management, human

Table 1.1: Comparison of GPRR data for Britain's 'big four' banks 2019–20

	HSBC	Barclays	Lloyds	RBS
Pay gap	47%	41.8%	33.5%	36.8%
Bonus gap	60.5%	42.8%	41.8%	44%
Women in the top 25%	35%	30%	37%	31%
Women in the upper middle 25%	52%	45%	53.8%	48.9%
Women in the lower middle 25%	61%	64%	67%	64.7%
Women in the bottom 25%	64%	67%	71.4%	69.3%

Notes: This table shows median figures for 2019–20, except for RBS, which did not report following the government's decision to suspend enforcement. RBS figures reflect its 2018–19 report. More recent reports are not included in this summary, as in 2021–22 Lloyds did not report bonus data and their 2022–23 report is not available. In their 2022–23 whole of business analysis, HSBC present a breakdown of women in each organizational third, not quartile.

Source: Contains public sector information licensed under the Open Government Licence v3.0. Gender pay reporting data available at: https://gender-pay-gap.service.gov.uk/

resources (HR), and employees and trade unions – help shape the trajectory of change. Entrenched norms and cultures inform how management defines and approaches the need for greater diversity and equality (Acker, 2006). Gendered workplace hierarchies, the power inherent in leadership, and the practical and ongoing effects of this within the workplace are therefore highly pertinent. In order to recognize these factors, the approach I have taken towards data collection adopts a range of methodologies.

Interviewing as a method gives an appreciation of how the GPG is perceived and experienced, and how this may have changed/be changing. Interviewees were recruited from a range of banking and finance firms and occupations. The experiences of participants in relation to hours worked, pay, bonus, progression and workplace culture shows the perfunctory reality of the transparency afforded by the GPRR. The key topics that participants discussed provide the framework for how this stream of analysis is presented, as shown in Figure 1.2.

Through a process of manual coding I identified key themes in the interview transcripts. Focus was progressively achieved, as patterns and common elements were identified and abstracted. Through these searches, the usage and frequency of word groupings across transcripts became clear. Interviewees regularly used terminology such as: brutal/battle/fight/ bullying/accusatory/toxic; care/flexibility/part-time; risk taking/risk averse; pay transparency/secrecy/hidden; politics/power (Basit, 2003; Saldaña, 2015). I then categorized these topics with reference to the architectures model. Untangling the relevance of each theoretical component further exposed the interrelationship between them, how they have shifted, and the consistency of barriers woven between them. This qualitative stream

Figure 1.2: Thematic approach to qualitative analysis

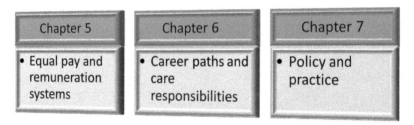

of analysis helps reveal how vision on the problem and, correspondingly, the pursuit of greater equality and diversity remains peripheral and partial.

Research design and construction of the architectures model

The introduction of the GPRR signalled an improved approach to pay transparency in Britain and requires investigation. This research examines how the GPRR and broader legal and organizational initiatives have impacted GPGs, and why progress is slow and prone to stalling (see Figure 1.1) (Hochschild, 2003; England, 2010).

Additional sub-questions help flag the obstacles to equality at the institutional macro level by considering: how legislation and case law is used to approach the problem of the GPG and to what effect. Organizational meso-level enquiries consider: what the gender pay reports tell us about the current situation; and how organizational processes and policies are tackling gender pay inequities and the factors that contribute to them. Finally, at the individual micro level, they tell us how policies and processes are experienced by women in the workplace and what impact they have.

I have constructed this multilevel research design to afford different insights on the problem, which, when considered in their entirety, offer a holistic lens through which to gain greater clarity on impediments to progress. Traversing disciplinary boundaries, the utility lies in the dialogue between the data streams. Each element progressively draws upon key themes and, in so doing, builds a richer understanding of the problem. The various empirical threads are concerned with related, yet different, aspects of the same occurrence and so different sources and approaches to data collection are adopted. The research design offers alternative and discreet explanations, not intended to objectively verify one or the other, but constructed around one another to build a stratified comprehensive understanding of pay gaps within finance. When considered in their entirety, the points of overlap and interaction more fully address the research questions and explain why progress has stalled (Yauch and Steudel, 2016).

Figure 1.3: Framework for a multilevel analysis

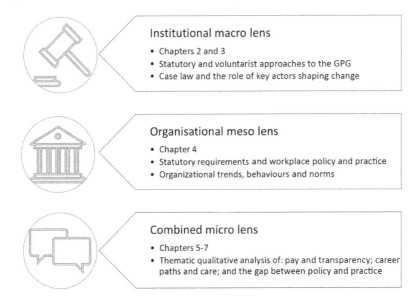

The structure of this analysis is shown in Figure 1.3.

This layered thematic analysis and the theoretical explanations pertaining to the topic lend themselves to the architectures metaphor. To conceptualize the development of the GPG and the barriers to change I have assembled these perspectives as architectures of inequality, as shown in Figure 1.4.

The architectures of inequality model extends the thematization proposed by Rubery and Grimshaw (2015) in an original and imaginative way. In addition, Franzoni and Sánchez-Ancochea's (2016) policy architectures concept is developed to recognize the interaction and interrelationship between legal rules, workplace arrangements and the individual worker. These approaches are combined to create a new analytical tool.

The model adds to the literature on the topic in several ways, first, by presenting a new way to understand and visualize how change is prevented from achieving its desired objective. We see how each explanatory approach is discreet, while at the same time interdependent. By considering these theoretical approaches (institutional, organization, sociological and economic perspectives) at the macro, meso and micro levels, we can observe how the problem persists, despite ongoing extension and development. The slow progress towards eradicating GPGs is rooted in systemic architectural features, increasingly visible through this multilevel analysis. Inequality is insulated from change at the regulatory or firm level, for instance by the lack of transparency concerning pay, or by the workplace norms and values they encounter. Each component part of the architecture has the potential to destabilize progress.

Figure 1.4: Architectures of inequality model

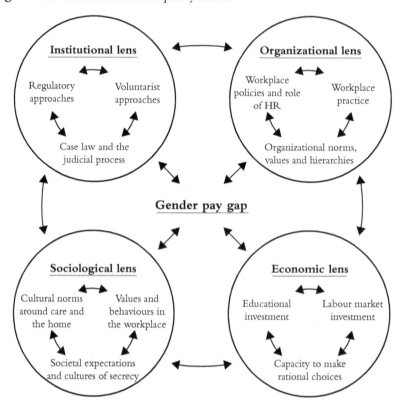

Second, analysis demonstrates there is constant dynamism in the model. Rubery and Grimshaw (2015) contend that once a remedy to resolve one of the factors impacting GPGs is pursued, the goalposts shift. This momentum is a feature of the architectures reflecting how the theoretical explanations operate alongside one another, helping to account for the persistence of GPGs. Understanding this dynamism also indicates where the most promising capacity for future change lies. To illustrate, the organizational policy architecture is defined by factors such as the public/private sector differential and then further still by normative sectoral behaviours and trends (Franzoni and Sanchez-Ancochea, 2016: 13). The model can be applied to different sectors of employment to illuminate how impediments to change operate and shift, and account for sectoral variability in GPGs. The inconsistency of inequities across industrial sectors is an inevitable outcome of the free market regulatory approach in Britain, regardless of institutional developments such as the GPRRs. This helps us to examine the relationship between stasis and change, building upon Acker's (2006) regimes of inequality. The construction of the architectures model provides a useful way of evaluating the change that has occurred, the barriers to it, and the lack of linearity in this progress.

Structure of the volume

Empirical examination of this multilevel research design involves both quantitative and qualitative methods and is subdivided into eight chapters as follows.

Chapter 1: Laying the architectural foundations

This chapter introduces the research, outlining the various thematic perspectives on gender pay inequity and specifying the research questions addressed in this volume. The finance sector is proposed as a relevant and apposite case study, given the inequities therein and the continual transformation within the industry. The architectures of inequality model is assembled, providing the groundwork for later chapters to develop, demonstrating how, while legal and organizational reforms are continuously built upon, underlying foundational principles reinforce inequality, and breathe through the building.

Chapter 2: Regulating equal pay in Britain: 1970–2010

The macro-level institutional component of the architecture is constructed by charting the historical development of the law, related to gender pay inequity. The passing of the EqPA70 was a watershed moment. The gradual extension of gender equality legislation since that point is presented in a phased legal analysis. The legal research incorporates an analytic periodization and evaluation of statute and case law, alongside a socio-legal analysis that adopts a feminist methodological lens. The key actors that have both impeded and encouraged these macro-level legal developments are described. Ongoing movement and tensions in the conceptualization of equality demonstrates the multifaceted way that resistance to pay equity has operated, and the unequal foundations undermining the potential for progress. This assessment is complimented by a parallel assessment of change within the finance sector, demonstrating the distinct yet interrelated nature of developments within the industry.

Chapter 3: Regulating equal pay in Britain: the Equality Act 2010 and beyond

The conceptualization of equality shifted with the passing of the Equality Act 2010 (EqA2010). Important transformative developments contained within the Act are contrasted with factors impeding their implementation and effectiveness. These legal arrangements are positioned as a component part of the architectures model, within which inequalities are seemingly insulated from change. Just as institutional approaches struggle to eradicate the problem, the relationship with other elements in the social subsystem helps illuminate why progress remains so slow. Regulatory change and technological innovations within the finance sector provide an illustrative backdrop for understanding these tensions.

Chapter 4: Evaluating the Gender Pay Reporting Regulations

The GPRR are introduced as part of Britain's evolving legal framework marking an improved approach to transparency to target gendered pay inequities. The size and shape of gendered inequity within the finance industry is described, given the particularly high pay gaps therein. A sample of firms is constructed and the first six years of largely untapped GPRR data are examined. We see how institutional and organizational frameworks are discreet and yet interact, revealing the strength of architectural foundations. This serves as a critique on the GPRR and the limited potential afforded by increased institutional and organizational focus on the problem. Notable areas of contestation within this interaction, such as a lack of transparency and preference for voluntarist approaches to governance, combine to keep inequalities hidden in plain sight. This helps illustrate how organizational trends impact at the meso level, contributing to the stalling of progress.

Chapter 5: Pay practices and inequalities

Qualitative interviews with women working in a range of banking and finance roles reveal their lived experiences of both legal institutions and commercial organizations at the micro level. The key topics discussed are thematized in this three-part stream of analysis. Chapter 5 focuses on pay and bonus systems. Shrouded in secrecy, the culture of silence that surrounds them limits women's capacity to appropriately position themselves at the point of job change and when negotiating uplifts. Critically, interviewees describe how a broad lack of transparency restricts their ability to challenge pay inequities. Pay reporting and voluntarist requirements are also considered, illustrating the practical constraints experienced around both hard and soft law approaches. The analysis illustrates how the macro-level institutional architecture is experienced within the workplace. This shows how rights at work and women's voices are inhibited by pay systems and the lived reality of legislative entitlements.

Chapter 6: Career paths, care responsibilities and contingent choices

The second stream of qualitative analysis examines women's reflections on career paths and the effect of career interruptions. The interview data evidences the myriad of factors impacting upon women's capacity to make rational choices and the subsequent translation of these choices into outcomes. This assessment reinforces how gender identities, derived from both the workplace and the home, impede efforts to reduce existing inequalities. The value ascribed to typified female characteristics, gendered networking environments and the reproduction of existing power structures help to contextualize the trajectory of progress. Economic and sociological explanations for the GPG are explored revealing the dynamism perpetually reinforcing the architectures of inequality.

Chapter 7: Organizational norms, HRM and the gap between policy and practice

The thematic interview analysis concludes in Chapter 7, as women working in the finance industry reflected on the impact of organizational policy: does it walk the talk, or do women experience these efforts as merely window dressing? Interviewees discussed promotion and flexibility policies, acknowledging both areas of progress and resistance. This illustrates how attitudes in different parts of the sector and the cross-national perspectives of some global firms on British equality requirements contribute to the persistence of GPGs. While union membership may be limited, interviewees described how the role of unions and social movements still holds some potency to drive change within the workplace. This reveals the interface between the macro and meso levels in the architectures of inequality, and the pivotal role of organizations in understanding gender pay inequity.

Chapter 8: Contradictions of transparency

Conclusions are drawn in Chapter 8 concerning: how the pay gap is experienced; what awareness employees have of the legislative entitlements afforded to them; and the interrelationship of factors impacting on this decades old problem. Application of the architectures model to the wicked problem of the GPG helps highlight the effectiveness and limitations of legislation and organizational approaches to gender pay inequity. Two key findings are presented from this examination. First, the utility of this approach reveals how common blind spots, such as the thorny issues of transparency and accountability, remain central to the persistence of the GPG. Second, the dynamism in the architectures of inequality demonstrates how the impediments to alleviating the gap are in constant flux, exerting continual pressures on any potential progress. By observing these interactions and paying close attention to the data, best practice can be identified. Within this model, the slow movement of legislative development suggests eradicating the GPG is an elusive legal ambition; at the same time, the organizational dimension currently offers the most likely potential for traction.

Conclusion

To fully assess the effectiveness of the GPRR, this book constructs a picture of the full lifecycle of gender pay provisions, from macro-level legal developments to the stories of individual women within the workplace. In this chapter I have set out why building a stratified understanding of the developing approaches to the GPG can offer an empirically robust and constructively critical analysis of current efforts intended to tackle it. Policy is rationalized by the various elements of the employment system, accounted for in this research by macro, meso, and micro levels of analysis and the interactions between them (Franzoni and Sanchez-Ancochea, 2016: 49–50; Gallie, 2007b; Rubery and Hebson, 2018). Accordingly, as legislative approaches to target the GPG have been extended, the capacity to address gender pay inequity seemingly remains just as remote.

The architectures of inequality model assembles the law and organizational policy, alongside economic and sociological analyses, as component parts of a dynamic structure. As this analysis develops, barriers to progress, foundational to the architecture, become clearer. Underlying embedded inequalities are shielded by light-touch governance and contradictions of transparency. Subject to continual extension these underpinning factors provide the footing for persistent inequities. Efforts to *see* inside organizations and gain greater clarity on the processes associated with GPGs reveal all the aspects that remain obscured from view (Menéndez-Viso, 2009).

The GPG and the factors that impact upon it are multi-layered and ever shifting. The linearity of progress towards gender pay equity is continually disrupted as COVID-19, Brexit and developments related to automation and AI demonstrate. The pruning back of legislative requirements, such as the removal of GPRR compliance when the pandemic first unfolded, was accompanied by an increase in the intensity of domestic duties for women. The prospect of ongoing economic uncertainty will inevitably continue to clash with efforts to address inequities.

With these tensions in mind, we turn now to focus on legal developments since the 1970s in Chapters 2 and 3.

2

Regulating Equal Pay
in Britain: 1970–2010

Introduction

An equality norm was first signposted in British law with the EqPA70 and, upon joining the European Economic Community (EEC) in 1973, the Treaty of Rome 1957 (ToR57). The law has since been progressively broadened. Macro-level legal requirements form the institutional component of the architectures model. This chapter explores legal arrangements alongside developments in the finance sector to examine the trajectory of gender pay inequity and understand the barriers limiting progress. Three phases in the conceptualization of equality are defined. This draws on Hepple's (2011) generational approach and distinctions used by Fredman (2011) and Dickens (2007).

- Phase I, 1970–84: formal conceptualization of equality as sameness.
- Phase II, 1984–98: recognition of the importance of difference.
- Phase III, 1998–2010: proactive developments.

This chapter highlights the slow-moving, incremental development of the law, recognizing its disruptive and pre-emptive potential, drawing on the work of Deakin et al (2015). Legal measures have evolved as the law has been constructed, applied and extended, resulting in gradual changes in the GPG over time. Governments, business, unions and social movements are presented as key actors that contest the parameters of the legal framework, alongside the momentum of decisions encapsulated in case law.

This analysis is underpinned with a parallel assessment of transformation within the finance sector. Changing approaches to equality are mapped alongside regulatory reform, increased competition and consolidation within the industry. In a state of continual flux, emergent work formations and organizational norms perpetually legitimize seemingly immovable inequities in terms of pay (Acker, 1990; Skuratowicz and Hunter, 2004; Britton and Logan, 2008).

This continuation of the periodized analysis exposes the constant movement of both legal and organizational approaches. The architectures model is a useful way to observe and understand the interrelationship between them. The British preference for a laissez faire style of governance, reflects an ongoing priority afforded to the needs of business, as more stringent equality approaches are refuted as costly and burdensome. The law is characterized by a lack of transparency concerning the requirements needed to access legal entitlements and address inequities. The law is critically examined with reference to these barriers. Understood as foundational architectural components, they insulate the deeply embedded inequalities upon which legal arrangements have been constructed. What becomes clear is the need to consider architectural arrangements in their entirety, beyond the institutional level.

Phase I, 1970–mid 1980s: equality as sameness

The legal system and the key actors that catalyze change

This chapter first outlines Britain's relationship to the EEC and how this has contributed to the changing conceptualization of equality in the law. The external influence of the EEC has been central to the British approach to equality since the outset. The new and developing Common Market stated, in Article 119 of the ToR57: 'Each Member State shall ... ensure and subsequently maintain the application of the principle that men and women should receive equal pay for equal work.' Under section 2(1) of the European Communities Act 1972 (ECA72), EEC law automatically became part of British domestic law.[1] In addition, ECA72 section 2(4) stated that courts must interpret domestic legislation in line with EEC provisions and could not enact contrary requirements. *Van Gend en Loos* (1967) applied this principle and confirmed that Article 119 would have direct effect, independent of any national provision, or lack of (a summary outline of all cases is provided in Appendix 1). The case established the criteria that so long as requirements were clear, precise, unconditional, and capable of giving rise to an individual right, then they could be relied upon in Member States. Should requirements conflict, European law would prevail. Reference could be sought from the European Court of Justice (ECJ) if needed, often prompting progressive and purposive judgements.

The EEC's inclusion of equal pay in the ToR57 was largely due to French concerns over other Member States gaining a competitive advantage (Burri and Prechal, 2013: 2). France had already enacted its own equal pay provisions and feared cheap labour elsewhere would put them at a disadvantage. This economic motivation was extended to include a social goal, as per the judges' interpretation of the ToR57 in the case of *Defrenne v Sabena* (1976).

However, despite recognition of the social aim, this economic rationale has remained central in Britain (Dickens, 2007). In response to EEC requirements, Britain's preference for a laissez faire approach to governance reflected the impact of government and business, acting to stall or restrict the approaches pursued (Gallie, 2007a). In addition, other key actors were also catalyzing change, as the influence of unions and case law illustrates.

Alongside and prior to EEC membership, there was increased political attention and mounting collective pressure to address inequality within Britain. The Labour Party (1964, 1966) made a commitment to equal pay in their 1964 and 1966 election manifestos. The women's movement for equal pay gathered steam during the post-war years, supported by Barbara Castle, Secretary of State for Employment (*Hansard*, HC Deb., vol. 795, cols 914–15, 9 February 1970). Industrial action and campaigning, particularly by the Ford sewing machinists at Dagenham, the Women's Liberation Movement and National Joint Action Campaign Committee for Women's Equal Rights, critically provided the internal backdrop for the implementation of the EqPA70. The GPG, in 1970, stood at 36.2% for full-timers and 48.5% for part-time workers (Perfect, 2011: 8). The current 14.9% overall GPG demonstrates the marked yet slow progress that has occurred over the intervening 50 years (White, 2022).

Alongside these political, industrial and organizational pressures, there were profound changes in the economic structure of the home (Jenkins, 2013). Larger numbers of women were working in both full- and part-time roles, alongside sharp increases in women entering higher education. These shifting patterns impacted on the conventionally established architectures of gender inequality that were emerging from the late 1960s and early 1970s.

The way that the key actors described here (governments, both in Britain and the EEC, businesses, trade unions, social movements, and those within the judicial process) constantly contested the conceptualization of equality illustrates why progress to eradicate gender pay inequity has been incremental and slow. This accords with the process and characteristics of 'layered change' that Streeck and Thelen describe (2005: 24).

Conceptualization of formal equality in the law

As a result of the combined forces of key actors, the Wilson government passed the EqPA70 just prior to the election in 1970. The EqPA70 represented a formal approach to equality, requiring equal pay for work that was the same, broadly similar, or equivalent (section 1(4) and (5)). The hidden complexities of this individual claimant-centred approach required to pursue equal pay underline another aspect of the power imbalance. The law prohibited less favourable treatment in pay unless there was a genuine material difference. To bring an equal pay claim a woman needed to identify a male comparator in the same employment, with whom they could be compared. If the courts found the work to be the same, broadly similar or equivalent to the comparator, they then had to consider whether there was a genuine material factor for the difference. The difference could not be directly discriminatory. If it was, then it had to be objectively justified.

The EqPA70 came into force in 1975 as employers were given time to make the salary adjustments that were required. The initial impact of the law on the GPG was marked, prompting a 10% reduction in the GPG 1971–77, followed by a lull as those inclined to adjust pay had done so (see Figure 1.1).

Barbara Castle introduced the Act to the Commons stating, "We are witnessing another historic advance in the struggle against discrimination in our society ... This goes beyond anything in the law of other major countries" (*Hansard*, HC Deb., vol. 795, cols 914–17, 9 February 1970). However, legal development was constrained by underlying business considerations, such as cost and bureaucracy, that both required and legitimized the pace of change (Dickens, 2007). Assertions made by the Confederation of British Industry (CBI) flagged the potential burden on business of the proposed inclusion of equal value to the EqPA70, ultimately contributing to its more limited scope and the five-year period allowed for adjustments to be made.[2] While broadly equivalent went further than the ToR57, the notions of equal value and equal treatment in pensions were not included. Castle went on: "the phrase 'equal pay for work of equal value' is too abstract a concept to embody in legislation" (*Hansard*, HC Deb., vol. 795 col. 916, 9 February 1970), with which the CBI agreed. Dickens (2007) has argued that this demonstrates the economic underpinnings of the law. To further illustrate these competing tensions, ten months prior to the EqPA70 coming into force the EEC approach had developed to include equal value.[3]

As a result, while the sewing machinists in Dagenham were one of the triggers for the Labour government to pass the Act, the factor that prompted them to strike in 1968 was not addressed by the legislation: although their pay was increased the nature of their work was not recognized as skilled. The gendered template and power imbalance upon which the law was constructed failed to recognize the importance of value. Given the marked occupational segregation at the time, this demonstrates how embedded foundational inequalities restricted the effectiveness of the EqPA70. The Dagenham workers took further industrial action following the Equal Value Amendment 1983 (EqVA83) that ultimately regraded their work as skilled. This highlights how key actors have both enabled and limited development: the EEC's role was more progressive; conversely, within Britain the lack of political will and deference to the needs of business were limiting. Within this context, the British tendency to 'stall, divert or dilute' EEC legal measures was a continued feature of its membership (Fagan and Rubery, 2017: 16).

This period was witness to a growing body of legislation concerning inequality in Britain, within which the core architectural features of governance and transparency were notable. Alongside the recognition of inequality in pay, the concept of discrimination was given legal voice by the Race Relations Act 1965 (RRA65). In 1975, the Sex Discrimination Act 1975 (SDA75) was passed, intended to 'compliment' the EqPA70 by prohibiting discrimination in employment, education, and training (*Hansard*, HC Deb., vol. 889 col. 515, 26 March 1975). Much like the EqPA70, the SDA75 requires consistency in the treatment of men and women.

The SDA75 defines direct discrimination as less favourable treatment and indirect discrimination as the disproportionate impact of a provision, criterion or practice, unless justified. The inclusion of the concept of justification within the SDA75 encompassed the potential to capitulate the principle of equality and accede to the needs of business, again highlighting the laws economic underpinnings (Dickens, 2007).

Prior to the passing of the SDA75 and EqPA70, separate pay structures for men and women had been commonplace (*Roberts v Hopwood* (1925)). By virtue of these Acts, direct and indirect discrimination became prohibited and the legal entitlement to equal pay enshrined (Hepple, 2011). This period of formal equality was characterized by the pursuit of equality as sameness. Case law is illustrative of the barriers women as individual claimants experienced.

Case law and the pursuance of legal rights

The notion of judicial precedent is fundamental to the development of British law, as decisions of higher courts must be adhered to. Legal discourse, in this way, can highlight key areas of difficulty, allowing for the law to be challenged and extended. Analysis here focuses on the individualized claimant–centred approach of legal entitlement and the shortcomings of equality as sameness, with reference to hours worked and pregnancy.

The legal right to challenge any discriminatory or unequal pay structures could be pursued by individuals with assistance from organizations, such as trade unions and the Equal Opportunities Commission (EOC). The EOC was established to help tackle discrimination and promote equality, with the power to investigate and support cases, alongside providing advice. In addition, the Central Arbitration Committee (CAC) had an adjudicatory role (Deakin et al, 2015: 383). The need for such institutional support mechanisms highlights the foundational power imbalance, lack of transparency and existing inequalities upon which legal measures have been constructed. Case-law analysis shows how the formal conceptualization of equality embedded this opacity and cultural ideas about gender.

To pursue an equal pay claim, a female claimant would first have to identify a male comparator. The tribunal would then assess whether the work carried out by both parties was the same, broadly similar, or equivalent to require equal pay. Contestation in the courts, concerning the investment of time and hours worked, helped to highlight the difficulties of this early conceptualization, demonstrating gaps in the legislation and sowing the seeds for future reforms. To illustrate, in *Dugdale v Kraft Foods* (1977) and *Electrolux v Hutchinson* (1977) contractual overtime, night and Sunday working requirements were held not to be sufficiently different in terms of contractual obligations. The work was found to be broadly similar and the equal pay cases were upheld.

However, a different interpretation of time was considered appropriate for part-time work. In *Dugdale* and *Electrolux* the choice of day of the week or time of day worked did not impede the requirement for equal pay. However, in *Handley v H. Mono Ltd* (1979) the more restrictive British courts found that part-time hours did constitute a genuine material factor difference, despite the work undertaken being the same. The concept of sameness as a standard for equality was seemingly based on a full-time contract, with no reference to productivity.

After referral to the ECJ, the case *Macarthys v Smith* (1980) confirmed that employment need not be contemporaneous to require equal pay. Having established that a comparator need not be employed at the same time, the court went on to state that performance of the same job (albeit on part-time hours) could require equal pay, seemingly supporting *Dugdale* and *Electrolux*. However, this purposive judgement left the matter open to the national courts to consider upon the facts of the case. This demonstrates how the contestation of legal rules, including reference to the European courts, has helped illustrate how inequality works and, in turn, extend the scope of the law. These cases highlight the variability in judicial interpretation while both revealing and clarifying the ways that unequal pay may be obstructed from view, sometimes in plain sight.

The limitations of this rigid formal approach to equality as sameness, based on a male legal norm, were also highlighted in cases concerning pregnancy. In *Turley v Allders* (1980), a claim of discrimination arising from pregnancy was not considered less favourable treatment, as there was no pregnant male comparator. To alleviate these concerns, Smith's minority judgement introduced the idea of illness. While *Hayes v Malleable Working Men's Club* (1985) did not follow *Turley*, Smith's reasoning from *Turley* was applied. A pregnant woman was likened to a sick man needing an extended period off work. The foundational gendered cultural template on which this early conceptualization of equality law was both applied and interpreted, clearly limited its capacity to recognize and resolve inequities. This demonstrates how macro-level regulations interact with organizations and women's experience in the workplace.

Formal equality and legal compliance in the finance sector

The structure of the finance sector and the jobs and career paths within it have also undergone fundamental change, reflecting these institutional level architectural changes. Assessment of sectoral developments demonstrates how organizations reconfigure themselves, while progress is similarly frustrated by foundational inequalities, governance structures, and lack of transparency.

London's role as a financial centre was strengthened during the 1960s and 1970s (Crompton, 1989; Davies and Richardson, 2010: 322). The sector was not an area of graduate employment at this point, but one in which school-educated men could expect on-the-job training and a job for life (Crompton and Birkelund, 2000). The volume of women working in banking was considerable and increasing, but did not offer the same career path. Pre-automation, the bank branch and cheque-clearing functions required manual clerical work (Bird, 1990). By 1980, women formed 57% of total bank employees in the UK (Cressey and Scott, 1992: 85), very much confined to these low-level and often part-time clerical occupations.

The legal framework inevitably affects the policies pursued within organizations. During this period the organizational equality focus was on legal compliance and equal opportunity (Oswick and Noon, 2014). Inequalities were kept hidden from view as banks implemented differentiated grade structures. In this way the marked occupational segregation within the sector was largely not troubled by the narrow approach of sameness embodied in the law. Critical of how management time was being diverted in the face of what they considered to be more pressing wider economic difficulties, the Bank of Scotland lambasted the apparently onerous requirements of the SDA75 (Adams and Harte, 1998: 801). These reactions demonstrate how firms may respond disingenuously to legal boundaries, again demonstrating resistance from the business community, a theme that has continued unabated.

Limitations embedded in inequality, governance and transparency

The limitations of the Phase I legal approach of formal equality as sameness were clear. The interrelationship between the component parts of the architecture, such as contestation in the courts, and corresponding developments in the workplace, are illustrative. Existing inequalities shaped the implementation of provisions and implicit bias and assumptions limited their application and effectiveness.

This analysis demonstrates the limiting architectural features of governance and transparency in Phase I. The preference for free market governance delayed and restricted legislative progress, somewhat tempered by the progressive role of the EEC and collective pressure within Britain. A lack of transparency in the prohibitive provisions that were adopted, characterizing equality as sameness, failed to recognize or be responsive to the inequities women were facing, such as occupational segregation in the work that men and women did.

The legal formulation of equality did not transition of its own volition, but because of combined and sustained pressures upon it. The variable roles of key actors helped lay the groundwork for legislative extension. The subsequent reform and reconceptualization of equality reflects 'layered change' as the law began to recognize difference and comparable worth in Phase II (Streeck and Thelen, 2005).

Phase II, 1984–98: recognition of difference

Key actors catalyzing change

The transition to a new conceptualization of equality within the law reflects the dynamism in the architecture model, a gradual shift in cultural ideas about gender, alongside ongoing contestation between key actors.

Relations between the EEC, government within Britain and trade unions illustrate how disputed the notion of equality was. Britain's failure to comply with the Equal Value Amendment Directive is illustrative of the resistance to address the disparities in the types of work men and women did at both the institutional and organizational level. In *EC v UK* (1982) Britain was found to have failed in fulfilling its obligations to the EEC, as per the ECA72. The EqVA83 was subsequently implemented, accompanied shortly thereafter by the Sex Discrimination Act 1986 (SDA86).

Despite these provisions, the prevailing political agenda of Phase II was marked by a free market preference for deregulation, characteristic of Thatcher's conservative government (1979–90). The increasing deference to business needs, during the 1980s, typified the institutional reluctance to consider equal value. Dickens (2007: 477) notes how British courts and judges adopted a more restrictive approach to the social aim of equal pay legislation when compared to the more purposive recognition shown by the ECJ. This was accompanied by an increasing Euroscepticism within government, as proponents suggested the EEC relationship was infringing British sovereignty.

Alongside this laissez faire approach to governance from parliament and the courts, the changing structure of employment, declining unionization and increased privatization were further restricting the potential of legal apparatus to address the GPG. Having peaked in 1979, levels of collective bargaining and trade union membership fell sharply in the 1980s, accompanied by the implementation of anti-trade union legislation (Deakin et al, 2015; BEIS, 2018b). The architectures model provides a useful tool to understand these competing tensions and how they impacted the GPG trajectory.

Alongside the changing industrial climate, the government repealed the CAC's institutional power to intervene and adjudicate. The preventative capacity the CAC had, going beyond the individual remedies available to claimants, was deprioritized due to concerns over bureaucracy (Fitzpatrick, 1987: 942–7). In addition, the EOC's role was redefined as advice-focused, further limiting access to and support for remedial justice. While legislative developments had enhanced the legal legitimacy to challenge inequalities in pay, this declining ability to access and use these entitlements demonstrates one of the contradictions of transparency. The means to access justice became increasingly remote.

These changes reflected Thatcher's prioritization to "roll back the frontiers of the state" and ensure legal requirements were not too onerous for business (Dickens, 2007). This concern was not extended to the individual and their capacity to navigate assertion of their legal entitlements. Despite the EqVA83 recognizing the different spheres in which men and women work, the complexity of the legislation, combined with the impact of these changes, inevitably added to the barriers faced by potential claimants. The architectural features of light-touch equality governance and a lack of transparency in the pursuance of legal entitlement acted as impediments to the law's evolution and its utility once it had. The continual momentum of opposing forces in government, the limited recourse to collective support, and shifts in the labour market help to explain why progress remained slow in Phase II.

Equality: sameness to difference

Phase II recharacterized equality to recognize the importance of difference, enabling occupational segregation and the variable value ascribed to roles to be recognized. The EqVA83 enabled claimants to identify a comparator doing work of equal value, with reference to effort, skill and decision-making. The ebb and flow of legal development and effect can be seen in the GPG reduction following the implementation of the EqVA83 (Figure 1.1). As the meaning of pay was widened, the variegated impacts of pregnancy and the family were also beginning to be acknowledged. This shows a gradual shift from formal standards and equal treatment to a more substantive approach to equality.

Case law subsequently tested the impact and reach of the EqVA83, demonstrating that, while legal rules can be reactive, the tendency is for slow-moving incremental progress as parameters take time to bed in.

Case law and contestation in the courts

The contestation of case law demonstrates the importance of combined pressure driving the development of policy. The themes of hours worked and pregnancy are returned to, demonstrating how legal discourse has helped to highlight deficiencies in the law, alongside actors such as the ECJ and collective mobilization driving change.

As described in Phase I, the notion of hours worked was troublesome for the courts. A significant example of this was the ECJ ruling in *Bilka Kaufhaus v Weber von Hartz* (1986). The court ruled that the German company had indirectly discriminated against part-time employees, who were excluded from their occupational pension scheme available to all other employees. The UK made numerous alternate submissions to the court stating that pensions were not pay and, therefore, not covered by Article 119; however, the court found they were. The judgement in *Bilka* outlined a three-part test for objective justification and indirect discrimination, which required consideration of whether the means used were appropriate, proportionate and necessary.[4] This is a move away from the 'equal treatment formulation' as the male cultural template of a full-time contract was no longer the starting point (Dickens, 2007: 474).

The courts' approach to pregnancy again illustrates how equality provisions have grappled with the notion of difference. The ramifications arising from the ECJ's judgement in *Dekker v Stichting Vormingscentrum Voor Jonge Volwassen Plus* (1992) are illustrative. The case had been referred from the Dutch courts, who sought guidance on the Equal Treatment Directive (76/207/EEC). As only women could be dismissed on the grounds of pregnancy, this was held to be direct discrimination, with no need for a hypothetical male comparator. The *Handels-og Kontorfunktionaerernes Forbund i Danmark (acting for Hertz) v Dansk Arbejdsgiverforening (acting for Aldi Marked K/S)* (1991) judgement was given on the same day and also considered Directive 76/207. *Herz* reiterated the *Dekker* approach, that treating woman differently because of pregnancy is discriminatory, with no need for a comparator.

Legal actors within the British courts were reticent to adopt this interpretation, as demonstrated by the ruling in *Webb v EMO Air Cargo Ltd* (1995). The lower courts were unwilling to apply the rulings of *Dekker* and *Herz* (Millns, 1992). In *Dixon v Rees* (1994) and *Hopkins v Shepherd and Partners* (1994), two appeals brought regarding dismissals of pregnant women, the Employment Appeal Tribunal (EAT) again used the male comparator, despite *Dekker*. In *Iske v P&O European Ferries Ltd* (1997) the EAT did conclude, in referring to *Dekker* and *Webb,* that the hypothetical sick male comparator was not needed. This illustrates the competing factors impacting upon the application of equality law, as actors within different jurisdictions interpret requirements according to prevailing norms and standards. It also underlines the importance of exploring the development of gender pay inequity as part of the architectures of inequality. Case-law analysis demonstrates the lived reality of legal entitlement and highlights the interrelationship of theoretical explanations at the macro, meso, and micro levels. It also reveals the impact of the restrictive foundational inequalities upon which institutional legal entitlements are constructed and interpreted.

Accompanying this sluggish institutional recognition of difference, the importance of unions and representation from the EOC helped expose inequities at the workplace. Both *Enderby v Frenchay* (1991) and *British Coal Corp v Smith* (1996), were group litigation cases. Part of a growing movement of public sector multiparty equal value claims in Britain, claimants sought equal value for roles across large organizations. In *Enderby*, the separate Whitley Council bargaining agreements in the National Health Service (NHS), covering speech therapists and pharmacists, were ultimately held to be discriminatory. Equally, in *British Coal Corp*, female canteen workers and cleaners were able to successfully identify surface mineworkers as comparators in their equal value claim. With the financial support of their unions, and in *Enderby* the EOC, the cases took over ten years to resolve. Given the cost and timescale associated with these lengthy resolutions, the importance of collective representation in enabling claimants to access justice is evident. Just as the value of women's roles within the public sector was under scrutiny, transformation was also underway in the finance industry.

Finance sector restructuring and the introduction of diversity management

During Phase II, the finance sector underwent fundamental change and restructuring. Fluctuations in the work were prompted by the 'Big Bang' in 1986, a phrase coined to describe the sudden deregulation of financial markets. The subsequent implementation of the Financial Services Act 1986 and increases in electronic trading resulted in a 7% growth of financial services, from 1980 to 1990, and an overall output increase of 125% for the sector (McDowell and Court, 1994a; Harkness, 1996).

As home banking and card-based transactions grew, retail banking branch closures were accompanied by a shift in the purely clerical roles for those working there, moving away from the clearing of cheques done centrally in London (O'Reilly, 1992; Daniel, 1999). As the market was reshaped there was a growing focus on marketing in the face of new competition, to take advantage of the opportunities that electronic communication afforded. The role of the bank branch was being reimagined as financial products were increasingly brought and sold, and existing inequalities were reconfigured. The resultant requirement for increased interpersonal skills in branch work, including management, represented a skill set associated with women, and one that they were able to exploit (Bird, 1990). Women began entering more senior positions within the branch, requiring greater expertise, but at the same time, those roles were increasingly given less authority, status and pay (Adams and Harte, 1998). The role of bank manager, as a high-status job for life, was being eroded as work became more centralized and cost cutting led to a reduction in terms and conditions (Crompton and Birkelund, 2000; McDowell, 2008). Alongside these shifts in branch roles, new specialized head office functions were emerging, concentrated in larger central hubs (McDowell and Court, 1994b). Just as the law recognized the ability to compare value and women had entered higher status roles, those roles were devalued.

Alongside these changes there was an increasing interest in gendered inequality in the sector (Crompton, 1989; Metcalf and Rolfe, 2009: 4). Diversity management was introduced as an addition to legal compliance and organizations increasingly adopted equal opportunity policies, as both the moral and commercial benefits to addressing inequities were acknowledged (Oswick and Noon, 2014). All four of the main clearing banks appointed equal opportunity managers in 1986 (Adams and Harte, 1998: 804). This shift was accompanied by wider developments in HRM (Dobbin, 2009), and the strategies pursued created new tensions. Paternalistic and hierarchical approaches, previously common in the sector, were replaced by less transparent performance-related pay (PRP) systems and the need for increased flexibility (Cressey and Scott, 1992: 94–5). These commercially driven responses acted to re-legitimize existing inequalities. The architectural foundations of laissez faire governance and lack of transparency are again reflected in these workplace trends.

Architectural features and limitations

Alongside these examples of sectoral transformation, key collective actors and the changing political, economic and industrial climate are pertinent to the evaluation of the EqVA83. Thatcher's Conservative government ultimately limited the capacity of unions to address unequal pay (Bauld, 2017: 153). Policy measures were designed to increase economic independence and boost the private sector, while undermining the role of trade unions (Moon et al, 1986: 341). The considerable political and organizational change of the time, in this way, obstructed women's ability to access justice and assert their legal rights. The ability to compare the value ascribed to certain skills and areas of employment, fundamental to decreasing the GPG, was, in effect, diminished.

While attempts had been made in the public sector to address inequalities, via the use of job evaluation schemes, this was typically not the case in the private sector. Much like in the finance industry, the usage of PRP schemes was increasing (Rubery and Grimshaw, 2015). Increased privatization in this way supported the tendency for inequalities to be kept hidden. *North Yorkshire CC v Ratcliffe* (1995) helps illustrate how this impacted the pursuit of equal pay. A group of school midday supervisors challenged the council's attempt to dismiss and re-engage them, on lesser terms and conditions. Their successful claim referenced the male council employees, with whom they had established equal pay, that were not put out to tender. However, the pressures of private finance allowed jobs to be downgraded, once outside the scope of this comparison (*Lawrence v Regent Office Care Ltd* (2003)). The potential for equal pay claims was in this way obstructed, as services were increasingly outsourced (Whitehouse et al, 2001).

These trends demonstrate how wider political and economic developments undermined institutional structures and the potential for increased transparency. This phased legal analysis shows how recognition of difference critically broadened the notion of equality alongside key actors contesting those boundaries. However, the pace and momentum for change was slowed by the preference for light-touch governance, the ongoing contradictions of transparency, and foundational inequalities. As institutional approaches developed, this process continued into Phase III.

Phase III, 1998–2010: proactive developments

Key actors and catalysts shaping change

Phase III was marked by a resurgence of interest in addressing inequality as key actors again helped catalyze change. The emergence of no-win-no-fee group litigation during this period highlighted the systemic nature of inequality and signalled the need to review public sector pay and grading systems (Deakin et al, 2015). The conceptualization of equality moved beyond difference to embrace a more proactive approach, with policies such as Gender Mainstreaming (GM), the Open Method of Communication (OMC), and the Gender Equality Duty (GED). However, despite increased liability for failure to address inequality, these approaches were subject to competing tensions. Architectural foundations and structural tensions again help us to understand this broader ongoing process of change and resistance.

GM was adopted as a new European Union (EU) strategy and given binding effect in Member States by the Treaty of Amsterdam in 1999.[5] GM requires the proactive promotion of equality and has been defined as 'the (re) organization, improvement, development and evaluation of policy processes, so that a gender equality perspective is incorporated in all policies at all levels' (Shaw, 2005: 260–1).

The Charter of Fundamental Rights in 2000 underlined the EU commitment to a universal value of equality, with provisions requiring Member States to act accordingly. The OMC was introduced to deepen the EU approach to equality and represented another more proactive, purely soft law approach to the problem. It was applied in the European Employment Strategy in 1997, initially intended for employment policy, though later given a wider remit. Both GM and the OMC incorporated the use of mutual learning, the sharing of best practice and common targets alongside benchmarking and peer review (Beveridge and Velluti, 2008: 3). These measures were intended to work in tandem with the existing hard law framework, where legal obligations are binding for Member States.

These changes prompted Britain's decision to adopt GM as a new strategy to address gender inequality (Squires, 2005). The political climate had shifted with the advent of New Labour in 1997 and their focus on social justice and labour market reform (Buckler and Dolowitz, 2000). However, there are conflicting views over how effective GM and OMC have been. The British preference for soft law approaches has been cited as a means of avoiding more stringent requirements (Beveridge and Velluti, 2008; Fagan and Rubery, 2017: 5). Even in changed political times, the shift to a more self-regulatory voluntarist approach by the EU accorded with Britain's typically laissez faire style of governance (McLaughlin and Deakin, 2011). To illustrate, in 2001 the EOC reported that the UK's combined GPG was the largest of all EU states and had only reduced by 2% over the preceding four years (Parker, 2001). The report recognized a lack of transparency and made a series of recommendations, including that employers be compelled to carry out regular equal pay reviews and that the tribunal procedure be simplified. Following resistance from the business community these EOC recommendations were pursued in an entirely voluntarist capacity (Parker, 2001). These failed attempts at greater transparency highlight how the utility of soft legal rules is invariably impacted by the degree to which key actors accept them or not.

Correspondingly, and with reference to governance, there was an increasing recognition of the economic imperative for change operating alongside the changeable structure of employment. As discussed in Phase II, the need to harmonize pay had been starkly illustrated by the liability in *Enderby* and *British Coal Corp* (1991). This was enhanced by *Magorrian v Eastern Health and Social Services Board* (1998). The case concerned indirect discrimination for part-time workers' occupational pension rights and ultimately extended the maximum compensation for equal pay claimants from two to six years. The impact of this extension can be seen in the number of no-win-no-fee lawyers who subsequently entered the market (Deakin et al, 2015).

In addition to this drive for reform, historical and systemic inequities were also being recognized in other areas. Following the Stephen Lawrence enquiry and Macpherson (1999) report, Britain acknowledged institutional racism, prompting the creation of the Race Equality duty. Introduced in 2001, this attempted to challenge cultural disadvantage and discriminatory attitudes, both within organizations and the services they provide. The Gender and Disability duties followed in 2007. They represented a new understanding of how inequality pervades society and social structures and critically introduced a more proactive approach to tackle systemic organizational failures.

A more proactive and voluntarist conceptualization

Phase III actively targeted disadvantage in its conceptualization of equality (Dickens, 2007: 473). This involved recognizing how apparently neutral practices can have disproportionate outcomes and the need to go beyond equality of opportunity (Barnard and Hepple, 2000: 564). This more comprehensive conception of equality is now discussed with reference to the GED, developments related to the reconciliation of work and family life, and the increased workforce participation of women (Rees, 2005).

The GED was perhaps the most striking of the legislative developments. It signified an attempt to embed gender equality into the heart of public services, implicitly recognizing the detrimental effect of embedded foundational inequalities. This statutory duty represented GM in operation and a shift away from reliance on the individual claimant, to a more positive pre-emptive approach. Public sector bodies needed to establish gender goals and review progress in areas such as occupational segregation, recruitment practices and service delivery.

During this period, regulation such as the Employment Relations Act 1999 (ERA99) and the Employment Act 2002 (EA02) was passed acknowledging the need for a family-friendly discourse within the law and embedded inequalities surrounding care.[6] Measures included therein had the potential to introduce greater flexibility and fairness to some key areas of disparity impacting gender inequities. For instance: the introduction of two weeks' paid paternity leave, alongside 13 weeks' parental leave; increases to maternity provisions; rules regulating the use of fixed-term employees; and the introduction of an equal pay questionnaire. When introducing the measures to the Commons, Alan Johnson stated: "We are extending the safety net of basic employment protection rights to reflect the diversity in today's work force" (*Hansard*, HC Deb., vol. 337 col. 591, 5 November 1999).

The increased gender diversity of the workforce had been firmly established through the 1990s, as women increasingly returned to work after maternity leave. The percentage of returnees in the UK rose from 40% in 1990 to 80% in 2005 (Brannen and Lewis, 2000: 103), illustrating how not only legislation but the challenge confronting it had changed (Smeaton and Marsh, 2006: 3). Regulations were constructed and extended surrounding this shifting gendered cultural template. The competing demands of work and family life were gaining legal voice in this phase of legislative development, visible in this active targeting of inequality.

The development and application of these legal protections demonstrates how key actors responded.

The legal process and case law

The contestation of case law has helped reveal how the law needed to evolve. Tensions often involved overlapping themes, concerning the format and type of work and the difficulty of reconciling with family life. Phase III again illustrates how potentially pre-emptive legal developments were impacted by key actors and the architectural features of transparency and governance. My analysis focuses on part-time work, public sector regrading and collective litigation, and how the legal discourse they generated altered the dynamics of the problem.

In recognition of the inequities concerning hours worked, the Part-Time Work Regulations 2000 (PTWR00) were implemented, prompted by the EU framework agreement for part-time work. They were intended to ensure that part-time workers are treated no less favourably than their full-time counterparts. To use the PTWR00, a part-time claimant needs to identify a full-time comparator. Subsequently the employer can put forward justifications to objectively justify any differential in treatment, which must be legitimate, necessary and appropriate. This introduced a separate stream of protection, additional to the SDA75, for the largely female part-time workforce.

Consideration of how the law was constructed and applied reveals the persistent centrality of existing inequalities, the tendency for free market governance and an undermining lack of transparency. The Labour government chose to apply the PTWR00 to casual workers, going further than the EU Directive, despite political resistance echoing business concerns over competitiveness (*Hansard*, HL Deb., vol. 613 cols 557–64, 22 May 2000). However, the PTWR00 did not allow for hypothetical comparators, which, given the gendered occupational segregation of part-time work, severely restricted their scope (Busby, 2001). Women occupied 80% of the six million mostly low-paid part-time roles in the UK in 2000. It was anticipated that by requiring a comparator, the PTWR00 would only cover one million of those (McBride, 2000). This further emphasized a full-time contract as the standard norm through which other employment should be referenced, despite part-time workers representing a quarter of the UK's workforce (Kilpatrick, 2003: 143; Bell, 2011a: 257).

Article 5 of the Directive also stipulated a two-fold purpose, requiring accompanying statutory guidance intended to improve labour market flexibility and facilitate greater access to part-time work (Bell, 2011a).[7] However Britain chose not to legislate for this soft law proactive element. The combined tensions of key actors in government and business prompted reversion to a more formal rather than substantive approach to the inequality the PTWR00 were attempting to address (Busby, 2001: 346).

The role of key actors in government and competing pressures arising from Phase III's more proactive conception of equality is also evident in the swathe of no-win-no-fee cases already touched upon (Deakin et al, 2015). This increased litigation was, in part, prompted by the introduction of large-scale pay and grading reviews. The Single Status Agreement 1998 (SSA) was introduced in local government and the Agenda for Change 2004 (AFC) in the NHS, to address the inequities between jobs of equal value across the public sector. The collective implementation of these regrading exercises highlighted the historical inequalities of bonus payments, shift enhancements and pay discrimination, and the inherent bias in job evaluation schemes.[8] The EO02 introduced new workplace dispute resolution procedures to encourage disputes to be resolved at the workplace, intended to reduce the cost and burden on the tribunal service.

However, solicitors like Stefan Cross and unions were able to capitalize on the opportunities presented by public sector regrading. Local authorities found themselves liable for eye-watering settlements (*Abdulla v Birmingham City Council* (2012)), demonstrating the transformative impact of multiparty litigation in this area (Deakin et al, 2015).

This also led to the role and liability of unions being challenged, given the pay protection arrangements agreed for male employees, alongside the limitations on back pay for female members who had been underpaid (*GMB v Allen* (2008)). Again, the pervasive relevance of existing inequalities and the contradictions of transparency are evident. By 2008, only half of the local authorities covered by the SSA had fully implemented the agreement (Wright, 2011). While liability ensured that local authorities could not ignore the matter, women were routinely not fully compensated for unequal pay, and cases took many years to resolve. The cost of implementation and remedying historic grading inequalities was not centrally funded, resulting in councils prioritizing stark anomalies in pay while phasing others in over time (Conley and Page, 2018: 293–4).

While regrading was intended to eradicate deeply embedded foundational inequalities, change has remained slow and incremental. This was aptly illustrated in Glasgow 2018 with the occurrence of Britain's largest equal pay strike to date (Brooks, 2018). Resolution of the 12-year regrading, pay protection and equal value claim for over 6,000 local government employees was finally agreed in 2019 (BBC, 2019) (see Chapter 3 for further discussion).

The outsourcing of public sector jobs further limited the potential of regrading to address inequities (Rubery and Grimshaw, 2015). Women in the private sector were not afforded the same protection, job evaluation is significantly less common and the utility of collectivism to address pay anomalies may only just be coming to a limited fruition (Deakin et al,

2015; Butler, 2021) (see Chapter 3 regarding ongoing retail cases). This demonstrates the continual reconstruction of inequalities and ongoing movement within the architectures. To further illustrate, analysis of a sample of equal pay cases from 2000 to 2010 revealed that fewer than a quarter of employing organizations had transparent pay structures (Ware, 2012: 4). This demonstrates the importance of collective opposition in the change process and how individually enforceable rights remain limited and limiting without it. Legislative rights and equality norms take time to embed, are variable according to the organizational context and are themselves subject to emerging challenges and repositioning by key actors. Developments may be uneven across the institutional and organizational spheres, illustrating the utility of the architectures model as a framework for analysis. Movement that counteracts potential progress is not only possible but inevitable. This is further illustrated as developments within the finance industry demonstrate.

High performance and risk taking in the finance sector

Further restructuring throughout the 1990s saw the core banking functions being expanded and new players entering the financial services market (McDowell and Court, 1994a). The increasingly global financial marketplace brought greater competition and choice for the consumer and, with it, ironically, more precarious employment. Technological innovations and automation were in the process of transforming the way that work was done and resulted in job losses across the sector as bank branches were not required in the same way (Daniel, 1999). There was huge growth in automated teller machines (ATMs), customer databases enabled new forms of marketing, and services were diversified, with banks entering those markets (Watkins, 2000: 65). The impact on women was significant, given their concentration in clerical grades undertaking transactional roles, those being the most affected by new technologies. The emergence of new jobs and subsequent regendering illustrates Acker's (1990) theory of gendered organizations in practice. This shows the complexity of the GPG and ongoing interactions between component parts of the architecture as existing inequalities are perpetually reproduced.

The sector was changing as larger merged organizations were created, alongside some smaller new banks during the 1990s and 2000s (Walby, 2009; De Ramon et al, 2017: 20). The evolution of more complex financial institutions saw key banking functions being supplemented by services such as insurance activities and investment banking. Interaction across the global financial markets, enabled by increased electronic communication, required specialized head office roles to be at work to deal with these demands at either end of the working day. The economy became more reliant on these bigger, highly leveraged organizations within which risk-taking cultures were commonplace, further emphasizing the preference for market-driven governance (Annesley and Scheele, 2011). The emergent global financial marketplace, in these ways, enabled existing inequalities to be reconstructed, maintained and legitimized (Davies and Richardson, 2010). This demonstrates dynamism in the architectures as existing patterns of gender inequality were reproduced in relation to what women could achieve in these new organizational structures.

Progressive legal developments recognizing the need to embed equality were matched within the sector by a widespread prominence of equal opportunity policies, although the practical implementation of them was limited (Hoque and Noon, 2004, Özbilgin and Woodward, 2004; Healy et al, 2011). Metcalf and Rolfe (2009) note that equality issues within finance were under less scrutiny than in Phase II (1980s–90s). HRM and organizational ideologies were concentrated on the need to gain a competitive edge, with less concern for the equality implications of pursuing these goals. The wider political economy shifts towards deregulation and free markets saw the broad management discretion within finance override the importance of value added through diversity of thinking (Özbilgin and Tatli, 2011). This again shows how architectural trends continued to impede change and the value of applying a holistic lens to examine the problem.

The trajectory of legislative and GPG development highlights the ebb and flow of layered change throughout this phase. The trend for securing political support and gaining judicial momentum in particular areas of contention was tempered by business arguments and approaches to governance, invariably countering progress and limiting potential. While factors affecting the GPG were increasingly recognized in Phase III, the counterbalancing influence of key actors, alongside the architectural features of limited transparency and light-touch regulation, impeded their potential, representing the ongoing dynamism in the model (Di Torella, 2007: 328).

Conclusion

This chapter has presented an historic account of the periodized legal developments since the passing of the EqPA70 up until 2010, as shown in Table 2.1.

This phased approach has explored how the conceptualization of equality has been determined according to the contestation of key actors, operationalized in law, and then evaluated through the judicial process. This assessment has shown the layered incremental nature of legislative change mapped alongside developments in the finance industry.

This analysis of the efficacy of equality law pertaining to the GPG has demonstrated the obstacles that legal developments and potential claimants face. This has shown how the combined tensions arising from key actors

Table 2.1: Mapping the development of equality law: Phases I–III

Conceptualization of equality	The law and legal discourse	National and industrial politics	The economy and labour market
Phase I: 1970–84 • Equality as sameness • Formal approach to equality • Prohibitive standard • Legal remit firmly focused on the public sphere	**Operationalized by:** • Article 119 ToR57 • ECA72 • EqPA70 • SDA75 **Implications and developments:** • Direct effect (*Van Gend en Loos*) • Social aim of equal pay (*Defrenne*) • Biological difference (*Turley/Hayes*) • Occupational/sectoral segregation	**National politics:** • Joining the EEC • Labour and Conservative administrations • Advent of Thatcherism, deregulation, privatization and free market approach **Industrial politics:** • Widespread trade union membership and bargaining • Mass strikes (Dagenham) • Collectivism of women's movement	**Social and economic junctures:** • Financial crisis • International Monetary Fund (IMF) bailout • Complete overhaul of pay systems • Women entering the labour market • Finance sector manual clerical work for women
Phase II: 1984–98 • Difference • Substantive approach to equality • Equality of opportunity • Focus on public sphere	**Operationalized by:** • Directive 75/117/EEC (*EC v UK*) • EqVA83 • SDA86 **Implications and developments:** • The need for comparators (*Herz & Dekker*) • Objective justification (*Bilka* three-part test) • Multiparty claims beginning	**National politics:** • Thatcherism, deference to market forces, rolling back the state • Purposive judgements ECJ **Industrial climate:** • Sharp decline in trade union membership and collective bargaining • Collective representation of EOC and CAC restricted	**Social and economic junctures:** • Outsourcing and privatization • Women's increasing workforce participation • Growth in PRP • Big Bang and deregulation of financial markets • Growth of specialized finance roles away from bank branch

Table 2.1: Mapping the development of equality law: Phases I–III (continued)

Conceptualization of equality	The law and legal discourse	National and industrial politics	The economy and labour market
Phase III: 1998–2010 • Equality of outcome • Transformative • Institutional inequality • Duality of approach • Implications for the private sphere	**Operationalized by:** • EU: Treaty of Amsterdam, GM, OMC • PTWR00 • EA02: flexible working/maternity and paternity rights **Implications and developments:** • Race and Equality Duty • Public sector regrading (SSA, AFC) • Increase in back pay (*Magorrian*) • Public sector litigation	**National politics:** • New Labour: combined market forces and social justice **Industrial climate:** • Declining trade union membership • Resistance from unions and no-win-no-fee solicitors through multiparty cases	**The economy and labour market:** • 2007–08 financial crisis • Recession • High unemployment • Growth of atypical work • Diversification of finance industry • Emerging global financial marketplace

simultaneously drive and resist the pursuit of gender equality. Further, the capacity of the law to promote change has been impeded by the architectural features of transparency and governance. In Phases I–III, a lack of transparency made accessing legal rights remote, time consuming and costly for potential claimants. Alongside this, the ongoing deference to the apparent needs of business stymied the development of British law.

Positioning this macro-level legal analysis within the broader architectural framework affords a multidimensional view of how factors at the meso and micro level further contribute to the GPG. The legal rules of the game do not represent a level playing field. They are invariably impacted by other factors, such as: pay structures and grading systems; differential growth in public and private sector provisions; and the levels of collective bargaining and union organization in various industries. Legal rules may be applied differently, with variable recourse for individuals, or have different meaning, resonance and applicability.

This socio-legal analysis has shown how societal gender norms have slowly changed, demonstrating the dynamic struggle within each constituent part of the architectures. They are inexorably connected, as legal rules are translated to normative realities.

It is with that in mind that Chapter 3 picks up and develops the feminist socio-legal analysis, investigating the current conceptualization of equality in Phase IV.

Notes

[1] Some types of EU legislation are directly applicable (that is, Regulations and Decisions) while others (that is, Directives) require enacting legislation within Member States. Measures such as Guidelines and Recommendations are not legally binding but present persuasive authority for Member States to act.

[2] The CBI lobbied for a seven-year period of adjustment while the TUC campaigned for two years.

[3] The EEC Equal Value Amendment was raised in February 1974 in the *Official Journal* and by February 1975, Directive 75/117/EEC had been agreed.

[4] Subsequent ECJ cases (*Douglas Harvey Barber v Guardian Royal Exchange* (1991) and *Dietz v Stichting* (1997)) helped further refine Britain's approach to part-time work, ultimately leading to the inclusion of pensions within the concept of pay.

[5] The EEC was incorporated into the EU and renamed by the Maastricht Treaty in 1993.

[6] These provisions implemented the framework agreement on parental leave Directive 96/34/EC and the pregnant workers Directive 92/85/EEC.

[7] Clause 5 of Directive 97/81/EC required 'measures to promote employment and equal opportunities … [and] a more flexible organization of work'.

[8] *Redcar and Cleveland BC v Bainbridge* (2008) and *Middlesbrough BC v Surtees* (2008) are illustrative examples.

Regulating Equal Pay in Britain: The Equality Act 2010 and Beyond

Introduction

The passing of the EqA2010 marked another reconceptualization of the legislative approach towards equality, and the start of Phase IV. Transformative mechanisms have become embedded alongside the streamlining of equality processes, with the capacity to increase both vision on gender pay inequity and the accessibility of the law. This current phase demonstrates another remodelling, building upon the proactive potential of Phase III while, at the same time, being undermined by counterbalancing architectural features.

First, the initiatives introduced and refined within the EqA2010 are outlined. The effectiveness of these potentially transformative provisions, in terms of both streamlining and increasing the accessibility of equality measures, is considered alongside the role of key actors, the judicial process, and the architectural constraints that surround them.

Second, legal developments beyond the EqA2010 that contribute to and are associated with the GPG are examined, highlighting the increasing preference for voluntarist and reflexive requirements. Those targeting the reconciliation of work and family life demonstrate how the architectures of inequality interact to limit effectiveness and restrict change.

Having critically evaluated legal developments and the key actors impacting upon them, I then turn to explore the impact of political, economic and societal shifts. The current legislative space is, in this way, considered alongside the threats, challenges and opportunities that it faces. Developments within the finance sector are mapped to illustrate the interrelationship with the institutional and organizational limbs of the architecture.

Finally, as cultural ideas about gender continue to change, a further reconceptualization of equality and the shift to Phase V is mooted. As the legal contestation of equal pay extends to the private sector and broader societal and economic junctures, such as Brexit and COVID-19, threaten to destabilize progress, the determining effect of key actors and architectural trends remain pervasive.

This chapter places the law firmly within established architectural constructs, highlighting the interrelationship with other social sub-systems. The points of interaction between the different explanatory approaches, arising from foundational inequality, governance and transparency, underline the need for this multilevel evaluation. It is within and around these points of contestation that the goalposts surrounding the aim of achieving pay parity continually shift. This indicates why progress to address the GPG has remained so slow and stalled and helps to suggest pathways to more effective measures in the future.

Phase IV: the Equality Act 2010

The EqA2010 was passed in October 2010 and marks another reconceptualization of equality. The characteristics of this approach are first outlined, followed by an examination of the proactive duties and improved approaches to transparency included within it.

Reconceptualizing equality

The need to update the disparate nature of equality law and recognize the changing nature and understanding of equality in society culminated in the introduction of the EqA2010 (Hepple, 2000). The proposed Equality Bill had included provisions to: tackle socio-economic inequality (section 1); promote equality within the public sector (section 149); and publish GPGs (section 78). However, the inclusion of these provisions in the EqA2010 did not always result in their implementation.

Prior to the Act's passing, Britain's equality laws were spread across 116 separate legislative provisions. These had developed in a piecemeal way, reflected in the inconsistency and complex nature of their approaches. The EqA2010 successfully updated and consolidated existing provisions and, in so doing, provided some much-needed consistency to the law. The EqA2010, in compliance with the EU's better legislation programme, intended to make the various equality strands more readable, accessible and transparent.

The EqA2010 harmonized and reformed the law, introducing new provisions, and reconceptualizing equality in potentially decisive ways. The UK is relatively advanced in its framework of equality and anti-discrimination measures, in part attributable to advances made in the passing of the Act (European Agency for Fundamental Rights, 2019). It attempted to recognize the need for more affirmative action, building on the measures outlined in Phase III, and has been described as 'transformative' (McLaughlin and Deakin, 2011). Part 11, Advancement of Equality, acknowledged that equality law is not just about treating everyone the same, but taking additional steps to level existing inequality. Proactive measures were introduced that attempted to reposition the claimant-centred approach to equality law, specifically acknowledging the need to take positive action to address historical disadvantages (Bell, 2011b).

The section 149 Public Sector Equality Duty (PSED) illustrates this new conceptualization of equality by requiring organizations to pre-emptively change and challenge inequalities (Hepple, 2011). The new single equality duty incorporated the old GED, and required public authorities, and bodies who exercise a public function, to have due regard to the need to advance, rather than merely promote, equality of opportunity (Wadham, 2012). The PSED represented an attempt to embed equality considerations into the public sector provision (GEO, 2013: 15). Demanding change before discrimination occurs demonstrated the shift in direction that efforts to address inequality underwent (Fredman, 2011: 423).

Some equality functions have been devolved to the Scottish Parliament and Welsh Assembly, meaning that the responsibility for determining how the PSED applies now lies within these separate administrations (Women and Equalities Committee, 2019: 6; Pyper, 2020: 15). As a result, the PSED has been used, to varying degrees, as a tool to target the GPG. For instance, in Scotland the PSED required that public bodies publish GPG information and detail on equal pay and occupational segregation, prior to the implementation of the GPRR (Pyper, 2020: 17–18). In Wales the PSED includes an obligation to publish strategic equality plans with consideration of the need to reduce inequalities in pay (Pyper, 2020: 17). This demonstrates the variability in institutional approaches and underlines the importance of the detailed sector-specific focus presented here.

Case law has subsequently confirmed the importance of the duty (*R (on the application of Essex CC) v Secretary of State for Education* (2012). Commentators have noted: 'The courts have developed a jurisdiction that enables them to give extremely close scrutiny to … equality issues' (Hickman, 2013: 343). The PSED has helped to make the principles of equality central to public services (Duggan, 2010: 9).

The transformative effect of the PSED on the way public authorities approach equality issues has been acknowledged; however, the impact on outcomes has not been so clear (GEO, 2013: 15). It has been noted that the requirements of the single equality duty are less prescriptive and potentially diluted the previous duties (Bell, 2011b). It was, and remains, only applicable to the public sector and, given the limited compliance mechanisms in place when local authorities do not comply, is 'virtually unenforceable' (Hepple, 2011: 142).[1] Fredman (2011: 411) further asks why there is only a 'due regard' to remove discrimination in the Act, when an 'express duty' is clearly more appropriate. Foundational architectural tensions are seemingly ever present.

The section 78 GPRR represented a significant legislative development, requiring employers to recognize their own GPGs. This demonstrates the incremental progression of the law and a change from the previously reactive and individualized scope of institutional arrangements. The provision shifted the focus from the individual employee/claimant, to enable vision on the site at which inequality occurs.

Other aspects of transparency in pay were also included in the EqA2010. Section 138 introduced the questionnaire procedure, enabling employees to ask questions to find out whether pay differences were discriminatory. This made pay structures potentially more transparent and the process of challenging inequities more accessible. In addition, while pay secrecy clauses are still legitimate, section 77 rendered them unenforceable when an employee is seeking a relevant pay disclosure. Under section 124, tribunals were given powers to make recommendations to benefit the wider workforce. This power enabled rulings to be given not just in favour of the claimant but relating to the whole workforce. For instance, in *Tantum v Travers Smith Braithwaite Service* (2013) the Employment Tribunal (ET) recommended the company implement diversity training for all their staff. This represented a development away from the wholly claimant-centred reach of the outcome. More broadly, these provisions demonstrate how the most recent phase has challenged the architectural barrier of transparency.

The importance of the multiple identities that people hold and the 'intersectional' way that inequalities operate was first labelled by Crenshaw (1989). Inclusion of the section 14 dual discrimination provision indicated acknowledgement of intersectional inequality. The section 1 socio-economic duty was intended to highlight and address the impact that factors such as housing, education and social status can have on an individual. The provision required public bodies to consider the impacts of public policy decisions on socio-economic markers. In so doing it had the capacity to recognize the multifaceted ways that inequality works and address their marked occurrence. Despite the importance and potential of these provisions, they have not yet been brought into force.

Positive action in recruitment and promotion was enabled by section 159. This acknowledged that additional support might be required by those with protected characteristics, to address unequal representation in the workplace.

If fully implemented, these provisions highlight how the EqA2010 could help address the obstacles claimants face in a more proactive way, broadening access to the law and enhancing its impact. The effectiveness of these measures and their enactment is now considered.

Foundational architectures and resurgent limitations

The adjustment of institutional arrangements and the shifting dynamics within the architectures model were again slow and stalled. Potentially transformative provisions met with resurgent limitations as key actors impacted the effectiveness of this Phase IV conceptualization. This demonstrates the continued relevance of both government and business and how they operate according to architectural constraints.

The incremental development of legal structures and barriers to implementation can be observed when assessing the development of these provisions. The socio-economic duty and dual discrimination elements were not brought into force by the incumbent coalition government. Prohibitive costs, increased bureaucracy and the burdensome effect on business were cited, reflecting Britain's ongoing preference for light-touch governance (Bell, 2011b; GEOa, 2013).

In 2012, the government went further and repealed some requirements already in force (GEO, 2012; Bazeley, 2019). Powers for wider recommendations were removed, meaning that employers are no longer compelled to address liability in relation to their wider workforce. While the potential for collectivism was already limited, given the declining strength of trade unions, this again restricted the courts' reach to the individual claimant. The questionnaire procedure was repealed and the planned PSED review was brought forward (GEO, 2013). The wider repositioning of the public sector and the PSED's limited application suggests an ambivalence in its aims. The government's reiteration of light-touch governance did nothing to encourage private sector employers to follow suit and embed proactive and transparent measures to address inequalities.

Similarly, the newly elected coalition government did not enact mandatory pay reporting, pursuing voluntary measures in the first instance, despite increasing recommendations from the EU and EOC. In 2011, the government devised 'Think, Act Report' to encourage employers to voluntarily report on gender and equality issues. Enacted by the Equality Act (Gender Pay Reporting) Regulations, the requirement finally came into force in April 2017. This provision (examined in Chapter 4) requires annual publication of pay and bonus gap details and marked a significant shift from voluntarism to compliance. The consultation it has since prompted, with reference to the publication of ethnicity and disability pay gaps, demonstrates the transformative nature of the wholesale approach to equality that is afforded by the EqA2010 (Adams et al, 2018).

These examples demonstrate how the government agenda and business interests have responded to architectural barriers, reflecting the underlying preference for a limited regulatory burden, alongside the multi-level resistance to greater transparency (Dickens, 2007). Even the significant development of the GPRR is limited by the lack of granularity in bonus and quartile reporting and the lack of compulsion surrounding the accompanying narrative (Murray et al, 2019). The fundamental relationship of key actors (government, business, the judicial process, unions, and social movements) with legislative development is evidenced by the political inclination in these decisions. The equality agenda has been promoted, retrenched, reversed, or failed to implement, to varying degrees (Riddell and Watson, 2011). This presents the objective of the EqA2010 as a constantly shifting paradigm, whereby the conceptualization of equality, in terms of how proactive it is, is varied and contested.

Another central objective in the passing of the Act was the goal of simplifying equality legislation to make it more accessible, though effectiveness here is also debatable (Feast and Hand, 2015). Case law and collective resistance provide illustrative examples.

Contestation in the courts and collectivism

The difficulties of pursuing an equal pay claim, in terms of knowledge, access and support (see Chapter 2), continued in Phase IV. When dealing with an equal pay claim, Lord Justice Mummery said: "The situations presented to the tribunals can sometimes hover on the verge of non-justiciability" (*Audit Commission v Haq* (2012): para. 13). Mummery LJ noted the high cost and unpredictable nature of equal pay cases but, in so doing, recognized the difficulties of simplifying this task. The very essence of the problem is a significant clash between employer and employee. The intricate and embedded nature of the problem being addressed, and the imbalance of power in these relationships, makes attempts to resolve inequities equally troublesome.

The issue of accessibility and the potential of the law to address embedded and historic inequalities can be illustrated with reference to the Glasgow multiparty equal pay case, first referenced in Chapter 2. This protracted saga, involving over 6,000 claimants, illustrates how the translation of legal rights to individual realities is overwhelmingly complex. At issue in *Glasgow City Council v Fox Cross Claimants* (2014) was the question of whether female employees, who had been transferred from their city council employer, could be construed for comparison purposes as working for an associated employer. The court held they were, and the equal pay claim progressed. A subsequent and associated claim, *HBJ Claimants v Glasgow City Council* (2017), found a job evaluation scheme, introduced because of the SSA, invalid. While the matter was seemingly on the verge of being resolved, as the council decided not to appeal to the Supreme Court in 2018, negotiations to conclude a settlement between unions and employers then broke down (Brooks, 2018). Consequently, Britain's largest equal pay strike took place at the end of October 2018. The conclusion of the case in

2019 has since resulted in further contestation over the settlement of legal fees, given the variety of unions and no-win-no-fee solicitors involved in the dispute (BBC, 2019).

The Glasgow case illustrates how some of the difficulties, first highlighted in Chapter 2, remain: cost; the complexity of multiparty actions; the substantial length of time for cases to proceed and reach conclusion; the difficulty of undertaking regrading agreements; and the embedded nature of the underlying problem. These factors allow resistance to creep in at various levels. This 12-year battle clearly demonstrates the gendered template, both in terms of the unequal value claimants were subject to and in the choice to pursue regrading at nil cost. The lack of transparency in pay practices and the inaccessibility of the judicial system remains obstructive and cumbersome for equal pay claimants, undermining the potential to resolve inequities. This is further highlighted by the potential pending equal pay case against Dundee City Council (Livingston, 2021).

Having noted the intractable difficulties of the legal pursuit of equal pay and the restrictive role of some key actors, conversely unions and lawyers in multiparty cases have exerted a positive influence. This also demonstrates the incremental potential of the law in shifting normative values. In *Asda Stores Ltd v Brierley* (2021) claimants are challenging gendered disparities within their pay. Here several factors have been contested, though the legal battle continues. The case has already considered the question of whether pay rates achieved through collective bargaining for the well-organized male warehouse and distribution workers can be compared to the rates paid to the typically less-organized female shop floor staff. In addition, the Supreme Court has held that, while the comparator for the shop floor claimants does not work at the same physical location, the common terms requirement has been established. Conclusion of the matter is likely to be some years away, however the ramifications of the case across a spectrum of retail organizations is already significant (Leigh Day, 2023). To date, around 44,000 claimants from Sainsburys, Co-op, Tesco, Morrisons and Next are part of the wider claim, with liabilities estimated at around £8 billion (Butler, 2018). This demonstrates the complexity of unpicking the notion of value when foundational inequities are so ingrained. It also highlights the importance of the architectures model in understanding the interrelationship between institutional arrangements, meso-level organizational structures, and the micro-level norms and values that impact upon both.

Understanding this interaction and the potential for equal pay rules to become more embedded is relevant not just for this new era of private sector cases, but in the continued volume of them. For example, in 2018–19, equal pay claims were the second most common to be lodged at tribunal. Figure 3.1 shows the level of claim receipts and disposals.

Figure 3.1: Equal pay cases lodged and disposed of at employment tribunal 2007–20

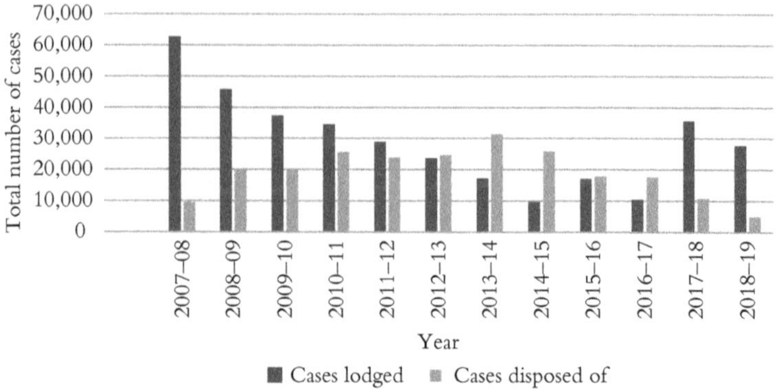

Source: Author's own analysis of Ministry of Justice Tribunal statistic data, available at Tribunal Statistics Quarterly: October to December 2020 – GOV.UK (www.gov.uk). Contains public sector information licensed under the Open Government Licence v3.0.

The lack of relationship between cases lodged and then disposed of demonstrates the time taken for any resolution. The mismatch between the two also demonstrates the consistently high level of cases that are withdrawn. The lack of visibility in how these matters are concluded, and the tendency for this to occur, speaks volumes about the individualized processes associated with taking a case and the pervasive lack of transparency that engulfs the problem (Scott, 2019). This also underlines the difficulty of simplifying and addressing the inaccessibility of equal pay provisions, as illustrated by the *Glasgow* cases and the potentially pending Dundee case (Livingston, 2021). In recognition of these difficulties, the Fawcett Society has set up an advice service to assist women attempting to resolve equal pay disputes (though this does not support litigation).[2]

While the prevalence of cases is, on the one hand, shocking some 50 years on from the EqPA70, the resurgence of the matter in recent years has inevitably assisted in the recognition and definition of some pay gaps as unequal pay. High profile cases, such as *Ahmed v BBC* (2020), have combined with the GPRR to help highlight the need for a more progressive approach.

The impact of key actors is starkly highlighted by the reduction in claim receipts in 2013–14, reflecting the government's introduction of tribunal fees. Despite the supposed intention of the EqA2010 to make equality law more accessible, the introduction of this measure, as part of the government's austerity drive and reflecting architectural governance trends, had a hugely detrimental effect. It further reiterated the notion of equal pay as an individual concern, for which wider societal responsibility was not necessary or required. Yet, as Figure 3.1 and the case law discussion here and in Chapter 2 have shown, this is at odds with the experiences of claimants.

The graph also indicates how other key actors have refined their approach. Law firms have continued to act independently but alongside trade unions, so a lack of union membership has not necessarily been a barrier in terms of accessing legal support. For example, the *Glasgow* local authority claim has seen unions and no-win-no-fee lawyers working collaboratively to represent claimants (BBC, 2019). This shift has also assisted the potential for multiparty actions for private sector claimants in large organizations with similar job roles, as per the retail example. Claimants from Asda are being represented by law firm Leigh Day alongside the GMB union's legal department (Prescott, 2021). Further evidence of this move can be found in the US, where long-running group litigation against Goldman Sachs has achieved an equal pay settlement of $215 million (Franklin and Miller, 2023).

The importance of the role of organized labour was also highlighted by litigation challenging the implementation of tribunal fees. A judicial review case, brought by UNISON (*R (on the application of UNISON) v Lord Chancellor* (2017)), highlighted the discriminatory impact of the fees, and led to the abolition of the measure. However, aside from this initial cost, the difficulties faced by claimants and the fundamental power imbalance in the system remain restrictive.[3]

The capacity of the legal system to address gender pay inequity extends beyond the EqA2010. This Phase IV conceptualization can be further evidenced by these associated measures and their relationship to architectural limitations.

Beyond the Equality Act 2010
Potential transformations and restrictive foundations

Surrounding the EqA2010, potentially transformative and proactive provisions have developed. Analysis now considers those targeting the intersection of work and family life, how key actors reproduce foundational inequalities, and the interrelationship of the broad architectures of inequality that surround these policies.

The effect of parenthood and childcare on GPGs is well understood. The tendency for women to take on the majority of childcare is inevitably impacted by the legislative and cultural landscape. For instance, maternity leave had, at this point, developed without state support of any alternative (Datta Gupta, 2018). Explicit reference to this wider cultural landscape was debated in several cases around the time of the EqA2010's passing. Cases such as *Hacking and Paterson v Wilson* (2010), *Cooper v House of Fraser* (2012), and *Chandler v American Airlines* (2011) concerned restrictions on working hours and the impact on women as carers, ultimately helping to prompt legislative development surrounding the EqA2010.

Britain's regulatory response to the EU Directive on parental leave in 2010 was illustrative of the shifting and yet distinctive response of key actors within the existing legal framework in Britain. The Directive set out minimum requirements intended to help reconcile work and family life. The Shared Parental Leave (SPL) Regulations, subsequently enacted in 2014, unusually went further than the Directive mandate (which did not require the leave to be paid).[4] This represented a significant legislative development, potentially enabling men and women to share parenting, while recognizing and attempting to accommodate the changing shape and needs of families. The shift in direction reflected increasing pressure for greater equality within government from the Women and Equalities Select Committee (2018) and organizations such as the TUC (2015), Fawcett Society (2018a) and Working Families (2018). However, its effectiveness is inherently limited. The mother is required to forgo her maternity leave and have employment status in order that parental leave be shared. In addition, the rate of pay once eligibility is established is low.[5] An annual international review of leave policies finds the 'UKs parental leave is amongst the weakest' lagging behind other European countries (Moss and Koslowski, 2021).

The SPL financial differential and entitlement for men and women has been contested. Case law has questioned the level of pay men can receive, alongside concerns over the threat of levelling down and losing existing rights for women. The charity Working Families intervened in *Capita Customer Management Ltd v Ali* (2018), where the purpose of maternity leave (ML) was discussed.[6] The tribunal found that ML is for the health and wellbeing of the mother and so cannot be a comparator for SPL. This highlights some of the binary gendered cultural boundaries associated with care and the persistence of foundational limitations. It also underlines the need to approach parenthood as a shared endeavour. Consequently, the bound together entitlement of SPL, rather than providing a standalone addition to ML, reinforces the notion of the mother as primary carer, 'eschewing gender equality for the idea that women should be the main carers of young children' (Moss and Koslowski, 2021).

The complexity of the SPL Regulations, a lack of understanding, awareness and promotion within organizations, limitations over who can apply and, critically, the question of pay, have all been mooted to account for the low take up (Taylor, 2017; BITC, 2018). Government estimates this at between 2 and 8%, while Maternity Action suggests it is between 3% and 4% (Dunstan, 2021; Scully and Miliband, 2021). Analysis by the TUC (2023) finds that one in four parents do not take any paternity leave, as they are unable to afford it. This demonstrates how legal requirements, organizational policy and women's normative investments in the workplace and the home are distinct and overlapping components of the architectures of inequality. Societal norms concerning care are pervasive and foundational to the architectural model insulated here by the lack of opacity in the regulations.

Despite the transformative potential of the EqA2010, and associated legislation such as the SPL Regulations, the resurgence of these foundational limitations helps account for the slow movement in the GPG. While the legal architecture has been extended, sociological aspects, such as cultural norms and values, limit its effectiveness. Within this context, the preference for voluntarist light-touch governance legislative approaches is now explored.

The development of combined approaches

The development of legal provision from Phases III–IV indicated a greater proactive capacity alongside an ongoing reluctance to proscribe and enforce change. This highlights the relevance of the architectures model, as institutional arrangements were very much dependent on commitment to engage at the organizational level. This is now demonstrated by the variable success of the Women on Boards initiative and gender pay reporting (BIS, 2015; EHRC, 2018).

In 2011, the EU created a non-binding Resolution concerning corporate gender imbalance. This followed efforts, most notably by Britain, to block more prescriptive legislation and quotas (Guerrina and Masselot, 2018). The Resolution outlined steps that should be taken by Member States to address the imbalance, with a Directive to follow, should voluntary measures prove unsuccessful (Fagan and Rubery, 2017: 15, Guerrina and Masselot, 2018).[7] These EU developments prompted Britain's pursuance of measures in this regard, most notably the Lord Davies report (BEIS, 2011), establishing the Women on Boards initiative, and, more recently, the Hampton-Alexander Review (BEIS, 2017). These combined voluntary and business-led approaches have targeted development and, to a degree, successfully mobilized a changing attitude. For example, the 2015 Lord Davies report target of 25% women on FTSE 100 boards was achieved, and the 33% Hampton-Alexander for the FTSE 250 was met by the end of 2020 (BIS, 2015; BEIS, 2017; BEIS, 2020; Hampton, 2021). This represents a degree of change in Britain, whereby the ambit of self-regulation has in some cases aligned the business case for equality with an element of corporate social responsibility (McLaughlin and Deakin, 2011: 1).

A much less successful attempt at voluntarism can be demonstrated by the 2011 'Think, Act, Report' initiative. This required companies to think about gender equality issues in the workplace, take action to improve them, and report on progress. Given the coalition government's preference for this voluntary approach, the section 78 pay reporting provision was not initially enacted. 'Think, Act, Report' encouraged companies to publish their own pay data, highlighting the potential benefits of retaining and developing quality staff, the reputational effect of increased gender awareness and the opportunity publication would afford to promote good work. However, after three years only five companies had reported their GPG (Wintour, 2015). As such, the GPRR were brought into force, with the EHRC setting out compliance procedures since March 2018 (EHRC, 2018). The narrative accompanying the report is not specifically required. It can therefore be perceived as a combination of voluntarist proactive principles, alongside a regulatory requirement for monitoring and compliance.

Analysis has demonstrated how architectural trends and key actors have impacted the scope, shape and implementation of legislative measures. Key actors impact inequality by exerting influence in complex ways, both shifting the debate forwards and obstructing progress. The importance of a multilevel understanding of how rights, organizations and societal norms interact is further illustrated by the economic and societal junctures that have impacted inequality.

Key actors, economic junctures and change

The political choices made in the aftermath of the 2007–08 financial crisis highlight how key actors in government shape the effectiveness of legal approaches to inequality. The crisis prompted significant repercussions resulting in a deep recession, both within the UK and Europe, and the government's programme of austerity (Clarke et al, 2011; Taylor-Gooby, 2013: 3). Discussion now addresses how the crisis impacted legislative interventions.

The electorate had lost faith in the Labour Party, with blame for the crash in part attributed to their light-touch approach to governance and lack of financial regulation (Diamond, 2013: 95; Jackson, 2018). Following the 2010 election, a Conservative/Liberal Democrat coalition was formed and chose to address the government deficit through austerity politics and an unprecedented reduction in state spending (Taylor-Gooby, 2013; Alston, 2018). This approach impacted equality measures in several ways.

Welfare spending was overhauled with the application of more stringent eligibility criteria, the freezing of some social security payments, the introduction of a benefit cap, alongside pay freezes applied across the public sector (Albertyn et al, 2014; Lambie-Mumford and Green, 2017; Macleavy, 2018). Despite the adoption of GM (see Chapter 2), and the commitment to pay 'due regard' to the need to advance equality of opportunity as per the PSED requirements, changes were implemented without any reference to the inequality of impact they may have. It has since been widely noted that this package of measures led to increasing inequalities, felt most by women and those with 'intersecting disadvantages' (Taylor-Gooby, 2013: 12; Rubery,

2015; Sanders et al, 2019). Durbin et al (2017) note the double disadvantage of austerity policies, given the limitations placed on mechanisms designed to promote equality that accompanied the cuts.

Despite the growing preference for reflexive legislation, demonstrated by GM and the PSED, austerity served to deprioritize equality. There were no equality impact assessments (EIAs) carried out on the programme of government cuts; the 'need' to reduce national debt legitimized associated impacts (Conley and Page, 2018).

This shift in gender relations is further reiterated by the subsequent abolition of EIAs, part of David Cameron's intention to reduce unnecessary government bureaucracy (Pyper, 2018: 22). This was part of a series of measures, known as the 'Red Tape Challenge', introduced in April 2011 (Cabinet Office, 2011). This demonstrates the vital nature of the relationship between law and society, not only in the introduction and application of legislative measures, but also the varied interpretation and abolition of them.

From May 2014, associated employment law reforms were also progressed, including: extending the qualifying period for unfair dismissal rights from one to two years; the introduction of tribunal fees, as already flagged; and mandatory early conciliation (Dickens, 2014).[8] These measures were intended to give employers greater freedoms and reduce the cost of tribunals (Pyper et al, 2017). These reforms illustrate how the 2007–08 economic crisis, and the approach pursued in its aftermath, shifted gender relations (Albertyn et al, 2014: 423).[9] Having legitimized cuts in spending as necessary, women bore a dual burden in terms of impact. Benefit reductions and the increased stringency of eligibility led to an increase in the unpaid care burden. This was accompanied by the shrinking public sector, in which a significant proportion of women work, putting largely female-supported services beyond the remit of the PSED (Taylor-Gooby, 2013: 14–16). Gender equality was not a key priority in this time of crisis, with policy development in Britain and Europe brought to a 'quasi-halt' (Masselot, 2015: 350). This 'fair weather' (Dickens, 2005: 189) approach to equality is again evident in the wake of the pandemic, given the decision to suspend enforcement of the GPRR. The architectures model provides a useful way to visualize this change, demonstrating how extensions in one area may be counterbalanced or offset by developments elsewhere.

The preference for light-touch equality initiatives can be understood within this context, given the capacity of other factors to diminish their importance. The blame for the financial crisis was partly attributed to the lack of diversity in the sector. As such, on the one hand, business can acknowledge the problem while retaining the ability to determine its own approaches, at the same time they can legitimately maintain the freedom to deprioritize efforts, should the 'need' arise. The restrictive effect of embedded inequalities, a lack of transparency and this deference to business needs continually relegitimize GPGs. Efforts to counter them are positioned as 'nice to have' add-ons. Application of the architectures model helps to demonstrate how the ever-shifting role of key actors continually reconfigures inequalities in this way.

There has been a revived focus on GPGs underlining the importance and momentum of collective resistance driving change, despite the declining remit of unions (Deakin et al, 2015). The #timesup and #metoo social media campaigns have prompted a widespread public narrative about the experience of harassment and abuse for women, challenging these societal norms and behaviours. Coinciding with the implementation of the GPRR in Britain, these social movements undoubtedly helped redouble their impact. The furore surrounding gender pay inequities at the BBC, the Gracie and Ahmed equal pay disputes, and their subsequent target of a 0% pay gap by 2020 are illustrative (Kentish, 2018). However, a public forum for debate around victims of inequality is not a panacea and does not, of itself, signal meaningful change. What it has done is starkly highlight the multitude of ways that inequality pervades society and social interaction. This reiterates the historic lack of transparency surrounding the problem and the importance of openness.

The interactions between the combined elements in the architectures of inequality are central to understanding resistance and the potential for change. The organizational willingness to voluntarily publish reports in 2020 may also be read in this light. It seems the reputational impact of engagement with the problem is now operating beyond legislative compliance (see Chapter 4).

Analysis of the finance sector during this period provides another perspective from which to assess institutional development and the effect of key actors in the workplace.

Voluntarism and regulatory change within the finance sector

The financial crisis prompted a huge financial bail-out amounting to 80% of GDP, as banking organizations were deemed by the government to be 'too big to fail'. The crisis resulted in significant spending cuts, across the economy as a whole and within the sector itself (Prosser, 2011; Taylor-Gooby, 2013). Between 2008 and 2010 up to 186,111 jobs were lost within the finance industry (Gall, 2017: 2). For those remaining in post, there was restructuring to cut costs, which, in turn, led to increased workloads, emphasizing a long-hours culture.

Regulatory changes were pursued to offset future risk, prompting further repercussions at the workplace. An Independent Commission on Banking (ICB) was established to promote financial stability and avert the risk of financial crises in the future. Recommendations were made for structural separation, in the form of ringfencing requirements between retail, wholesale and investment banking (Korotana, 2016). Measures were introduced to ensure banks are better capitalized, restricting highly leveraged banking practices (ICB, 2011). The resultant Banking Reform Act 2013 intended to contain the risks that had manifested in the earlier crisis (Parise and Shenai, 2018).

Alongside the ICB's focus on the regulatory framework, recognition was given to the causative impact of the lack of equality and diversity, particularly at senior levels (Treasury Committee, 2010). Blame for the crash has been attributed to the widely favoured entrepreneurial masculinities and risk-taking culture within the sector (Walby, 2009; Annesley and Scheele, 2011). The lack of group think has been flagged as contributing to ineffective decisions, such as an increased willingness to lend and the pursuance of risky returns (Wilson, 2014; Guerrina and Masselot, 2018). Interestingly, the EHRC (2009) focus was purely through a gendered lens. The importance of intersectional sensibilities to understand how women navigate organizational settings, and the barriers they face, was not considered relevant (Acker, 1990; Acker, 2006; Britton and Logan, 2008). The lack of recognition of race, socio-economic status and other protected characteristics in the various post-financial crisis reports concerning inequities is marked (EHRC, 2009; Metcalf and Rolfe, 2009; Treasury Committee, 2010). This one-dimensional approach to the inequities in the sector is at odds with the apparent need for diversity of thinking.

Alongside the combined and business-led approaches already described, a similar inquiry was launched specifically within finance to address the lack of women at senior levels. As a result, in 2016 HM Treasury launched the Women in Finance Charter (WiFC) (HM Treasury, 2016).

Pressure from key actors at both the institutional (EU and UK government), and organizational level (firm based) to implement initiatives has combined to both create and limit change. The level of WiFC signatories certainly suggests that there is organizational pressure to conform, as does the commitment to targets visible in the GPRR accompanying narratives (see Chapter 4). This voluntary measure requires organizations to set self-determined targets for women's representation in a self-defined management population. The fifth annual review of progress to date notes the broad remit of organizational ambitions, with nearly 50% of companies hoping to achieve 40%+ representation of women at senior level. The review also shows that, while two thirds increased or maintained their proportion of senior women, one third reported a decline (Chinwala et al, 2022: 6). There is a clear divergence across the industry. To illustrate: global and investment banking firms reported only 26% of women in senior roles in 2021 (up from 25% in 2019); gender balance in senior management increased from 31% in 2019 to 33% in 2022; these firms typically have the lowest ambition and lowest average target (31%) (Chinwala et al, 2020; Chinwala et al, 2022: 10).

While the annual reviews show an increased level of compliance with WiFC commitments, over 30% still did not publish the required update, resulting in 14 signatories being removed by HM Treasury in 2020 (Seddon-Daines et al, 2019; Chinwala et al, 2020: 21). A continually challenging aspect of the charter, the publication of progress demonstrates the trend for policies that do not walk the talk is ongoing (Dickens, 2005) (see Chapter 7). In 2021, 59% of firms did not publish an update (Chinwala et al, 2022: 23). This demonstrates the impact of the continued preference for voluntarism and the competing mechanisms in operation in different parts of the sector. These tensions between continuity and change indicate where combined, collective and sustained movements of key actors are needed to challenge the status quo and remodel the blueprint (O'Reilly et al, 2015). This examination shows how the targeting of change is inevitably framed by the architectures of inequality that surround it: developed and legitimized by existing management structures, by normative values at the sectoral level, and by the wider institutional framework.

The one-dimensional focus on diversity can also be understood within this context. The narrative surrounding inequities within the finance sector have mostly been described as a problem of gender equality, and one that has largely focused on the representation of women and less on the gendered equality of pay. While initiatives such as the Race at Work Charter (introduced in 2018), and the consultation over race and ethnicity reporting, were encouraging, any regulatory reform and a thorough intersectional analysis of the sector remain to be executed (CRED, 2021).

The support for such measures is growing. In September 2021 a petition to introduce mandatory ethnicity reporting reached more than 130,000 signatures, alongside a joint call from unions, business leaders and the UK's equality watchdog to publish a timeframe for implementation (Dray, 2021; TUC, 2021). Despite the growing public visibility of the problem, levels of voluntary publication remain limited. In 2021 only 13 of the FTSE 100 published their ethnicity pay gaps (Roach, 2021). Likewise, achievement of the voluntary targets for boardroom diversity, as set out in the Parker Review, demonstrate the inadequacies of a non-mandatory approach (Parker, 2020). More research is needed, as exposing the issues that are obscured from view is an important step towards addressing them. To illustrate, analysis by the Bridge Group (2023: 5) has shown that women from a low socio-economic background face a 'double disadvantage' in terms of efforts to reach seniority and the speed at which they do so. Understanding these kinds of intersectional impacts is another critical development in the conceptualization of inequality.

As the finance sector continues to evolve, occupational segregation and resegregation persists (Skuratowicz and Hunter, 2004). The gendered substructure remains pervasive, as emergent roles continually re-establish structural inequalities (Acker, 2012). The repositioning of gender within organizations demonstrates the importance of both sector and occupation-specific analysis (Burchell et al, 2014). This phased historical analysis has shown the growing divergence between the status and pay of those in the branch network and those in head office, as terms and conditions, such as pension benefits, have been reduced (Gall, 2017). Weil (2014) suggests that this process will continue as the sector mirrors the process of fissuring and polarization that has been seen in other industries. Fissuring occurs as the trend for higher profits and erosion of mid-level jobs is accompanied by a growth in less stable work and conditions for those at the bottom of the income scale. Reorganization typically occurs during periods of economic decline and instability, which has been a characteristic of the post-financial crisis period.

This goes beyond the well-documented outcomes of globalization, lower union density and technical innovations. While the changes outlined within the sector were undoubtedly propelled and impacted by the financial crisis, Gall (2017: 183) goes further, suggesting that offshoring, automation and branch closures would have taken place regardless of the crash. The introduction of ringfencing requirements (post financial crisis) and, as described in Chapter 4, the varied classification of financial services across different standard industrial classification (SIC) codes, are an example of how this fissuring makes it increasingly difficult to map the development of the GPG within the sector: companies separate highly lucrative and high-status services from more routine operations into distinct organizational structures. Underpinned by sociological sensibilities and cultural ideas about gender, new manifestations of the same problem mark the ongoing movement in the architectures model, while at the same time demonstrating how foundations remain firm.

Understanding these historic trends and current intransigence is useful in anticipating the trajectory of the GPG as we move towards Phase V.

The emergence of Phase V

The impact of the financial crisis, and the political and economic uncertainty in its aftermath, has been linked in this chapter to the deprioritization of gender and increasing levels of poverty and unemployment in Britain (Goodwin and Heath, 2016). As such, a changed governance model, resulting from Brexit, alongside the impact of shifts in the world of work and the potential effects of the pandemic, are now considered, with reference to how equality measures are evolving beyond Phase IV.

The UK's EU Referendum was held in June 2016 and, while gender was not a determining element in voting trends, socio-economic factors such as class, education and generational distinctions were significant (Goodwin and Heath, 2016; Hobolt, 2016; O'Reilly et al., 2016). While any gendered effects of leaving the EU are yet to manifest, it is appropriate to acknowledge, given the spectre of shifting goalposts in Britain's equality landscape, that this will lead to a shift in gender relations (Macleavy, 2018: 1–2). Women, and women's issues were marginalized throughout the debate, from the Referendum campaign to the leave negotiations (Guerrina and Masselot, 2018). This deference to other apparently more important factors was underlined by the lack of women involved in the negotiation process. Given the model of the previous chapter, and the themes identified and continued in Phase IV, it is also worth recognizing the potentially tenuous basis of legislative developments thus far. The implications of Brexit, in terms of lack of recourse to developments within the EU and the ECJ, suggest another reconceptualization of equality is imminent. The post-Brexit risk to equality rights in the UK has already manifested as the vulnerability of the 'single source' test illustrates (BBC, 2023). On the contrary, within the EU pay transparency requirements have progressed. After ten years of stalemate a 40% mandatory quota for women at boardroom level has finally been agreed (Wigand, 2021; Rankin, 2022). Alongside these developments, in the UK a voluntary pay transparency pilot scheme was launched in March 2022, with participating employers committing to publish salary details on job adverts (GEO, 2022). However, analysis by Adzuna (2022) shows that the level of jobs advertised in the UK with salary details has been falling over the last six years: from 61% in 2016 to 44% in 2022. Unsurprisingly, disclosure of remuneration in senior roles is lower still.

Alongside these political shifts, the world of work has also undergone change. Atypical working patterns underwent a sharp increase in the post-financial crisis period (Clarke and Cominetti, 2019). The growth of precarious work in Britain's job market is expected to continue and projected to exacerbate existing inequality of income (Caruso, 2018). Women occupy the majority of zero-hour and casual contracts in the UK (Mandl et al, 2015; Meager, 2019; Verdin and O'Reilly, 2020). The lack of security and benefits, such as sick pay and holiday pay for non-standard workers, highlight the inequities inherent within precarious work arrangements. This has been recognized by the government in the Taylor Review, and with stark consequences during the pandemic (Taylor, 2017; Hendy, 2020; Paul, 2020; Wong, 2020). All the while, the 'deafening silence' from government to address these issues remains (Partington, 2021).

While organizing these workers industrially is challenging, emerging forms of organized labour demonstrate the importance of unions to address inequalities (Però, 2020, Staton, 2020, Joyce et al, 2022). In addition, progressive development has been afforded by the courts in the absence of government action to reconsider legal categories of employment (*Pimlico Plumbers v Smith* (2018), *Uber BV v Aslam* (2021)), and recognize the importance of intersectionality (*O'Reilly v BBC* (2010), *Hewage v Grampian Health Board* (2012)).

Since 2020 the most prescient of these challenges is undoubtedly the pandemic. Foundational and entrenched gendered and intersectional inequalities have been brought to the fore: highlighted as a result of school closures during the British national lockdowns, and visible for keyworkers and those more likely to work in shutdown sectors (Queisser et al, 2020; Summer, 2020). In addition, the absence of women in the response to the crisis has been noted within Britain and globally (Fuhrman and Rhodes, 2020; Norman, 2020; Wenham, 2020). Britain's COVID-19 response plans were shaped without women's experiences in mind. The subsequent and disproportionate impact of care demands on women's productivity and career development has been evidenced as a result (Landivar et al, 2020; Toyin Ajibade et al, 2021).

The trend to deprioritize equality provisions due to economic forces and the need to maintain competitiveness has continued. The burdensome nature of the GPRR was used as the rationale for withdrawing the compulsion to report in 2019–20. The announcement of a six-month extension to the reporting deadline for 2020–21 again demonstrates a deference to the needs of business, and equality as a secondary concern (GEO, 2021).

That said, despite suspension organizations demonstrated a willingness to voluntarily report (see Chapter 4). In addition, there are voices within government supporting the increased need for gender equality measures (Fawcett Society, 2020). The visibility of these voices will be fundamental in shaping the next inevitable reconfiguration of the problem. In turn the architectures of inequality will no doubt continue to counterbalance developments.

Conclusion

Gender pay inequity is a socially constructed problem. This analysis has shown how the conceptualization, operationalization and implications of legislative approaches have been shaped by key actors, restrictive foundations and resurgent limitations. The pressures exerted by government, both in Britain and the EU, the interests of business, the role of the judicial process, and collectivism in its various forms have been fundamental to both the development and scaling back of legal initiatives. This shows that the difficulties encountered and discussed in Phases I–III are still apparent, albeit in refracted forms. This periodized analysis is summarized in Table 3.1.

This shows how the law is a site of both constriction and enablement, in terms of its own design and when considered alongside its interrelationship with wider economic and social junctures, at the workplace and at the level of individual entitlement.

Table 3.1: Mapping the development of equality law: Phases IV–V

Conceptualization of equality	The law and legal discourse	National and industrial politics	The economy and labour market
Phase IV: 2010–current • Proactive potential • Increased transparency, monitoring and compliance	**Operationalized by:** • Equality Act 2010 (PSED, GPRR) • Tribunal fees • National Living Wage 2016 • SPL **Implications and developments:** • UNISON v Lord Chancellor – tribunal fees abolished • EU/ECJ developmental, but recourse due to be limited • Ahmed and BBC equal pay cases • Need to acknowledge more fluid definitions of gender • Intersectionality in the courts Bahl, O'Reilly and Hewage • Taylor Review • Cases concerning worker status Uber and Pimlico	**National politics:** • Coalition and Conservative • Austerity • Conservative landslide 'levelling up' • COVID-19 **Industrial politics:** • Collectivism – new world of work/precarity • Lack of regulatory protections.	**Social and economic junctures:** • Post-financial crisis recession • Resurgence of interest • #timesup #metoo • Expectations variable according to sector of employment • Economic – sectoral pay secrecy/ wide pay bandings/PRP • Ringfencing requirements
Phase V: Imminent • Intersectionality • Reformulation of legal definition of worker • Enhanced preference for voluntarist approaches	**Yet to be operationalized**	**National politics:** • Brexit and COVID-19 – women's voices marginalized **Industrial politics:** • New forms of organized labour	• COVID-19 – homeworking, school closures, risk of reversal of gender gains • Recession and high levels of unemployment • Increasing levels of inequality • Increasing use of technology and AI

While the EqA2010 and associated measures were potentially transformative, much of this promise, with reference to gender pay inequity, has not materialized. It is perhaps more pertinent to think of the process of legal reasoning as gradually embedding normative values around equality, as well as accommodating those that are changing in society regardless of the machinations of the legal system. The institutional regulatory and legal framework is slow-moving, incremental and inherently vulnerable to the push and pull of key actors and the foundational structures that continually reconfigure and legitimize inequities.

Phase IV is characterized by a deepened understanding of inequality in pay, yet has been limited by the seismic political and economic shifts discussed. This indicates the importance of understanding inequality as part of a broader dynamic. The restrictive trends and key points of contestation are visible within each level of analysis. To illustrate, beyond the legal boundary, the legislative framework can catalyze productive developments in the organizational sphere. The GPRR are not transformative of themselves, though they have forced organizations to comply. The potential to be transformative arises from what is done with the information. As organizations seek to understand their particular problems, through the accompanying narratives, they may reassess how to achieve pay equity. The need for greater transparency surrounding pay, particularly in the private sector, and the contradictions that emerge when efforts at transparency are improved, reflect how embedded this architectural feature is. This is compounded by the preference for light-touch governance in Britain, as described within each legislative phase and illustrated by the public/private sector differential and the growing trend for voluntarist approaches.

Despite the architectural features of transparency and governance, the dynamics are shifting. This discussion has shown that legislative blind spots and political and economic dynamics, such as intersectionality and changing labour markets, are continually evolving. Framing the eradication of the GPG as a business imperative, not merely a legal problem, has been ongoing in the diversity literature (Healy et al, 2011). The increased recognition of the business benefits achieved through greater diversity has become more central. The depth to this imperative and the added scrutiny that the GPRR provides is crucial. Widening the motivation and responsibility for addressing the problem is therefore an interesting development, echoing the work of Dobbin and Kalev (2016) and again demonstrating how the different explanatory approaches overlap.

However, the risks to this reformulated business imperative, greater pay transparency and reframed gendered cultural template, are writ large by the pandemic. As the world of work evolves and awareness of intersectionality increases a further reconceptualization of equality seems imminent.

The phased analysis has shown legislative approaches can tip into new models, according with the process of incremental layered change described by Streeck and Thelen (2005: 31). Within this context, a further reliance on voluntarist approaches seems likely, demonstrating how law and organizations can and often do catalyze each other (Streeck and Thelen, 2005: 19).

Given the number of moving parts within the architectures model, innovations can become derailed at various points and so moving goalposts are inevitable and continuous. The law is an integral part of this ongoing and ever-changing relationship. The organizational element of the architecture is again refined through normative values, with existing inequalities and occupational hierarchies informing the approaches sanctioned for use. These conclusions inform the subsequent analyses as the research moves onto consider the GPRR and organizational aspects of the architecture in Chapter 4. The multidimensional vision that is ultimately achieved helps to envisage how these interactions seem poised to change and, in so doing, suggests where future pathways may be best positioned to assist change for the good.

Notes

[1] The EHRC is responsible for enforcement of the PSED by first encouraging compliance and then moving to compliance mechanisms. The EHRC and/or organizations (that is, trade unions or charities) may institute judicial review proceedings to identify whether a public body has acted lawfully in respect of its obligations. The use of judicial review by the EHRC has been limited, a fact undoubtedly enhanced by funding cuts since 2010 (Doward, 2016; Women and Equalities Committee, 2019: 10, 13 and 25).

[2] https://www.fawcettsociety.org.uk/equal-pay-advice-service

[3] The need for and use of crowdfunding campaigns, such as https://www.crowdjustice.com/case/equalpayforall/ further illustrates these difficulties.

[4] EU Revised framework agreement on parental leave Directive (2010/18).

[5] The 2023 statutory weekly rate of both SPL and statutory maternity pay (SMP) is £172.48 or 90% of earnings, whichever is lower. SMP is paid at 90% of earnings during the first six weeks. The question of discrimination has arisen as employers often offer enhanced maternity pay. Those on zero-hour contracts, agency workers and the self-employed cannot claim.

[6] The case of *Snell v Network Rail* (2016) also concerned SPL and the differential between shared parental pay and the enhanced maternity package offered by the company. The tribunal found the two could not be compared. However, the company subsequently levelled down their enhanced maternity package, underlining the need for caution, as presented by Working Families in *Ali*.

[7] The proposed Directive was to improve the gender balance among non-executive directors of companies listed on stock exchanges and related measures. This proposal was pursued after opposition, most notably from Britain, with regards to the prospect of quotas (Traynor and Goodley, 2012).

[8] As per the Unfair Dismissal and Statement of Reasons for Dismissal Order 2012, the Employment Appeal Tribunal Fees Order 2013 and the Employment Tribunals Regulations 2014.

[9] Enacted by the Deregulation Act 2015, intended to reduce 'red tape' during the 2010–15 parliament.

4

Evaluating the Gender Pay Reporting Regulations

Introduction

The GPRR operationalized a potentially transformative aspect of the Phase IV conceptualization of equality. This chapter examines the introduction of compulsory gender pay reporting in 2017 and the first six years of comparable new data that it has produced. Some years are limited due to COVID-19: enforcement measures were removed two weeks prior to the 2019–20 reporting deadline and enforcement of the 2020–21 reporting window was delayed until October 2021.

The increased focus afforded to the finance sector's GPG in the post-financial crisis period prompted greater traction. However, this was variable and the pace of decline remained slow (Healy and Ahamed, 2019). The GPRR as a monitoring tool adds to this focus, presenting both opportunities and limitations. By identifying the stark reality of reported figures, organizations can begin to understand them and strategically target approaches for change. Nevertheless, there is a growing awareness of limitations in the collected data, such as reporting thresholds, calculation errors, and lack of compulsion surrounding the accompanying narrative (Dromey and Rankin, 2018; HoC, 2019a).

First, the variable roles of the key actors who shaped the implementation of the GPRR are considered, building on themes discussed in Chapters 2 and 3. An overall review of the data is then given, detailing measures required, compliance and the need for sector-specific review. The evidence is used to critically assess the requirement, noting the impact and limitations of the architectural features of governance and transparency.

Second, a sample of finance sector firms is constructed to compare the progress of reported variables, demonstrating the persistence of large GPGs within the sector. Additional manually coded variables of organization type, nationality and age add scope for further comparison. A review of the narratives accompanying reports is then given, demonstrating policy measures commonly pursued alongside those routinely disregarded.

This chapter builds upon the legal analysis, while constructing the organizational component of the architectures model and demonstrating the interrelationship between the macro and levels. This quantitative examination evidences the contradictions of transparency surrounding the GPG with reference to sectoral norms and organizational policy blind spots. As the initial shock of organizational pay reports has subsided, coupled with the disruption arising from COVID-19, it is now critical to ensure lack of progress is not legitimized and momentum remains. Observing the machinations within the architectural framework demonstrates that, while progress is slow, organizations have shown a willingness to comply. Attention must be paid to ensure accountability for gender equality and the pursuit of it in the workplace is not merely perceived as a 'nice to have' add on.

Gender Pay Reporting Regulations 2017

Key actors and enactment

As part of the evolving legal framework, the implementation of the GPRR was driven by key actors in government, business and feminist activists. The EU was increasingly focussed on driving pay transparency among Member States. Following the limited take up of a European Commission recommendation in 2014 regarding pay audits, there was a growing inclination from Brussels to mandate quotas to address GPGs (Hofman et al, 2020). There was a wide remit of measures in operation across Europe as some countries have implemented mandatory quotas with tough sanctions for non-compliance (Seierstad, 2011), while others have opted for more voluntary approaches (Arndt and Wrohlich, 2019). This has led critics to suggest that the GPRR were implemented in Britain to offset any mandatory requirement arising from the EU (Fagan and Rubery, 2017: 5). A general political reluctance to mandate change in this area was also evidenced in the resistance to implement quotas to increase women's representation on boards (Traynor and Goodley, 2012: 10; BIS, 2015). The increased use of voluntarism in Britain's legal framework reflects the architectural trend of light-touch governance (see Chapters 2 and 3) (Dickens, 2007; McLaughlin and Deakin, 2011; Milner, 2019). The resistance of key actors in business and government led to the section 78 pay reporting requirement in the EqA2010 remaining inactive for seven years (GEO, 2015).

Interestingly, since Brexit the EU is in the process of ratifying a Directive to address various aspects of pay transparency alongside mandatory board-level quotas, both of which are due to be introduced by 2026 (Wigand, 2021). Conversely, the UK government launched a voluntary pilot scheme in 2022 to encourage greater pay transparency with a focus on job adverts (GEO, 2022). However, at the time of writing they were yet to report on the scheme and analysis by Adzuna (2022) shows the level of salary disclosure in the UK has been declining.

That said, alongside these developments within Britain there has also been increasing recognition of the importance of diversity and inclusion among the business community. The CBI acknowledged the business benefits and importance of mandatory measurement to help drive necessary change (Fairbairn, 2018). McKinsey (2016) quantified the substantial economic benefits of enabling women's full participation in the workforce, in their 'Power of Parity' report, flagging a potential increase of £150 billion to UK GDP by 2025. They propose unlocking this financial imperative by increasing the number of women who are economically active, increasing the number of hours they work, and encouraging the employment of women in sectors with higher rates of pay.

A shifting political will was also emerging as cross-party feminist activism increasingly supported a mandatory approach (Milner, 2019: 126–7). Prior to the 2015 election, Labour introduced a ten minute rule bill to address the failures of 'Think, Act, Report', which finally enacted the compulsory reporting recommended in section 78 of the EqA2010 (Perraudin, 2014). It has also been suggested that Prime Minister Cameron's low popularity among female voters prompted the Conservative 2015 manifesto commitment to implement the GPRR (Milner, 2019). These increased and combined pressures from political actors and feminist activists drove the implementation of the section 78 provision.

Reporting requirements

The detail and data required by the GPRR, enforcement mechanisms, compliance levels, and sectoral trends are now examined to understand how they have contributed to reducing the GPG.

Since April 2017 the Regulations oblige all private and voluntary sector employers in Britain with 250 or more employees to publish six calculations of their pay gaps on an annual basis. This includes: both the mean and median hourly GPG; the mean and median bonus pay gap; the proportion of men and women receiving bonus payments; and the proportion of men and women in each pay quartile (25% band). Employers should publish this data on the government website within 12 months of the relevant snapshot date, the date determined by whether they are public, private, or voluntary sector organizations.[1] Employers can choose to provide an accompanying narrative, though they are not obliged to. Additional information can be included and employers with fewer than 250 employees can voluntarily report, should they so wish.

Measuring the mean or the median

The GPRR require the publication of two measures of central tendency, the median and the mean. The ONS and the ASHE use the median in their GPG analyses. When data is not symmetrical this represents the middle point in the salary range, with half of staff earning more and half less. Outlying values have the potential to skew the average mean value, which is relevant for this research given the typical right-hand skew of earnings in finance.

The Institute for Economic Affairs objects to the use of the mean (Andrew, 2017). They suggest that, given women's prominence in part-time work and the fact that it is lower paid, an average of wages of all men and all women presents a misleading picture. Combined with the level of CEO pay, they assert this measure is inevitably skewed and, as such, misrepresentative.

The Fawcett Society, on the other hand, calculate the UK's Equal Pay Day date using the mean gap data. Equal Pay Day is a national campaign to highlight the point in the year at which women, on average, stop earning relative to men. In addition, the EU and the UK Household Longitudinal Study use the mean value in their analysis. The mean represents the average calculated by the sum of values, divided by the count. It is impacted by high earners and, as such, is more sensitive to extreme scores in its calculation of the average value (Olsen et al, 2018). The mean value, in this way, highlights the high-paying practices found within the finance sector and lack of women in the most senior roles. Given the capacity of a small number of high-earning outliers to impact the average value, this may also conceal progress occurring within the pay range.

Using either the mean or the median reveals different aspects of the GPG, further reiterating the importance of acknowledging both figures and the inherent debate within the choice (Scholar, 2009). The analysis presented here typically uses the mean value, given the gendered inequities and high-earning outliers common in the finance sector.

Enforcement and compliance

Enforcement action can be taken by the EHRC if employers have not complied by the deadline (EHRC, 2018). The question of non-compliance was a matter of early criticism, given the uncertainty surrounding enforcement mechanisms and sanctions for breaches (BEIS, 2018a; Milner, 2019). This has since been clarified: the first stage involves a written request which, if unsuccessful, leads to the second stage of formal enforcement action involving a court order requiring the breach to be remedied, punishable by an unlimited fine (EHRC, 2019). Incomplete submissions are also subject to enforcement action.

However, despite some clear errors it is unclear whether and how the validity of pay reports is being checked. For example, statistically impossible gaps of over 100% have been reported each year. The 'unwieldy enforcement mechanisms' suggest a clearer, quicker resolution process is needed (Francis-Devine and Pyper, 2020: 32).

It is estimated that the GPRR cover 56% of employees in Britain (BEIS, 2018a: 13). The first year of reporting (2017–18) saw a surge of employers choosing to publish at the last minute: 90% of eligible companies submitted in the last three months. This led to speculation that the tactic was intended to 'bury the bad news' (Wisniewska et al, 2018) and the trend has continued (Webber, 2023).

Nevertheless, the level of compliance has been much higher than anticipated. Nine out of ten employers published their data by the first April deadline in 2018. Within four months of the deadline, all reports had been submitted (GEO, 2018a; Hofman et al, 2020: 19). A written warning was a sufficient prompt, without the need for recourse to court action by the EHRC. Similarly, year two also achieved 100% compliance, with a slightly lower level of late reports (down from 8% to 3%). This indicates that, by the second year, companies had set up their reporting systems more effectively to comply on time. However, the tendency for employers to voluntarily report additional information has steadily declined from 73% in 2017–18 to 58% in 2022–23 (see Table 4.1).

This level of additional reporting may have been evidence of employers attempting to ensure they were ready for any regulatory shift, given the enactment of the GPRR prompted consultation over ethnicity gap reporting (Adams et al, 2018). The government has since asserted that regulatory change is not pending, perhaps contributing to the trend for reduced

Table 4.1: Gender pay reporting levels 2017–23

Reporting year	Total number of firms reporting	Number of late submissions	Extra information
2017–18	10,577	885	7,805
2018–19	10,841	545	7,448
2019–20	4,962* (7,040**)	0 (enforcement suspended)	3,442* (4,731**)
2020–21	10,573	1,003	7,009
2021–22	10,283	469	6,657
2022–23	10,644	502	6,131

Note: * Refers to deadline date total, ** refers to total on 1 May 2023.

Source: Contains public sector information licensed under the Open Government Licence v3.0. Gender pay reporting data available at: https://gender-pay-gap.service.gov.uk/

additional information reporting (CRED, 2021). Commitment in the Labour manifesto to introduce ethnicity reporting for large companies, should they be elected, may well see this trend reverse (Warraich, 2023).

The government suspension of compulsory reporting in 2020, as a result of COVID-19, further underlines this tendency for organizational compliance. At the point of the announcement, there was up to ten days remaining until the reporting deadline (GEO, 2020a).[2] At this point, 26% of employers within the full population had reported, demonstrating the continued preference for late reporting. By the deadline, 46% had reported (see Table 4.1 for the deadline date figure, percentage based on the previous year's reporting total). The numbers of those reporting in the full population increased from 4,962 on the deadline date, to 7,040 by the 2022–23 reporting deadline.

There is a marked difference in the reporting levels in the finance sample reinforcing Healy and Ahamed's (2019) findings that increased focus within the sector has helped achieve greater traction. In March 2020 when the government announced suspension, 48% of companies within the sample had already submitted their reports, increasing to 80% by the deadline. These figures certainly suggest a willingness to comply and potentially reflect the establishment of automated systems to assist this process. The level of additional information reported (see Table 4.2) has not been subject to the decline observed in the full population (see Table 4.1), suggesting another positive effect of the additional scrutiny within the sector.

Classifying organizations

Organizational pay reports are given a SIC code that identifies the organization's business activity (see Appendix 2). This enables a sectoral analysis of differences and trends (as discussed in Chapter 1). It should be noted that these distinctions are not entirely accurate, as some companies

Table 4.2: Finance sample GPRR reporting levels 2017–23

Reporting year	Number of finance sample firms reporting	Number of late submissions	Extra information
2017–18	55	6	51
2018–19	53	5	49
2019–20	52	0	45
2020–21	55	3	48
2021–22	56	5	47
2022–23	59	2	49

Source: Contains public sector information licensed under the Open Government Licence v3.0. Gender pay reporting data available at: https://gender-pay-gap.service.gov.uk/

do not input a SIC code or classify different parts of the business under different codes. For example, within the finance industry 570 employers failed to submit SIC code data (Treasury Committee, 2018: 34). Bearing these limitations in mind, and consistent with ONS analysis, the GPRR data shows that pay gaps in the finance and insurance industries are among the largest (Smith, 2019; Francis-Devine and Pyper, 2020).

Having identified the compulsory elements and compliance with the GPRR, engagement with the voluntary aspect and a broad evaluation of the Regulations is now given.

Voluntarism and evaluating the effectiveness of the GPRR

The increasing preference for combined statutory and voluntary approaches in the law is reflected in the accompanying narrative element of the GPRR. Interestingly, despite the lack of legal compulsion, analysis of the 2017–18 data shows 83% of companies chose to include a narrative (Murray et al, 2019: 87). Private sector companies have been slightly less likely to publish a narrative (81%) than the public (90%) and voluntary (92%) sectors (Murray et al, 2019: 24). This demonstrates how organizations vary within the confines of the same legal apparatus. This reflects the importance of governance as an architectural feature, in terms of choosing the degree to which legal requirements are mandated and, in turn, the level of accountability within the workplace. Exposing trends and organizational variability is useful to help understand both the barriers and potential for change within the architectures of inequality. Understanding movement beyond the boundaries of legal requirement may help explain why disparities occur.

Within the narratives, there is inconsistency in the level of detail given. Organizations typically: define GPGs as distinct from unequal pay; refer to organizational and sectoral challenges; and outline how they have been addressing, or intend to address, the situation. Some companies have failed to provide one at all and/or simply provide a link to their company website where they reiterate what has been said in their report (for example, Bank of China and RBS).

Some companies use the narrative to defend their position, attributing gaps to the wider social problem within their particular industry (for example, Ryanair). At the other end of the spectrum, employers have used the narrative to provide clear, open and honest reports, with detail of their own organizational picture, the wider sectoral perspective, the initiatives they are pursuing and have pursued, and how these will be measured (for example, Barclays and Department for Transport).

Some organizations have chosen to publish additional information, such as ethnicity gap details (for example, RBS, Barclays and Nationwide Building Society). This highlights how some organizations are willing to go beyond the mandatory legislative aspect, indicating the proactive potential that they retain.

The human resource profession has been propelled by the increasing drive for equality and diversity since the 1960s (Dobbin, 2009). This has been accompanied by a growing understanding of the business benefits and economic imperative to improve diversity and GPGs (Healy et al, 2011; Oswick and Noon, 2014). The GPRR have sharpened the focus on gender pay inequity, further reiterating the need for commonplace best practice standards. For companies that have taken the time to publish meaningful narratives, they typically show an understanding of the complexities causing gender pay inequality, defining the organizational perception of the problem and the challenges of counteracting it. Without the narrative, the GPRR is simply an exercise in collating and publishing data. Understanding how organizations approach the voluntary aspects of the GPRR is therefore critical. This also demonstrates how the architectures of inequality model helps us to understand the relationship and movement between different theoretical explanations and how, within that, organizations retain the capacity to innovate.

The compliance levels described certainly suggest a degree of effectiveness of the GPRR. However, identification of regulatory limitations and the trajectory of GPG progress also indicates the confines of their success and whether this capacity to innovate has, in reality, occurred. Evaluation by a governmental select committee identified limits to the efficacy of the Regulations and prompted various recommendations to improve them (BEIS, 2018a). These included: making the narrative mandatory; recognition that the bonus calculation needs to be pro rata for part-time staff, as in its current format it fails to recognize the gendered nature of part-time work and skews the data; the threshold for reporting to be reduced to 50 employees; further granularity from quartile to decile reporting; publication of full-time and part-time figures; and to recognize and prompt action on other markers of inequality, such as disability and race reporting. Despite the consultation regarding race reporting, all recommendations have, thus far, been rejected by government. This suggests ambivalence in the aims of the GPRR and corresponds with the architectural trends identified (HoC, 2019a). However, the ability for other jurisdictions to learn from the UK experience is clear. Ireland introduced GPG reporting measures in 2022. While initially applying to firms with over 250 employees, the requirement will be extended to firms with over 50 employees by 2025 (Department of Children, Equality, Disability, Integration and Youth, 2022). Interestingly, Ireland have made the narrative compulsory as reports have to identify and disclose the causes of any pay gaps, alongside presenting the measures they are taking to address them. Within the UK it seems the financial and moral imperatives for change are seemingly less important than the perceived costs of mandating more effective and stringent legislative requirements.

However, despite these limitations, feedback from those that have submitted reports has shown that 24% increased their prioritization of gender pay inequality as a result of the GPRR, rising to 43% for those with gaps over 20% (Murray et al, 2019: 5). This meso-level impact highlights the potential of the GPRR as incremental legal development has prompted a wider dynamism in the organizational architecture.

Policies to bring about change

The GEO has provided an assessment of organizational actions that can be taken to reduce GPGs (GEO, 2018b, 2019a, 2019b). This guidance on typical policies describes a range of commonly used measures: those deemed 'effective', such as women on shortlists and salary negotiation with transparent ranges; those deemed 'promising', including workplace flexibility, mentoring and sponsorship; and those with 'mixed results', including unconscious bias training and diverse selection panels. This developing understanding of what is considered best practice in targeting the problem underlines a positive impact of compulsory reporting.

The translation and practical application of these recommendations highlights the relevance of considering the GPRR within the organizational context and the importance of the architectures model. Choices made within the workplace may follow sectoral best practice path-dependent norms, but there is also potential for change (Streeck and Thelen, 2005). However, analysis of reporting data demonstrates that increased awareness of the problem does not necessarily correlate to success in reducing inequities. The GPRR are, first and foremost, a monitoring and diagnostic tool. The proactive potential within them requires further activation at the firm level. Comparisons over time will ultimately indicate whether measurement and publication are both prompting action and delivering results. This is likely to operate in divergent ways across different industries, as priorities and actions vary as different sectors take up the challenge to varying degrees. This echoes the variability of legal requirements, such as the private/public sector differential discussed in Chapters 2 and 3. Understanding these trends and interactions is vital and requires the sector-specific focus that is now pursued.

Sector-specific analysis
The sample dataset

The 2007–08 financial crisis exposed the gender inequality within the finance sector, prompting firms to more explicitly address the problem (EHRC, 2009; Metcalf and Rolfe, 2009). Healy and Ahamed (2019) assessed the interventions subsequently implemented with reference to Labour Force Survey data. They found a greater reduction within financial services GPGs than in the wider population. Their research also highlighted greater degrees of reticence in certain parts of the industry with increasing gaps at the top of the wage spectrum. This reluctance within certain parts of the sector underlines the importance of understanding the sectoral variation of GPGs.

This analysis uses publicly available gender pay reporting data to explore some of Britain's largest GPGs by creating a sample of finance firms. Anomalies in definition, SIC code usage and errors in the data prompted the selection of a more limited sample for review. The small sample of representative organizations is not intended to be exhaustive but capable of highlighting indicative trends within finance (Benson et al, 2018). To construct the sample, all organizations reporting under Central Banking, Bank and Building Society SIC codes were selected. The resultant dataset contained 69 firms though, as Table 4.2 shows, the numbers reporting in each year is variable. Appendix 2 details how the dataset was constructed and Appendix 3 gives the full list of firms included in the resultant sample.

Having created the dataset, a further variable categorizing the age of organizations was added. The EqPA70 denoted the first legal requirement to systematically recognize and address pay inequalities; as such, reference is made to organizations operating either prior to or after this point. A further delineation marks the start of the financial crisis in 2007–08. When determining age, this was ascribed according to the creation of the financial group: organizational mergers (for example Santander), name changes (for example Cynergy Bank), or operations in new markets (for example Mizuho) have been disregarded. Organizations were also categorized according to the types of services they provide and, for larger global firms, the location of their headquarters. These additional dimensions enable the exploration of shifting normative values and cultural differences between organizations.

Pay reporting data from the selected organizations provides an opportunity to see how GPGs have changed since the Regulations were introduced and how the finance sector trajectory compares to the overall population. Direct comparison with ONS figures is not possible as there is a tendency for gender pay reports to show lower industry gaps than ONS longitudinal data. This is due to the ONS inclusion of employers with fewer than 250 employees, where GPGs tend to be higher (Colebrook et al, 2018). Consideration is given to any commonalities and differences in the organizational variables: type; country of origin; and age, with reference to pay, bonus gaps and quartile information.

A further complicating factor to note is the impact of ringfencing requirements. Ringfencing requires large banking organizations to separate their core retail banking services from investment and international banking services. The requirement was introduced in 1 January 2019, in the wake of the financial crisis, to offset the risks arising from large highly leveraged organizations. For instance, using HSBC as an example, they now report the retail and commercial part of their business (which includes around 21,000 employees), as HSBC UK, while the global banking and markets part of the business (which includes around 2,000 employees) is reported as HSBC Bank Plc. Within their narratives, they provide the aggregate UK-wide detail, but in terms of the individually reported data, it is important to understand the difference, given the impact this will have on the organization type variable. They note in their report that their global and market-based operation, while significantly smaller, has higher rates of pay and more men in senior roles than the other parts of the business. This is reflected in the figures. A similar situation is apparent with Barclays, Lloyds, RBS and others. This demonstrates a contradiction of transparency, as the effect of organizations fissuring their operations in this way obstructs the potential to compare year-on-year progress (Weil, 2014).

While smaller organizations are typically thought to have larger GPGs, the organization size detail reported in the GPRR is not explored further in this research. This is due to the size of the sample, the impact of ringfencing requirements separating organizational entities, and, as many of the organization's reporting are large global firms, their main employee base may be located elsewhere.

The reporting measures themselves, as discussed, also limit the capacity to make inferences about the wider finance sector and whole population. The variability and potential bias involved in bonus calculation, as discussed during interviews, means that bonus gaps could potentially illustrate bias and discrimination. Additionally, the prominence of women in part-time roles, particularly within the branch network, skews this data as bonus figures are not pro rata. Further, the lack of granularity in quartile reporting does not enable a focused analysis of women's seniority and areas of progress or retrogression. Interestingly, since 2021–22 HSBC assess occupational segregation with their accompanying narrative using organizational thirds (senior, middle and junior), not quartiles. However, the devil is very much in the detail, which is now addressed.

What the data shows

An overview of reported data within the sample dataset is shown in Table 4.3 revealing the scale of inequities.

To understand and evaluate this data pay gaps, bonus gaps, and quartile movement and progress are first assessed, before turning to consider the added variables of organization type and age.

Table 4.3: Comparison of reported data for sample dataset 2017–23

Variable	Sample dataset reported data					
Reporting year	2017–18	2018–19	2019–20	2020–21	2021–22	2022–23
Number of firms reporting	55	53	52	55	56	59
Median GPG	33.5%	31.9%	31.3%	32.1%	31.6%	30.1%
Mean GPG	35%	34.2%	33.8%	33.6%	31.9%	30.3%
Median bonus gap	46.2%	38%	46.8%	42.2%	37.7%	41.2%
Mean bonus gap	54%	50.7%	52.5%	46.6%	44.7%	49.9%
Women in top quartile	28.3%	28.8%	29.2%	28.8%	28.2%	29.9%
Women in upper-mid quartile	43.1%	44.6%	44.3%	42.4%	42.4%	43%
Women in lower mid quartile	56.3%	55.6%	56.9%	55%	54.4%	54.2%
Women in low quartile	63.8%	63.8%	62.8%	62.8%	63.6%	62.7%

Source: Contains public sector information licensed under the Open Government Licence v3.0. Gender pay reporting data available at: https://gender-pay-gap.serv ice.gov.uk/

Pay gaps

Within the sample dataset Table 4.3 shows that the GPG has slowly reduced. While this mirrors the glacial speed of progress observed in the full population, interestingly finance is one of the sectors seeing the biggest rate of decline (PwC, 2023: 7). This confirms Healy and Ahamed's (2019) contention that increased attention is prompting progress, highlighting the continued need for sectoral and organizational focus on the persistent problem.

The data is used here to help highlight the way inequalities move and to better understand where progress has occurred. Figure 4.1 shows the quartile spread of GPGs by reporting year, the trend for outliers at the top of the pay distribution and the stuttering progress that has occurred.

This is consistent with reports of 'diversity fatigue' and a kick back from some of the highest paying parts of the sector (PwC, 2019; Sheerin and Garavan, 2021).

Bonus gaps

A central feature of an employee's pay package in the finance sector is bonuses. The importance of the bonus culture in terms of pay inequities is well established in the literature (EHRC, 2009; Gall, 2017; Benson et al, 2018; Treasury Committee, 2018).

Figure 4.1: Mean range of GPGs in the sample datasets 2017–23

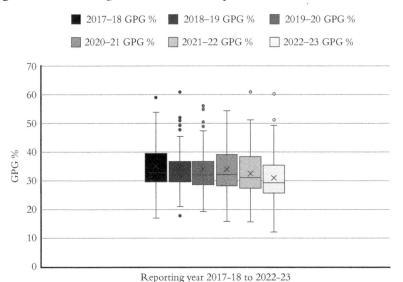

Source: Contains public sector information licensed under the Open Government Licence v3.0. Gender pay reporting data available at: https://gender-pay-gap.service.gov.uk/

A key criticism levied at the Regulations relates to the bonus gap figures (BEIS, 2018a). While quantitative research may be perceived as scientific and credible, this element of the reported data may be misleading. Women's prominence within the part-time workforce is well established. However, bonus gaps are not pro rata and so do not reflect fundamental and gendered differences in hours worked. Chapter 2 discussed how the early phase of equality law struggled to recognize difference in comparison to the male norm standard. Some 50 years on, the failure again of legislation to be alert to these differences may escalate bonus gap figures, where women are employed on reduced-hour contracts. This highlights how sociological norms remain foundational in the architectures model. In addition, it provides another example of the contradictions of transparency that limit the utility of the GPRR as a monitoring tool.

Despite failing to accommodate the impact of part-time workers, there is still a clear relationship between the pay gap and the bonus gap. As the pay gap increases, the bonus gap increases. The variability of pay gaps and broad trend for higher GPGs to be associated with higher bonus gaps is shown in Figure 4.2.

The payment of bonuses is a largely hidden process (see Chapter 5) which, as evidenced by the data, exacerbates pay inequalities. Yet, there is limited mention by firms of the impact of bonuses, despite the size of the gaps. This is all the more confounding given the entirely discretionary nature of how these payments are awarded and the strict secrecy associated with them. This illustrates one of the contradictions within which organizational approaches towards pay secrecy reside. Normalcy is afforded to this complete lack of transparency despite the potential for bias inherent within their calculation. It is, therefore, useful to reflect on this in relation to how the architectures of inequality are remodelled and adapted in light of regulatory change and organizational processes. Gender pay inequality is both exacerbated and legitimized by: the lack of take-up of the BEIS (2018a) recommendation to understand the impact of part-time staff on the bonus gap calculation; the disregard shown to bonus gaps in narratives as a result of this discrepancy; and the values awarded and associated with certain higher revenue-generating and highly gendered occupations.

Pay quartiles

Occupational segregation in the finance sector is described as a defining feature of pay inequity. Within the sample dataset women's employment in the top two quartiles has increased year on year (see Figure 4.3).

A bivariate correlation test showed there is a statistically significant inverse relationship (at 0.05) between the top and upper-mid quartiles and the GPG. As the pay gap increases, women's representation at the top and upper-mid

Figure 4.2: GPGs and bonus gaps within the sample datasets 2017–18 and 2022–23

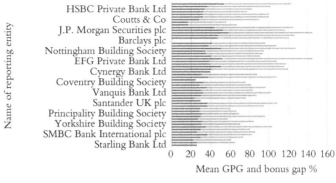

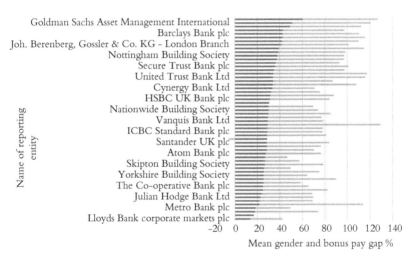

Note: A full and corresponding list of firms in the dataset and their respective gaps in 2022–23 is provided in Appendix 3.

Source: Contains public sector information licensed under the Open Government Licence v3.0. Gender pay reporting data available at: https://gender-pay-gap.service.gov.uk/

quartiles decreases to a significant degree, for all reporting years. This suggests there is enough evidence to imply a relationship between these two variables in the finance sector. This reiterates the importance of organizations focusing on the promotion of women to more senior roles, statistically, for fairness, and ultimately to improve in terms of gender pay inequality. That said, increases have been small and the limitation of lack of granularity in the quartile measure is clear. A resistance to further transparency here also

Figure 4.3: Sample dataset pay quartile analysis 2017–23

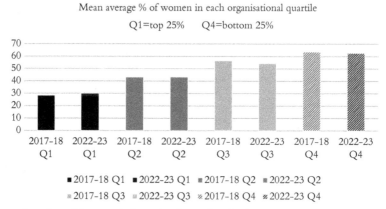

Source: Contains public sector information licensed under the Open Government Licence v3.0. Gender pay reporting data available at: https://gender-pay-gap.service.gov.uk/

speaks volumes in terms of the existing inequalities and power imbalance that efforts are trying to address.

The decrease in women in the lowest organizational quartile is also of interest. Figure 4.3 shows movement is also occurring at the bottom end of the pay scale. Bringing more men into these lower paid roles is another way to reduce the GPG.

Organization age

An assessment of GPGs, with reference to the organization's age, shows a trend for smaller gaps in newer organizations (see Figure 4.4).

The post-2007–08 financial crisis category comprises organizations that have emerged since the focus on gender inequalities within the sector arose. This incorporates newer challenger banks. However, the limited number of organizations within the sample (and across the sector) that fit within the category is small (n=7) impacting the ability to find statistically significant results. It is also of note that, within the sample dataset, the organizations that fit into this category are UK retail banks. As per the organization type analysis, the services they provide are limited and do not operate in parts of the business associated with higher pay and larger gaps. Unfortunately, the impact of ringfencing requirements, and the operation of global firms with different arms of the business operating under different trading names, mean that an analysis of organization size does not offer any additional insights on this theme.

With reference to age, it is perhaps more surprising that organizations that have emerged since 2007 already have pay gaps in excess of 25%. They

Figure 4.4: GPG according to age category of firms in sample dataset 2022–23

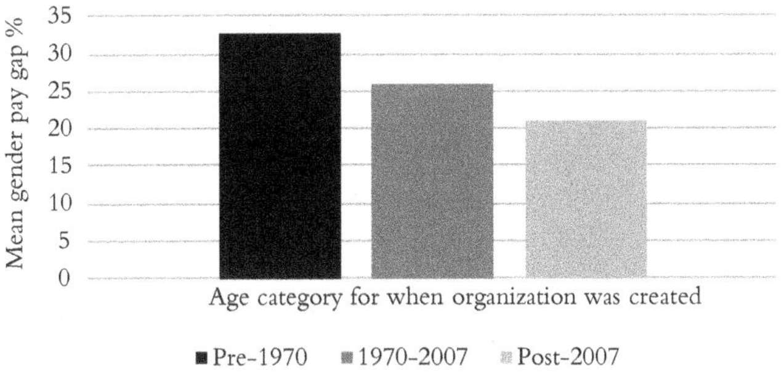

Source: Contains public sector information licensed under the Open Government Licence v3.0. Author's own analysis of gender pay reporting data available at: https://gender-pay-gap. service.gov.uk/

do not have historic GPGs to remedy yet find themselves drawn into pay practices associated with the sector, revealing how pervasive foundational inequalities can be. As discussed during qualitative interviews, the pressure to match or better salaries at the point of recruitment means that organizations may inherit pay anomalies, unless systems are robust enough to counter this tendency.

These findings underline the importance of using the architectures model to understand the intransigence of GPGs. While the institutional framework was well established and understood when some of these firms were created, its limitations are evident. The potential that workplace practices, norms and values add to pay inequities demonstrates the insights gained through this multilevel approach.

Organization type

Within the sample dataset comparison of gaps according to organizational type indicates several trends (Figure 4.5).

For firms engaged in the highest revenue-generating activities, such as asset management, investment and private banking (n=16), GPGs are larger. Similarly for global banks (n=22) this may reflect the wide remit of operations they are engaged in, including those associated with higher pay. These findings may also indicate the effect of exposure to less stringent regulatory frameworks in other jurisdictions. Correspondingly, the graph shows that currency, payment and credit firms have significantly lower gaps, with the variability reflecting the small size of the sample (n=5) and the more limited services they provide. Likewise, smaller UK banks (n=16) do not engage in the trading and global aspects of the business typically associated with higher GPGs and their gaps are lower. While building societies

Figure 4.5: GPG by reporting year and organization type in sample datasets 2017–23

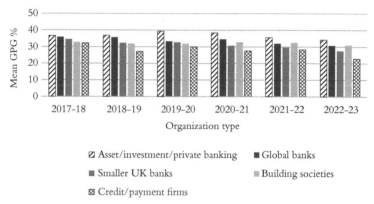

Source: Contains public sector information licensed under the Open Government Licence v3.0. Author's own analysis of gender pay reporting data available at: https://gender-pay-gap. service.gov.uk/

(n=10) also focus on lower revenue-generating services, their mean GPG has seen limited progress. This may in part reflect the trend for smaller firms to have larger GPGs. The size of the sample limits the potential for statistically significant results; however, analysis by Benson et al (2018) and PwC (2022) confirms these organization-type trends.

This analysis has shown how, despite working within the same legal statutory compliance framework, gaps can persist or vary between organizations. Exploration of the efforts that organizations choose to address inequities and, importantly, those they do not, is therefore highly relevant.

Accompanying narrative analysis

Monitoring and understanding the causes of gender pay inequality and the myriad of ways that it operates are key to changing it. The reflections and actions that accompany pay reports are therefore critical. As such, the raw presentation of reported gaps is further enhanced here by an analysis of stated organizational priorities. A systematic review of the accompanying narratives demonstrates areas of focus and the level of ambition among firms in the dataset. This is complimented in Chapters 5–7 by qualitative analysis to understand how women working for some of these organizations experience these initiatives.

The narratives for all companies in the sample dataset were reviewed each year, noting the types of initiatives stated. I categorized the initiatives described, according to the GEO (2018b) review of evidence-based actions for employers, which defines their outcomes as 'effective', 'promising' or giving 'mixed results'. More transparent and open approaches are typically referenced as effective actions. This seems logical given increased vision of the problem lends itself to an increased capacity to address it.

The range and frequency of approaches pursued by organizations is outlined in Table 4.4. This presents a combined assessment of approaches specifically referenced within narratives since 2017, categorizing their use as low (up to 33% of firms), mid-range (between 33% and 66% of firms) or high (66% +).

The most frequent description within the narratives asserts the company position that their GPG occurs because of occupational segregation and does not reflect unequal pay. It is from this starting point that organizational practices are described. The most common initiatives used relate to the targeting of change in terms of gender balance within the organizational quartiles. Nearly all organizations referenced commitments to the WiFC and internal targets to address the lack of women in senior roles. This accords with the major theme of the narratives that GPGs are the result of the lack of women in senior roles and concurs with the correlation of quartile progression and pay gap reduction, as described.

The respective targets organizations then set reflect the varying degrees of ambition within them and the varied positions they are starting from. Some organizations do not explicitly state goals in their reports. Some have been met with years to spare. Some are limited in ambition, while others are striving for full parity at senior levels. The following firms and targets are illustrative. Aldermore and Triodos bank are both WiFC signatories but do not divulge target details in their 2022–23 narratives. Goldman Sachs Asset Management met their 30% target in 2021 yet in their 2022–23 report have still not updated it. RBC Europe's target of 25% by 2020 has been extended to 2025. At the other end of the scale, some firms are targeting full parity in senior roles or management populations, for example Cumberland Building Society, Santander and RCI Bank (who voluntarily report) by 2025, while Yorkshire Building Society has already achieved 50% parity at senior levels. While some organizations have removed older narratives from their websites, preferring to just publish the most recent ones, others still display all the narratives.

What does appear consistent is that movement to meet objectives is slow. This suggests that subscribing to these policies and targets is for some organizations perhaps more important than the goal of achieving parity (see Chapter 7) (Hoque and Noon, 2004).

There is also variation in what defines the target population. This corresponds with interviewee reflections on the utility of WiFC targets, their comparability and the ability for organizations to shape them. The impact of voluntarist self-determined approaches to governance are determined by organizational ambition and interest and, in this way, are limited.

Table 4.4: Accompanying narrative analysis

Workplace initiative and usage

Evidential category					
Effective actions	Shortlists	Skill-based assessment	Structured interviews	Encourage negotiation by using salary range	Transparency of pay/reward/promotion
Referenced by	Mid	Low	Low	Low	Low
Promising actions	Flexible working	Shared Parental Leave - enhance and encourage	Returner programme	Internal targets	Networking
Referenced by	High	High	Mid	High	High
Mixed results	Unconscious bias training	Diversity training	Leadership training	Diverse selection panels	Performance self-assessment
Referenced by	Mid	High	High	High	Low

Source: Contains public sector information licensed under the Open Government Licence v3.0. Author's own analysis of narratives accompanying gender pay reports. Narratives coded according to GEO (2018b) guidance. Data available at: https://gender-pay-gap.service.gov.uk/

The second most commonly referenced approaches were workplace flexibility measures and networking opportunities. There has been a growing organizational commitment to improve and embed flexible and hybrid working, particularly evident since the COVID-19 outbreak. Firms such as Skipton Building Society have described efforts to enable branch staff to benefit from flexible working opportunities, while others describe embedding hybrid working practices. That said, the 'new normal' remains to be seen and there is variability in how finance firms are positioning their expectations (Moore, 2021). It is worth noting that improvements in flexible working were also noted during interviews conducted pre-pandemic.

The foundational limitation of underlying inequalities means developments here are critical, yet COVID-19 has shown how their application is also vulnerable to these embedded inequities. Understanding how flexibilities and networks may impact career development and the variability of provisions within organizations again requires greater transparency, a theme picked up in more sociological explanations for the intransigence of reducing the GPG.

The prominence of actions, such as unconscious bias and diversity training, are less apparent in more recent narratives. For example, Leeds Building Society referenced unconscious bias training in earlier reports, but since 2019–20 it has not been mentioned. This progression seems to highlight the positive impact of the GEO review, which suggested that these actions deliver mixed results (Bohnet, 2016; Dobbin and Kalev, 2016). It also reflects the development of trends in anti-discrimination strategies (see Chapter 2) (Healy et al, 2011; Oswick and Noon, 2014).

Correspondingly, in more recent narratives there seems to be a growing prominence of efforts to improve and equate parental leave, deemed promising. For example, in their 2022–23 narratives Handelsbanken describe their gender-neutral parental leave policy, Co-operative and Zopa bank both mention improvements to parental leave, NatWest group describes having 'market leading partner pay' while Santander commits to making its family-friendly policies publicly available. The importance of these developments was reiterated by interviewees.

Since 2020–21 there has been a notable increase in policies relating to menopause and women's wellbeing. Newer reports show a trend for efforts to debias the whole recruitment process alongside an increased number of firms addressing the pipeline issue by targeting the recruitment of women in areas like tech. These trends demonstrate the importance of sharing good practice and the role of HRM across the sector (Atkinson et al, 2021). This also demonstrates the similarity in the approaches firms pursue, illustrating the concept of layered change (Streeck and Thelen, 2005: 19). The incremental development of alternative approaches is gradually accepted over time, much like the developing conceptualization of equality in the law. Taking a holistic perspective enables consideration of these corresponding and sometimes divergent views and, in so doing, affords a more nuanced understanding of the problem.

Furthermore, these reflections are interesting given the actions that the GEO deem effective. While shortlists and diversity managers are clearly among the most popular effective approaches, the other initiatives they describe are strikingly less so. This may, in part, reflect the lack of specificity within narratives and the resultant difficulty in identifying these kinds of measures within them. However, it does also suggest a resistance and lack of willingness to address the question of transparency around pay, reward and promotion, a theme consistently described during interviews. The lack of clarity or inability to identify salary bandings inevitably impacts on pay outcomes, particularly if assertions around gendered disparity in negotiation ring true (Bohnet, 2016; Colebrook et al, 2018). This concurs with Acker's (2012) theory of inequality regimes.

The inability to identify salary bandings inevitably impacts on pay outcomes, particularly if gendered approaches to negotiation ring true, as suggested by more sociological explanations (Acker, 1991; Rubery and Grimshaw, 2015; Bohnet, 2016: 70–1). This stymies the ability of individuals to make equal pay claims, and also restricts the ability to assess whether organizational assertions around the lack of unequal pay are indeed true.

That said, the focus of narratives does seem to be changing. Reference to 'fair pay' and the use of equal pay audits has gradually increased. For example, there was more reference to fair pay in the 2020–21 reports than in all previous narratives combined. To illustrate, in their 2020–21 narrative Leeds Building Society highlighted their publication of a fair pay reference guide, while the Bank of America and SMBC used external firms to conduct fair pay analyses. Though still limited, this increased use has continued. For example, in the 2022–23 narratives Standard Chartered Bank described the implementation of a 'fair pay charter', Atom Bank the use of salary benchmarking and Clydesdale Bank a 'simplified' approach to salaries.

Notwithstanding these improvements the reluctance towards greater transparency remains stark, despite potentially being one of the most accessible and tangible means with which to target change. This analysis highlights the importance of focusing efforts on this aspect of the phenomenon, but also the counterbalancing reaction of some key actors who will invariably resist.

Chapters 5–7 assess the lived experience of the initiatives described, to help evaluate these findings. The capacity of individuals within the workplace to limit access to policies or interpret conditionality, both overtly and covertly, inevitably impacts the scope and uptake of organizational efforts and will be explored. The thematic insights garnered from both previous and subsequent chapters are, in this way, woven into this stratified mixed-methods approach and provide the blueprint from which the architectures model is constructed.

Conclusions

This chapter has examined the large GPGs within the finance sector through analysis of the GPRR. The level of reduction in reported pay gaps is greater within the sample dataset than in the full population, confirming the trend identified by Healy and Ahamed (2019). This variability highlights the importance of understanding the interrelationship of theoretical explanations and the utility of the architectures of inequality model. The slow positive change that has been critically evaluated demonstrates how architectural development and extension can prompt change, with the potential for further improvement apparent within the organizational dimension. Conclusions are also drawn concerning the contradictions of transparency, as improved visibility has shown the obstacles that transpire at the organizational level, the policy blind spots that have emerged through accompanying narrative analysis, and the limitations of the GPRR and governance trends.

The effectiveness of reports as a diagnostic tool has demonstrated that identification of the detail can certainly be used as a means to recognize inequities and target change. However, this is limited at the organizational level by factors such as pay and reward policies, and normative values and behaviours. This is evidenced through the bonus gap analysis and organization type trends discussed in this chapter. Reports of equality fatigue in certain parts of the sector, resulting in the increased visibility of organizations less willing to address the problem, support this finding (HoC, 2019b; Makortoff, 2019; PWC, 2019). The research has, in this way, demonstrated how, while remaining compliant with the GPRR, various points in the strategic pipeline can impede vision on the problem and disrupt efforts at progress.

A second central theme relates to the accompanying narratives. The terminology itself suggests an element of storytelling, distance and a predetermined course of events. The banking narratives generally reflect this in their assertion that GPGs are outside their control (Murray et al, 2019: 49). While the limited effect of policy to target change seemingly supports this, the increased improvement within the sector, as opposed to the wider population, suggests otherwise. As such, an alternative conclusion is that organizational efforts are not ambitious or far reaching enough. The evidence shows that organizations are myopic in their focus as discussion around pay remains taboo. The failure to include key issues, such as pay transparency, quite obviously central to understanding and targeting pay differentials, speaks volumes. While the GEO evidence-based assessment categorizes these actions as effective, this reticence is as illuminating as it is concerning (GEO, 2018b). Greater transparency is needed (BEIS, 2018a). Without full visibility of the problem, the capacity to eradicate it is invariably limited. The multiple ways vision of the problem is constrained reiterates the themes discussed in the legal analysis and more sociological explanations.

A final conclusion concerns the architectural feature of governance, the role of key actors in government and what is next for the GPRR. It is encouraging that, despite the 2019–20 government suspension of enforcement, companies still chose to report. This suggests either a genuine commitment to reporting or that systems were set up for compliance.[3] However, the suspension itself reflects the trend to deprioritize gender equality measures by key political actors, also observed in the aftermath of the 2007–08 financial crisis (Guerrina and Masselot, 2018: 327). The requirement itself is not new; companies had a year to prepare reports and systems were in place, yet suspension instead of a temporary delay was deemed necessary. Within this context, the effect of Brexit and the lack of compulsion to keep up with emerging EU requirements are also concerning (Wigand, 2021). The adoption of recommended changes, or additional efforts to address the lack of transparency, are unlikely, despite the financial imperatives for change (BEIS, 2018a; HoC, 2019a). While the reintroduction of the requirement for the 2020–21 reporting window is encouraging, the decision to offer a six-month grace period underlines the positioning of equality measures as peripheral (GEO, 2021). This evidence suggests that path-altering dynamics are currently more likely to occur at the organizational level.

What remains clear from this and previous chapters is that both institutional regulations and organizational responses contribute to the way the architectures of inequality is structured beyond its initial foundations, how it changes over time through statute, and how organizations respond to these regulatory changes beyond levels of compliance. Approaches to gender pay inequity are affected by the foundational principles of addressing gender inequalities in Britain, how these principles have changed with the passage of legislation, and how organizations have taken these up with varying levels of engagement.

This chapter has shown how the phenomenon of the GPG persists and evolves, as emerging firms in tech finance with large gaps have clearly demonstrated. Within this context organizations can still act in a decisive and influential way and retain the capacity to change. To make that more of a reality the challenge will be moving away from the language of lack of control over gaps, to confront the contradictions of transparency, fix the repositioning of equality as a business imperative and utilize the control mechanism of pay.

Examination of women's micro-level experiences of both legal and organizational approaches is now given as we move to the qualitative micro-level examination, focussing first on the topic of pay in Chapter 5.

Notes

[1]   https://gender-pay-gap.service.gov.uk/
[2]   Reporting deadlines are different for public sector organizations (31 March) and businesses and charities (5 April).
[3]   4,962 companies had reported by the deadline. By 25 January 2021 the total reports submitted for 2019–20 stood at 5,976.

5

Pay Practices and Inequalities

Introduction

The GPRR data starkly reveals that the gendered inequities pertinent to the financial crisis have not been resolved. This demonstrates that despite the widely recognized need for reform other interconnected factors, such as organizational practices, cultures, and behaviours, continue to help insulate the GPG from more wholesale change.

This micro-level phase of the analysis interrogates the semi-structured interviews carried out with those working in and around the finance sector. The empirical data from qualitative interviews are used here to understand the lived reality of some of the GPGs observed in Chapter 4 and the efficacy of efforts designed of offset them. This addresses the core research questions with reference to: how legal entitlements translate into a practical understanding and knowledge of rights; whether rights and institutional structures are accessible to workers; the factors relevant to accessibility; and how regulatory requirements are experienced in the context of the finance sector.

The EHRC (2009) and Treasury Committee (2010) examined the under-representation of women in senior levels in finance. Inequalities and GPGs in banking and finance have been attributed to how the sector typically organizes work, recruitment and pay, further intensified by informal mechanisms and the corporate culture (Metcalf and Rolfe, 2009; Atkinson, 2011: 250). Instances include: the unencumbered worker, still perceived as the ideal manager; the long-hours culture; the incompatibility of caring and parenthood with the requirements of senior roles, thus presenting barriers to those with additional responsibilities; the after-hours networking culture, modelled around masculine traits; gendered skill sets associated with certain high-paying roles and parts of the sector; and the structure of work that limits part-time roles outside the branch network (Liff and Ward, 2001; Harkness, 2004; Özbilgin and Woodward, 2004; Manning and Petrongolo, 2008; Wilson, 2014: 362). The embedded normalcy of these masculine cultures was shockingly illustrated by the Presidents' Club saga in 2018, which many leading financiers attended (Marriage, 2018).[1]

This series of chapters (5–7) draws on the lived experience of women working in various parts of the finance sector, to give voice to their experiences on a range of subjects material to the GPG. The analysis is structured according to the topics that interviewees discussed, those being: promotion, progression and caring responsibilities (see Chapter 6); organizational policy and practice (see Chapter 7); and starting here with the most significant for participants, pay. This analysis demonstrates how institutional, organizational, sociological and economic explanations contribute to the architectures of inequality within finance and the intractability of the GPG.

First, the methodological approach to participant recruitment is summarized and an overview of interviewees is provided.

Second, the pay and bonus systems interviewees described are examined with reference to annual uplifts and the discretionary nature of reward. The capacity for individuals to negotiate pay is considered with reference to out-of-cycle increases and job change. This reveals how impenetrable organizational pay systems are and the gendered differentials in how women position themselves with regard to pay.

Third, the capacity for interviewees to challenge disparities is assessed in terms of their knowledge of equal pay requirements and initiatives intended to support the drive for equal pay. What is evident from this analysis is how the law is obscured by organizational practices, such as hidden pay systems and the bonus culture, which dilute the strength of legislation seeking to redress gender pay inequity. While organizations are obliged to comply with statutory regulatory requirements, the architectural features of transparency and light-touch governance demonstrate how organizational practices, norms and power relations can obfuscate and retard the original intentions of the lawmakers.

To draw together the analysis, employees' experiences are considered with a particular focus on institutional theoretical explanations. Interviewees give voice to interesting dynamics in the impact effectiveness of key aspects of legislation at the micro level. While the accompanying narratives discussed in Chapter 4 claim that GPGs are the result of occupational segregation, the pay processes participants described undermine the strength of these assertions. What is evident is how, despite improved institutional approaches to transparency, the normalization of GPGs and the individualized approach to pay setting remain limiting. The murky relationship between equal pay and gender pay inequity further highlights the contradictions of transparency surrounding the GPG.

Participant recruitment

Interviewee recruitment was targeted at those working in and around the finance sector with no restrictions on age, seniority or length of service.

Interviewees were sought from three broad groups: firstly those in HRM involved in producing the gender pay reporting data; a second group targeted trade unions and those representing workers in the sector; and, finally, the main target population, women working within the sector. For this final group, given the size and slow progress in addressing gaps at the top of the earnings distribution, there was a focus on senior and management roles, which did, in part, drive the target population. While men's voices could also lend useful contributions to the topic, given the limited time and resource available, a decision was made to concentrate on women (see Appendix 4 for further details of recruitment and the interview process).

Given the sensitivity of the topic, HRM reluctance to engage with the research was anticipated. To alleviate these limitations a dual approach to participant recruitment was planned. Direct contact and a purposive sampling method targeted those listed on organizational gender pay reports, through email or LinkedIn, in an effort to recruit those in the first group. This approach failed to generate any leads.

As an alternative, I approached contacts in my professional and personal networks and pursued a snowball sampling method. As the snowball analogy suggests, this process took time to build up momentum.

Given the purposive sampling strategy failed to generate any leads, the intention to adopt McDowell's (1998: 2136) 'comparative research strategy' for interviews, whereby those in similar jobs across different organization types are interviewed, was not possible. Concern over the topic, possibly given the increased attention on GPGs, made gatekeepers hesitant to grant access via the purposive approach. (McDowell (1998: 2141) experienced these difficulties in similar circumstances.) The importance and relevance of interviewing is through identification of individual perceptions and experiences. Inferences about occupational groupings are still achieved through participant insights. It is also important to acknowledge the potential for self-selection bias, as those volunteering to take part may be more likely to feel that have something to say on the topic. However, the research is not intended to be definitive. The force of example, or the 'critical case', can be just as relevant and impactful and therefore is also generalizable (Aharoni, 2011). Interview findings form part of a stratified understanding of the problem. The different insights garnered help to build a dynamic reflection of the goalposts surrounding gender pay inequality in action.

Table 5.1 provides an overview of the pseudonyms ascribed to participants, employer type, age, family status and nationality.

Interviews were semi-structured and centred on matters such as: the impact of pay policy and how bonuses are distributed; how careers had developed and the effect of caring commitments; and their perceptions of workplace policies. These are all personal and emotive topics which the interviews opened up in various ways and to varying degrees.

Table 5.1: Overview of interview participants

Participant pseudonym	Seniority and organization type	Children	Age range	Nationality
Alice	Senior in corporate banking for global UK bank	Yes	50+	British
Belinda	Branch cashier for global UK bank	Yes	50+	British
Claire	Senior in leverage finance for global UK bank	Yes	40+	British
Ella	Mid-level HR for global Asian bank	No	30+	British
Faye	Branch cashier and union rep for global UK bank	Yes	50+	British
Greg	Trade union organizer in the sector	Not applicable	60+	British
Hilary	Senior director in corporate banking for global European bank	Yes	40+	British
Jacqui	Mid-level in risk management for global UK bank	No	40+	British
Jade	Senior HR for global investment management firm	Yes	30+	Australasian
Jane	Senior director in investments for global European bank	Yes	50+	British
Jean	Mid-level HR for building society	Not discussed	50+	British
Kate	Senior HR for global UK bank	Yes	50+	British
Kaye	Senior in commercial banking for global UK bank	No	30+	British
Krista	Senior in corporate banking for global UK bank	Yes	40+	European
Laila	Mid-level in investment for global UK bank	No	20+	European
Moira	Trade union organizer in the sector	Not applicable	60+	British
Nia	Senior in commercial banking for global UK bank	No	50+	British
Reshma	Mid-level in risk management for global payment firm	Yes	30+	Asian
Roy	Trade union organizer in the sector	Not applicable	50+	British
Sabina	Mid-level analyst in hedge fund	No	30+	European
Sally	Senior Director in commercial banking for global UK bank	No	50+	British
Sophie	Senior in corporate banking for global UK bank	Yes	40+	British
Sue	Mid-level in commercial banking for global UK bank	Yes	40+	British
Tali	Mid-level in global risk analysis for global UK bank	No	20+	European
Val	Mid-level in investment for global Asian bank	No	20+	European
Yasmine	Mid-level in commercial banking for global UK bank	Yes	50+	British

This series of chapters examines these topics, focussing first on pay and bonus.

Remuneration systems and the capacity to negotiate

Wage determination and pay policy ascribes value to the work men and women do (Rubery et al, 2005). It is well documented that large pay bandings and hidden pay and reward systems can mask and legitimize gendered valuations within occupations and between different parts of the sector (EHRC, 2009; Madden, 2012; Gall, 2017; Koskinen Sandberg, 2017). A lack of transparency around pay, beyond the pay reporting requirements, and the use of PRP systems are significant features of the finance sector's approach to remuneration (Gall, 2017: 14). This is despite the GEO (2018b) designating greater transparency an 'effective' action to combat pay inequity (see Chapter 4). Participant experiences of pay policy, which we turn to now, highlights how this broad discretion in the awarding of pay impacts within occupations, exposing the lived realities of the organizational blind spot surrounding remuneration.

Hidden pay systems, wide bandings and bonus

Despite the organizational assertion that GPGs are the result of occupational segregation, pay and reward practices were described by participants as another key factor in understanding gender pay inequities. While there may have been an element of self-selection in the recruitment process, as the women interviewed had agreed to participate in research on the GPG, the processes surrounding all aspects of remuneration were highlighted as relevant by most interviewees. They described their perceptions of and interactions with the pay systems used in their respective firms. Their overriding criticisms relate to a lack of transparency in these hidden approaches. This is now explored with reference to annual uplifts and wide pay bandings.

The communication of annual pay rises demonstrates how organizational approaches can undermine the law. Participants working in different roles for a variety of global banking firms described the notifications they receive outlining uplifts. These notices are accompanied by explicit instructions, or implied expectations, to keep the information confidential (Sophie, Sue, Yasmine, Belinda, Jade, Nia, Alice, Krista and Kaye).[2] Alice (senior in global UK bank) said, "the letter clearly states, 'you're not allowed to discuss this with your colleagues'". Yasmine (mid-level in global UK bank) noted, "we're very very actively discouraged from talking about it". Some participants went on to suggest that any such discussions would potentially be disciplinary offences: "I've heard it's a disciplinary offence to discuss your salary package … you would be seriously reprimanded if you did" (Sue mid-level in global UK bank); "while it's not necessarily a disciplinary event if you did [discuss your pay], you know it could be used as a reason to have a disciplinary event" (Claire senior in global UK bank).

Meaningful conversations about pay, performance and grading are, in this way, restricted. These organizational expectations are further underlined by the wider cultural norm that renders discussions around pay taboo. This organizational control and the employee response to it conflicts with the macro-level statutory right to request pay details, as per section 77 EqA2010, which will be returned to later in this chapter.

Finance sector approaches to pay are further resistant to challenge, given the voluntary and limited remit of collective agreements and the PRP system itself. Union density has been steadily declining in the finance and insurance sector, falling from 37% in 1995 to just over 10% in 2021 (Bishop, 2022). The role unions have in negotiating pay is limited to organizations covered by collective agreements: around 30% coverage of the sector in 2021 (BEIS, 2022). Agreements typically cover personal banking firms, such as large retail banks and building societies, where unions have the capacity to negotiate terms and conditions for those in low and mid-level roles. Unions are not able to address pay inequalities higher up the pay distribution via collective bargaining. Furthermore, the remit of union negotiations is limited to the pay pot, and not the subsequent allocation of that, which is apportioned according to PRP systems at the behest of managers.

Union participants described the way that organizational approaches and negotiations concerning PRP work (Roy trade union organizer in the sector and Faye cashier and trade union rep). The annual pay uplift is agreed according to a bell curve approach, which requires pay review outcomes to fit the agreed pay pot. This "highly subjective" system pre-designates how many 'satisfactory', 'good' and 'outstanding' performance reviews there should be (Roy trade union organizer in the sector). If managers have too many 'good' ratings, they need to recalibrate to achieve the required amount.

Participants talked about their experience of this subjectivity, citing instances of receiving 'excellent' performance ratings, yet limited pay increases. Jacqui (mid-level in global UK bank) noted the variable approach of managers when faced with ratings that do not add up. Val (mid-level in global Asian bank) described how the process does not operate like a "meritocracy" and is laden with bias. Union representatives explained how their capacity to address the issue is restricted, given their limited remit.

Participants frequently described a complete lack of understanding of the pay systems. Sue (mid-level in global UK bank) acknowledged, "our organization has no transparency with regards to pay scales, so I couldn't find anywhere what the minimum would be for someone at my grade".

Being uninformed in this way led to feelings of frustration for employees, echoing the costs of pay secrecy, described by Colella et al (2007). Alice (senior in global UK bank) described the vagaries resulting from large pay bandings.

> 'We need to be more transparent in terms of our pay within pay grades. Rather than have a pay range within a certain role, you can have a range and be more transparent about what that is, what that means. There's no point in publishing the bracket, it's so huge no-one knows what it means.'

The frustrations articulated by participants extended beyond annual uplifts and pay scales, to include all aspects of reward. The mechanisms that calculate and award bonuses were described as even more opaque. Heavily dependent on who your manager is, responses were typified by comments such as, "it's not an exact science ... it's very secret squirrel" (Sophie senior in global UK bank).

Interviewees revealed practices such as bonuses that stay with you even after leaving high income-generating roles. Nia (senior in global UK bank) described the bonuses a couple of her male colleagues, who had previously worked as traders, were still receiving. Despite now occupying jobs in her commercial banking team, they continue to receive comparatively high bonus payments associated with their previous roles. Her relatively low bonus figure and the inequality arising from these ongoing disproportionate payments was organizationally normalized. Historic pay differentials are, in this way, preserved and a disconnect between current performance and pay is legitimized. The architectures of inequality model provides a means to understand this disconnect as, despite the extension of legislation and organizational approaches targeting inequities, existing structures remain firm.

The allocation of pay and bonus is subject to management discretion, laden with potential for bias and defined as variable and uncertain. Participants described how the secrecy surrounding pay bandings and bonus restricts their capacity to position their expectations and negotiate uplifts, which we turn to now.

Out-of-cycle increases and negotiation strategies

The degree to which negotiation of pay is possible is also shrouded in secrecy. Characterized as part of the system, this legitimizes resultant pay gaps as individual failures of women to negotiate successfully and illustrates the 'doing of gender' at work (Martin, 2003; Acker, 2009). The uncertainty in pay bandings was described as enabling other factors to come into play. Participants raised interesting observations about out-of-cycle pay increases and pay negotiation strategies.

Tali (mid-level in global UK bank) described her experience of fighting to achieve an out-of-cycle pay increase to remedy her low pay. She was later told she would not receive her annual pay review, again rendering her pay below the market rate. The relationship between the legal entitlement to equal pay and organizational approaches to pay rates demonstrates the interaction and counterbalancing effect of each theoretical component in the architectures model.

Those with experience of either managing others, or from an HR and trade union perspective, noted how men are more likely than women to request out-of-cycle pay increases. Interviewees described how, in their experience, men were more confident than women about taking the risk of asking; they will shout the loudest and more commonly seek out uplifts driven by external job offers (Kate, Jean, Moira, Sally and Kaye). Sally and Sophie (both senior in global UK banks) conveyed their experience of awarding out-of-cycle increases to women in their teams, having realized their pay was too low. The women concerned did not drive the increases themselves, indeed they may not have known of the disparity. More broadly these interviewees acknowledged the well-documented trait that women do not negotiate as well as men (Blau and Kahn, 2017; Colebrook et al, 2018). Correspondingly, Tali (mid-level in global UK) suggested that she would like more support in how to negotiate. This reflects the theme in the literature that men are more confident in these situations (Niederle and Vesterlund, 2007).

HR respondents were also aware of these gendered differentials (Kate senior HR in global UK bank and Jean mid-level HR in building society). They described how they were in the process of looking into the impacts of out-of-cycle pay awards. The intention of their analysis was to inform the construction of organizational policy to offset gendered effects, supporting the work of Dobbin (2009). If higher rewards are partly achieved by shouting the loudest in asking, reducing the ambiguity around pay would support individuals in positioning their expectations and negotiations around what is achievable and expected (Bohnet, 2016: 70–1).

The effect of gendered assumptions and values, such as men's risk-taking appetite, is discussed further in Chapter 6. Of relevance to the discussion here is the way the secrecy inherent within PRP systems allows existing inequalities to reproduce, relegitimizing existing gaps. Evidence has shown the self-fulfilling impact of performance ratings: those for women being typically less developmental or less likely to find potential than those for men (Correll and Simard, 2016; Eden, 2017).

In each of these instances the potential for anomalies and gender bias was enabled by the culture of secrecy concerning pay. Val (mid-level in global Asian bank), summarized the impact of this: "there is no transparency at all, there is an equality problem". This demonstrates Acker's (2006) theory of gendered processes within organizations. This lack of clarity further impacts the negotiation of pay at the point of job change, which we turn to now.

Job change

The overriding lack of transparency around pay was significant for participants when joining an organization or when moving roles; it also highlights the changing shape of careers within finance (see Chapters 2 and 3). Excluding clerical or graduate trainee roles, all participants described salary negotiation upon joining an organization, or moving within it, as largely uninformed. They had no knowledge and no way of finding out the detail of often extremely wide pay bands or, within some organizations, non-existent ones. This resulted in the frequent response that job applications and pay negotiations were approached blindly (Sabina, Val, Claire and Krista). Yasmine (mid-level in global UK bank) commented, "I've never seen a salary advertised with a job". Nia (senior in global UK bank) reflected, "there is no choice or power really. You either want the job or you don't".

Nia (senior in global UK bank) noted a fortuitous occasion where, at the point of changing job, she happened to know a colleague working in a similar role: "That was pure luck as I knew someone who was willing to share. Otherwise, you just go in blindly. There is no choice or power really." Equally, Hilary (senior in global European bank) acknowledged how not knowing had affected her when she was appointed to a very senior post in corporate banking: "I didn't realize at the time, but I should've fought harder for a higher grade. I went in too junior."

This experience resonated with Ella (mid-level HR in global Asian bank), who had been suggested a rate of pay for a role by a recruitment consultant. She realized too late that the tip she had been given was below the market rate. These experiences highlight the different obstacles that women face in securing comparable rates of pay at the point of recruitment. The resultant inequities are then further embedded over time.

An evolving mechanism around maximizing pay can be seen in the now redundant concept of a 'job for life' within the sector (O'Reilly, 1992; Crompton and Birkelund, 2000). While historically the requirement for long service has been a factor associated with lower pay for women, now the frequency of change between roles and most notably between companies is significant. Participants described how 'job shopping' affords the potential to negotiate larger pay increases than those achieved by staying in a role, regardless of performance ratings (Manning and Swaffield, 2008). This again denotes a variance in the capacity to negotiate pay, in terms of women's ability to move. Analysis by the ONS also notes how factors such as the commuting gap impacts the GPG (Smith, 2019).

Annual pay awards were described as small compared to those achieved by changing company. Alice (senior in global UK bank) said: "You tend to find if you're moving roles then you can get more [money]." Sally (senior in global UK bank) agreed: "The only way to really negotiate salary is when you change jobs." Jade (senior HR in global investment management firm) elaborated: "If you're doing the same role then you get year on year a smallish increase. If you move to another role there's a bit of room to negotiate, but nothing like if you're an external candidate."

Relatedly, interviewees also revealed various factors limiting their capacity to change roles: wanting to keep existing flexibility arrangements (Kaye senior in global UK bank); the importance of trust and the known entity prompting them to stay with their current employer (Nia senior for global UK bank); career being on hold for kids, first in the expectation of having them, and then to be available for school drop-offs (Yasmine mid-level in global UK bank); and, finally, the frequency of job change being affected by typically gendered traits (Sally senior in global UK bank). Interestingly while senior or mid-level in their respective firms, these respondents all worked in retail or commercial banking and not the highest paying parts of the sector (see Chapter 6 for further discussion of the factors constraining career paths).

Kate (senior HR in global UK bank) described the implications of employers continually bettering existing packages. As men are more likely to move roles than women, firms inherit inequities and gaps increase. This, she reflected, results in the continual reproduction of GPGs. She went on to acknowledge the institutional requirement to ban conversations regarding salary history, utilized in parts of the US and Australia, and incorporated within a proposed EU Directive (Wigand, 2021). This legal tool prohibits employers from requesting the details of previous remuneration packages.

Throughout the career lifecycle, hidden pay and grading processes create practical barriers, impeding the eradication of GPGs and obstructing the right to equal pay. The undermining influence of a broad lack of transparency is now considered with reference to the statutory entitlement to equal pay.

Legal entitlement in practice

The interviews evidence how the lack of organizational transparency around pay enables inequities to arise, while at the same time concealing the detail needed to challenge them. A lack of clarity about pay structures to feel fully informed and able to contest pay inconsistencies was a common theme. Participant experiences demonstrate the need for and importance of a woman's 'Right to Know', a theme championed by the Fawcett Society (Bazeley and Rosenblatt, 2019).[3] In addition, nearly 50 years on from the EqA70's inception, Fawcett Society (2018b) research suggests that one in three working people still do not know that pay discrimination is illegal. In the case study interviewees were asked about their experiences and understanding of some of the institutional regulations outlined in Chapters 2 and 3. Their responses are now described, demonstrating the practical barriers the law faces, which may also be relevant to some of the gaps described in Chapter 4: first with reference to unequal pay and the difficulties participants faced in rectifying it; second, these difficulties are considered in terms of participant knowledge of legal entitlements; finally, participants' experiences of statutory and less stringent voluntarist measures are explored.

The right to equal pay at the workplace

Several interviewees identified gender pay anomalies. Sue, Val and Nia discussed specific instances of unequal base salary pay with male comparators, how they had challenged this, and how the organization responded. Interestingly, these participants did not acknowledge the potential illegality of the situation. This may reflect a lack of awareness of equal pay provisions, or reluctance to use them. While back pay was mentioned (by Sophie senior in global UK bank and Val mid-level in global Asian bank), inequities were resolved in all instances by an uplift in salary, albeit sometimes a significant period after the underpayment was first raised by the employee, without any compensation for lost earnings and not necessarily in full. Clearly, their employers may have had a material factor defence to claims of unequal pay, but the illegality is not what is of note here. What is of interest is why the applicability of the law in these situations was not even acknowledged, let alone a viable consideration for participants.

Interviewees talked about the practical reality of being treated unfairly and voiced a disconnect with legislative entitlement. Tali (mid-level in global UK bank) described her experience of trying to rectify unequal pay. Having spent a year challenging her level of pay, she was finally given an out-of-cycle pay increase to remove the difference. However, at the end of the normal pay cycle review, she was not given an annual uplift. She described the management response: "They told me the regulations say that if you've given [an out-of-cycle increase] then you can't give one again. But they gave it to me as I was underpaid. If I don't get it again then I'm underpaid again?! You reach a point where you can't fight anymore."

The suggestion that correcting pay disparities was a battle, rather than a clear statutory entitlement, was echoed by Val (mid-level in global Asian bank). She discussed her struggle over a two-year period while working in a leveraged finance team to bring her pay in line with a male comparator: "Eventually they increased my salary, they brought me up by £20k in the end and now I'm in line with male colleagues … You have to fight all the time, I'm there now, but it's hard."

Regardless of whether the employer perceives liability, the culture is one that seemingly does not enable employees to feel supported in asserting their legal right to equal pay. A fundamental power imbalance between interviewees and their employers illustrates one of the foundational aspects of the architectures of inequality. As Roy (trade union organizer in the sector) stated: "parties are not equal". The impact of these inherent inequalities was described on a practical level by Nia (senior in global UK bank):

'When you're in a room and you have HR, and your line manager siding with HR, that made me feel quite threatened. I felt that I didn't want to push it any further. You don't have any HR resource on your side. I didn't have any support. It felt like if I kept pushing the issue, I would come off the worse for it.'

Participants spoke about feeling exhausted by the fight to correct pay inconsistencies (Tali mid-level in global UK bank and Val mid-level in global Asian bank). It seems, in these instances, the legal right to equal pay was accompanied by a loaded choice. The viability of this choice was reflected on by participants who perceived that challenging the situation more formally constituted a risk. Workplace power dynamics, individual reticence to drive a claim and negative assumptions about the potential consequences are evident.

Disparity in pay was also identified with reference to bonuses. While a bonus is not a contractual entitlement, where it is paid it is included in the equal pay provisions in the EqA2010 and subject to the same equal treatment requirements. Sophie (senior in global UK bank) described a bonus payment error. A management miscalculation had occurred while she was on maternity leave: "A mistake was made while I was on maternity ... in my bonus calculation. My boss at the time hadn't realized it would be pro rata, the figure he put down, so I got half of what I should have got." However, Sophie went on to describe how, despite acknowledging their fault, the corporate banking team she was working in did not fully rectify and pay her according to her performance ratings and, presumably, in line with her male colleagues. Correcting their error was apparently too difficult and so she lost out. The lack of clarity and discretion in bonus calculation makes challenging them problematic. In addition, and for Sophie, the potential to challenge further and rectify fully was seemingly not an option. This echoes the resigned acceptance of inequities that others described and the practical barriers they faced when trying to assert their legal entitlement.

Awareness of rights and the culture of secrecy

The instances of unequal pay described show a disconnect with statutory equal pay provisions, but also section 77 in the EqA2010 (see

Chapter 3). This provision concerns pay secrecy clauses and an employee's ability to render them unenforceable, if seeking to make a relevant pay disclosure. This is potentially at odds with the lack of transparency and threats of disciplinary action for discussing pay, as already examined. The management expectation that employees will not talk about pay or bonus was commonly acknowledged by interviewees (Sophie, Sue, Yasmine, Belinda, Jade, Nia, Alice, Krista and Kaye). Jade (senior HR in global investment management firm) recognized a disconnect with the legal entitlement: "People are encouraged to keep quiet about their pay. I'm sure that within the Equality Act they are able to act, but that's not common knowledge."

While general discussions about pay are not covered by section 77, the typically British approach to discussing pay is closed (Jean mid-level HR in building society). The implied and explicit organizational norms further embed this cultural expectation and stymy efforts at enabling greater transparency. The inevitable impact of this lack of transparency is writ large in the experience of Nia (senior in global UK bank). She described the organizational reluctance to comply with section 77 after she had requested pay information, with reference to making a relevant pay disclosure. A colleague had shared his salary information with her, but she did not want to breach a trust, given the company position on this. Management pressed her into revealing her source and making her request a formal process, but her concern over the repercussions led her to drop the matter. Management did not remedy the inequity. She described a subsequent job move that achieved a 20% pay increase and brought her into line with colleagues. She was told her pay was, "embarrassingly low compared to my team" (Nia). This again demonstrates how legal entitlement to equal pay can be impenetrable and inaccessible for many; the alternative to finding a remedy within the organization was to leave.

The inability to speak up about inequalities at work is described here by participants in terms of the lack of support they experienced, the confused and variable pay systems in operation, and the pervasive nature of the culture of silence. The regulatory approach to pay transparency has been dramatically improved since the introduction of the GPRR. The impact and effectiveness of the measure at the micro level is now considered.

The Gender Pay Reporting Regulations and Women in Finance Charter

The long-held preference for a light-touch approach to regulation and avoidance of onerous regulatory burden in Britain was described in Chapters 2 and 3. Efforts to prohibit and mandate change have been limited by the competing pressures of business and tempered by government, reflecting the variable priority given to equality policy initiatives (Dickens, 2007). The statutory compulsion of the reporting elements in the GPRR marked a step change (see Chapter 4). The requirement has undoubtedly raised awareness of GPGs across all organizations with more than 250 employees.

A resurgence of interest in gendered inequities, partly because of the financial crisis, also prompted the introduction of the Hampton-Alexander Review, the Women on Boards initiative, and associated targets (BIS, 2015; BEIS, 2017). Within the finance sector, the WiFC, a voluntary commitment supported by HM Treasury, was introduced to address the large GPGs within the sector. It requires signatories to commit to four targets concerning gender equality at senior levels. It is now seen as normal practice within the sector to sign the charter. The resultant increase in interest and organizational focus on equality and diversity was recognized by participants during interview (HoC, 2019b). Research has found that the GPG within finance has reduced marginally quicker than in other sectors, suggesting that systems of institutional and organizational rules can help encourage progress (Healy and Ahamed, 2019: 321). The GPRR and the WiFC were discussed by participants in terms of their understanding of the requirements and the degrees to which organizations complied and engaged.

Participants were all aware of the GPRR, though they varied in how valuable they believed the requirement to be and whether they had read or shown any interest in their own employer's report. The most common response was that it had achieved an increased level of attention on the problem (Greg, Kate, Jean, Moira, Sally, Nia, Alice and Claire). While prior to the implementation of the GPRR gender inequities within the sector were well understood, the publication of pay data has helped focus attention underlining the need for change.

Participants did, however, express a divergence of opinion as to whether the GPRR and the WiFC will drive progress. For instance, compliance with the GPRR was considered less important than the resultant negative publicity and reputational impact prompted by a bad report (Jade senior HR in global investment firm). Sally (senior in global UK bank) described this differential: "It's [the GPRR] helped us to lobby and resource. Negative media has a much bigger impact for us than the regulator. What are they going to do? Fine us? They're never going to fine us enough to make a difference."

That said, Roy (trade union organizer in the sector) did not believe the GPRR, or the resultant bad publicity and increased attention, were sufficient drivers for change:

'They're embarrassed by the figures but they'll get over it. Embarrassment's not a problem, they're pretty inured to it now. I genuinely don't think they care. I don't believe this industry will change on a voluntary basis. The Regulations need to go further. I can't voluntarily decide to adhere to the speed limit, it's not just a guide. There's a reason why these things are mandatory.'

The limitations of the GPRR, given the widely understood and accepted inequalities within the sector, perhaps more aptly reflect the resigned acceptance and normalization of the problem. The most common reaction among those interviewed was a lack of response to the stark gaps that reports revealed. Despite most participants occupying mid to senior roles, and so potentially most affected by limited progression and/or pay inequities, only one expressed disappointment in her organization, given the size of its GPG. Sally (senior in global UK bank) said: "When the numbers came out, I went to my boss and said, 'for the first time I'm embarrassed to work here, how is it so bad?'"

Interviewees sensed that little had changed because of the GPRR and WiFC, emphasizing their assumption of organizational reluctance or inertia to address reported gaps (Jane, Roy, Sally, Faye, Jacqui, Ella and Krista).

Sophie (senior in global UK bank) mentioned a pay increase she had received prior to the GPRR being implemented:

'Before the report was published, I got an ad hoc pay review, completely out of the blue. The idea of that was to put me in line with my male colleagues, but it wasn't explained very well. Two weeks later the gender pay gap report was published. It was very nice at that point in time, but then I became suspicious, have I been paid £7k less than male counterparts and for how many years? There was no back pay.'

Interviewees' experiences demonstrate the inherent tensions between institutional efforts to reduce the GPG, such as the GPRR and WiFC, and their limitations, due to the setting of low targets and organizational acceptance of the persistence of gaps.

The importance of legislative development and change in the GPG over time, identified in Chapters 2 and 3, has been considered here with reference to the micro-level experiences of women working in the finance sector. Institutional explanations are now used to situate these insights within the architectures model to better understand the nature of progress and change.

Applying the architectures model to the thematic analysis

The law has been significantly extended and developed in relation to gendered pay inequity. This chapter has explored how long-standing rights and more recent developments have been experienced by women working in finance to understand the persistence of gaps in the sector. Barriers to legal entitlement in terms of access, power dynamics, and limited knowledge and recourse to the law have been described. This has highlighted the practical consequences of the broad lack of transparency surrounding all aspects of pay.

Attempting to isolate institutional rules for assessment at the micro level has shown how organizational elements, such as remuneration structures and pay grades, alongside sociological considerations, such as power and workplace hierarchies, are useful to contextualize interviewees' experiences. The architectural characteristics observed in both the macro-level legal analysis (Chapters 2 and 3) and meso-level organizational analysis (Chapter 4), of a blinkered approach to transparency, free market governance and underlying foundational inequalities, are again evident. The awarding of large salaries, legitimized by the need to attract the best talent, illustrates how organizational practices can present barriers to women's legal entitlements. Despite an improved regulatory landscape, the secrecy around pay and promotion demonstrates how component parts of the architecture interact to reproduce foundational inequalities.

The architectures model provides a useful way of understanding the persistence of the GPG. Despite the continual modification of institutional approaches, the broader framework helps us to conceptualize and evaluate the progress trajectory of the GPG. To assist this endeavour, an assessment of institutional explanations is now given to explore the limitations the law faces. This draws on the feelings of disconnect and lack of support in accessing legal entitlements that participants described. Their insights are explored in terms of the barriers claimants face: first with reference to transparency and access to the law; and then to governance, the role of trade unions and voluntarism. Conclusions are then drawn articulating how these architectural features inform the potential for future change.

Institutional explanations and the importance of transparency

It is first useful to recap what is meant by institutional explanations, with reference to the wider context of equal pay law. The practical reality of how the law operates demonstrates the restrictive factors impacting upon individuals and their ability to use it. The extent to which the legal developments discussed here reduce or hide GPGs demonstrates the contradictions of transparency described throughout the research.

The law is framed as a vehicle with which to challenge inequities. Litigation has been shown to still hold potency in its ability to drive change, as the public sector no-win-no-fee cases in the 2000s and the ongoing supermarket equal pay cases demonstrate (Deakin et al, 2015; Croft, 2019). Yet the pursuance of equality measures has been subject to deprioritization (see Chapter 3). The role of law, the positioning of it, access to it and the factors associated with that, such as cost and consideration of the knock-on effect of taking a claim, are also fraught with difficulties for would-be claimants.

Exploration of these factors within the finance sector shows, despite the size of GPGs and reports of the 'alpha-male' culture, that reports of cases reaching tribunal are limited (Treasury Committee, 2018; Ablan, 2019). However, there have been some notable exceptions. Recent high-profile cases concerning discrimination and unequal pay help to account for this disconnect by illustrating the difficulties claimants face (Szalay, 2019).

In *Macken v BNP Paribas* (2019) the judgement focussed on three key elements: (1) the variable and inherently biased approach to the awarding of bonuses; (2) the lack of set criteria against which to score candidates at the point of recruitment; and (3) the application of the McLagan salary code to the individual and not the role.[4] The *Walker v Co-operative Group* (2020) case, supported by the Fawcett Society, highlighted other pertinent issues for equal pay claimants coming from the finance sector: the time taken for cases to be resolved; the scale of legal costs involved; and the impact of adversarial legal interventions on the individual, both personally and professionally.

These cases demonstrate how the lack of formal pay structures, wide pay bandings and issues of accessibility mean equal pay provisions do not easily translate into the work environment. As also indicated by these cases, a combination of factors may place insurmountable obstacles in the path of those wishing to pursue claims. Costs associated with representation in equal pay and discrimination cases are high and can stretch beyond the outcome of claims, even if successful. In equal pay cases, back pay is limited to six years, does not include lost pension rights and compensation is taxable, again limiting the potential for fair compensation. In addition, future employment can be impacted, given the stigma associated with taking a case and the close networks within the 'small world' of finance. Indeed, *Macken* subsequently pursued a £3.4 million claim to address the detrimental impact her case has had on her career prospects (Fullerton, 2021).

The foundational power imbalance around which the law is constructed is reflected in factors such as the burden of proof and costs of pursuing a claim. Alongside this, the ever-present lack of transparency, in terms of individual pay and identification of comparators, demonstrates the interrelationship between the institutional and organizational aspects of the architectures model. Institutional approaches are further limited by the declining role of trade unions and Britain's preference for voluntary approaches in the pursuit of change, which we turn to now.

Institutional explanations and the role of governance

Counterbalancing some of the limits of institutional regulation in terms of access, knowledge and support, organizations such as trade unions can extend the reach of the law (Heery, 2006). There is a long-held preference in Britain for a voluntarist system of industrial relations, where unions are free to bargain collectively. However, as described, membership has steadily declined in the sector and density is low. There has also been a trend away from the pursuance of industrial action since 1997, with a marked unwillingness post-2006 (Roy, trade union organizer in the sector). This highlights how the impact of trade unions has receded, indirectly contributing, through the lack of redress available, to the persistence of inequalities (Gall, 2017; Conley et al, 2019).

However, in addressing unequal pay, unions have typically moved beyond bargaining and have co-opted the law to challenge and campaign for change, helping counteract the difficulties of cost and access described (Conley, 2014; Deakin et al, 2015).[5]

The importance of collective action in driving institutional regulatory change was recognized as a core strand of the different phases in Chapter 2. The declining remit of trade unions since the 1980s is therefore a contributory factor restricting the effective implementation of equality measures. The importance of union representation, no-win-no-fee lawyers in multiparty cases, and social movements driving change has been well evidenced. Bearing in mind the barriers discussed during interviews, ensuring workers have the means and support to access and understand legal entitlements underlines the importance of collective forms of opposition (see Chapter 7).

The collective fuel that social movements can provide has been demonstrated again recently with the increased visibility we now have of the problem. For instance, this is illustrated by the attention derived from the introduction of the GPRR, and the accompanying furore around the BBC's publication of the salaries of its top stars (Kentish, 2018; Ruddick, 2018). The subsequent surge of visibility around equal pay coincided with the mass online social media campaigns against sexual abuse: #timesup and #metoo. The increased exposure of the issue of equal pay and discrimination in the workplace is helping to provide a sense of collective opposition beyond the trade union movement. For example, the expense and isolation of raising pay inequities has been raised by campaign groups like the Fawcett Society, which, in conjunction with Yess Law, are now providing free equal pay advice and support for individuals earning under £30,000 pa.[6] The difficulties associated with a lack of transparency have been countered by women at the BBC as they have organized themselves into sharing salary information (Gracie, 2019). Initiatives like the Fawcett Society's 'Right to Know' campaign, championed by the claimants in the *BNP Paribas* and *Co-op* cases, demonstrate how collective voices can push for change (Bazeley and Rosenblatt, 2019). That said, the degree to which these kinds of initiatives are tempered by the changeable political climate, the pandemic, Brexit, and the digital transformation of jobs in the sector, remains to be seen.

Assessment of institutional perspectives also demonstrates the resonance of the ongoing deference to the needs of business. This is illustrated by how participants perceive the prohibitive measures around equal pay and initiatives, such as the GPRR and WiFC. Despite the statutory and voluntary requirements, action to remedy change is voluntary and interviewees commonly described the setting of low targets. Resigned acceptance of the status quo reflects the 'diversity fatigue' and 'resentment' that has been associated with the GPRR in the highest paying parts of the sector (Makortoff, 2019). This demonstrates the organizational potential to disconnect from institutional regulatory requirements that require going beyond the statutory need to report.

While there are clear benefits to the legal compliance required by the GPRR and the voluntary sign-up to the WiFC, the preference for letting organizations decide, thereby avoiding mandatory action plans and quotas, is a persistent architectural feature. It has been suggested that the Hampton-Alexander Review targets were implemented to avoid more stringent measures from the EU (Fagan and Rubery, 2017; Guerrina and Masselot, 2018).[7] Nevertheless, research shows that statutory requirements with tough sanctions are more effective, in terms of women's representation at senior levels, compared to the voluntary approach currently preferred in Britain (Arndt and Wrohlich, 2019). In this context, further decoupling from the EU equality agenda post-Brexit is therefore concerning, given the British preference to defer to the needs of business.

Conclusion

This research set out to interrogate the efficacy of equality regulations and understand the markedly slow progress trajectory of the GPG within finance. By drawing on interviewees micro-level experiences this analysis has shown the nature of the barriers and opportunities the law has encountered. Institutional regulations can and do impact on organizations and the way they deal with the GPG. However, as the evidence from the employees interviewed has demonstrated, there are architectural constraints placed on these developments in terms of how women understand, experience and access legal entitlements. While institutional regulations retain a disruptive potential, as the revived feminism prompted by the GPRR and the capacity to litigate show, this potency is diminished. The lived realities of combined statutory and voluntarist approaches, alongside the power retained by organizations, where the norms of secrecy and fear are prevalent, have limited the potential for more significant and lasting change to reduce GPGs.

While the GPRR has extended the regulatory model, this sits alongside existing and competing tensions where the foundations, dug deep, remain unchanged. Through the experiences of interviewees, described in this chapter, the interactions within the architectures model are evident. Meso-level organizational barriers, such as hidden pay systems, alongside micro-level norms, such as gendered character traits and the pay taboo, have been shown to contribute to how inequalities are constructed and reproduced. The practical barriers that the law faces demonstrate the utility of the multilevel approach pursued in this research. For instance, the drive to improve organizational performance through PRP systems can act as a barrier to realizing the business benefits achieved through gender equality. This demonstrates how work systems, designed to support businesses to achieve a higher bottom line, may be at odds with the drive for greater equality (Davies et al, 2015: 539). The tensions described highlight fundamental limitations. The value of visualizing these interactions according to the architectures of inequality model helps determine the sites at which contradictions of transparency occur. The light-touch approach to governance does little to dissuade organizations from pursuing existing pay and progression policies. These restrictive characteristics, as described by participants, also demonstrate how the foundational inequalities upon which legislative extensions have been constructed perpetually undermine institutional change efforts.

The most pressing point from this analysis concerns the sector-wide lack of transparency around pay. This is despite the centrality of hidden pay practices to the problem of gender pay inequality. The capacity of high GPGs shaming firms into action is limited given the normalized occurrence of these inequities across the sector (Bennedsen et al, 2019). The claim commonly made by organizations that they do not have an unequal pay problem is blindsided by the fact that processes to ascertain these values are so opaque and undefined. The lack of open communication around all pay processes creates uncertainty, ambiguity and mistrust (Colella et al, 2007).

In financial services, there is typically a 65% usage of PRP, compared to 25% in the private sector overall (Gall, 2017: 14). PRP systems are not open or permeable to challenge, yet are laden with the potential for unconscious bias. Policymakers need to confront that reality, instead of attempting to work around it. Further to this, the 'institutional vocabulary' that legitimizes the large GPGs in the sector positions them as arising from occupational segregation and the factors associated with this (Suddaby and Greenwood, 2005). The fact that this logic does not then address the contradiction of transparency around pay and reward highlights the intractability of the problem and the need for organizational architectural reform.

This exploration of women's micro-level experiences has evidenced the practical reality of how change is constrained. The way that interviewees navigated critical decisions around their career paths and caring responsibilities offers another dimension to understand these limiting factors and is now addressed in Chapter 6.

Notes

[1] The Presidents Club was a long-running men-only fundraising event. It came under the spotlight in 2018 following reports of attendees sexually harassing hostesses.

[2] The names given in brackets denote the source participant. Interviewees were ascribed a pseudonym. See Table 5.1 for a full breakdown of pseudonyms, and their associated characteristics of organization type, job category, age, family status and nationality.

[3] 'Right to Know' is a campaign for an enforceable legal right for women to know what their male colleagues earn, if they suspect pay discrimination. A draft Equal Pay Bill was awaiting scheduling for its second reading in the House of Lords, with cross-party support. However, the parliamentary session has been prorogued and the Bill will make no further progress.

[4] McLagan is a pay benchmarking code to determine salary ranges in jobs across the finance sector.

[5] The impact of cost is illustrated by the sharp decline in tribunal claims, most notably discrimination cases, after the introduction of tribunal fees. Their subsequent removal prompted an increase in cases, reiterating how cost impacts access to justice (see Chapter 3 and Figure 3.1).

[6] The Equal Pay Advice Service was set up following crowdfunding to the Equal Pay Fund, accompanied by donated backpay from the BBC's former China editor, Carrie Gracie https://www.fawcettsociety.org.uk/equal-pay-advice-service. Similarly, the Times Up Legal Defence Fund in the US, has been established to support women experiencing various forms of misconduct and discrimination in the workplace https://timesupfoundation.org/work/times-up-legal-defense-fund/

[7] Hampton-Alexander was a government-led initiative to increase the representation of women in senior positions (see Chapter 3).

6

Career Paths, Care Responsibilities and Contingent Choices

Introduction

Women's micro-level experiences at the workplace are used in this series of chapters (5–7) to better understand the intractability of the GPG. This chapter examines the interview data with reference to how women working in the finance sector described their career paths, care responsibilities and the contingent choices and cultures that shaped them. Interviewees revealed how these trajectories and decisions around care were limited, while at the same time reflecting on progress, such as the ability to balance work and family life. This builds on the themes discussed in Chapter 5 concerning legal entitlements and the institutional and organizational nexus. The empirical data shows how inequalities arise not just from pay systems and structures but according to embedded norms and cultures in the workplace and the home (Treasury Committee, 2023a).

This layered explanatory approach is a useful way to visualize and understand the ongoing reconstruction of persistent gender pay inequities within the finance sector. As the qualitative interview analysis develops, these chapters further demonstrate the interrelationship between each theoretical explanation in the architectures model and how the ongoing tensions between them obstruct the eradication of the GPG.

This chapter first examines how participants described their initial motivations to enter the finance sector and their subsequent career choices. Their reflections are considered in light of typical character traits associated with some male majority jobs, the concepts of workplace hierarchies and the ideal worker, and the occupations that are considered more resistant or less appealing to women (Acker, 2006, 2009). The interview data evidences how women align to workplace codes, the importance of networks and increasingly political power struggles to reach senior levels. This reiterates the foundational inequalities and underlying gendered assumptions upon which the architectures model has been assembled and subsequently develops.

Second, the effect of decisions around working time and the reconciliation of work, family and home life are addressed. Those interviewed described how they have navigated choices relating to work and care responsibilities, and the resistance they have encountered marked by factors such as: presenteeism; the organization's country of origin; and trends associated with the type of work carried out.

To draw together the analysis and locate it within the architectures framework, women's insights are considered with reference to economic and sociological explanations for the GPG. Application of an economic lens contextualizes the career choices interviewees made and the importance of education and training. The opportunities available, and the skills women bring to their respective organizations, are described as framed within contingent and gendered management expectations, shaping their chances to progress. Sociological explanations usefully highlight the importance of gendered hierarchies at work and the degree to which norms and values in both the workplace and the home impact upon the jobs that women do.

The empirical evidence presented in this chapter shows the shifting relevance of economic and sociological perspectives, reflecting the ongoing movement in the architectures of inequality. Understanding the factors that impacted the key decisions for interviewees, described in this chapter, shows how developments in one area are often offset by resistance elsewhere. For example, the effect of improvements in terms of flexibility are then subject to restrictions in terms of its availability, the sacrifice required in some parts of the sector and pervasive norms in the home. The dynamism observed through this multidimensional approach helps make sense of the progress trajectory of the GPG as extensions remain counterbalanced by architectural footings.

Career paths and stereotypes

Career choices, investments and progression

Interviewees' career paths and decision making are material to understanding the occupational segregation discussed in Chapter 4. Participants reflected on the ongoing and pervasive effect of deeply embedded and gendered assumptions within finance, from the point of entry into the sector to subsequent progression and promotion.

For some participants, their original choice of job was, in part, motivated by the higher wages they anticipated earning. They recognized themselves as ambitious and keen to achieve (Sophie senior in global UK bank and Jacqui mid-level in global UK bank). Kaye (senior in global UK bank) articulated this by describing how she had entered a graduate programme, "looking for roles that paid good money". However, more often women spoke of the importance of non-economic forces, such as interest in the work, social networks, and the 'fun' of working in the industry, as key determining reasons for their choice of career (Jane, Hilary, Sophie, Claire and Kaye). In addition, Reshma (mid-level in global payment firm) described her initial career choice to be the route of least resistance. As a young successful graduate keen on aeronautical engineering, she opted for her current career path believing it would be less challenging as an Asian woman.

The stimuli for subsequent career path choices demonstrates how these initial motivations were developed. Senior roles within the industry are known for high pay and, within that, income-generating roles, in areas like investment banking and asset management, tend to offer significantly higher financial rewards than retail and corporate banking. Despite the driver of money that had motivated some women to enter the sector, subsequent career moves reflected that the potential to maximize earnings was limited by other factors. Sally (senior in global UK bank) described the gendered consequences of the culture in the higher paying parts of the industry:

'The investment bank is worst for women breaking in, the culture isn't there yet, retail is pretty good, corporate is getting better … If you think about the trading floor, then it's "work hard play hard" … most trading floors you can count the number of women on one hand. It's a testosterone filled environment. Most women I know who've been in [such an environment] have opted out.'

Hilary (senior in global European bank) also acknowledged the motivator of money, while noting the importance of other factors: "Yes, it can be very financially rewarding, but that's not the be all and end all. There are much nicer, more respectful places to work."

These reflections demonstrate the norms and behaviours that participants expect in certain higher paying parts of the sector, inevitably impacting their decision making. The rational choices of women working in the sector are accompanied, and in part determined, by how these expectations are acted out in certain occupations. Jade (senior in HR in global investment management firm) discussed her perception of investment management, concluding: "The general appeal of the industry, it's never been attractive to women, from grass roots level." Further to this, Kaye (senior in global UK bank) described her motivation to change job from a role in capital markets and trading: "The culture was unpleasant, bullying and it drove me to think about moving … It was very aggressive, quite toxic, and accusatory."

Cultural expectations, norms and environmental factors were significant for the career lifecycle decisions these interviewees had made. The interrelationship between theoretical explanations and each component part of the architectures model can be seen in the complexity of factors that shaped their decisions.

The participant cohort largely comprises a very well-educated group of employees who spent a significant amount of time spent investing in in-work training, particularly those on graduate programmes. The speed and ability to progress was an attractive proposition for those who joined such schemes. However, the effect of this investment was variable for interviewees. For example, Nia (senior in global UK bank) became aware of a GPG with a male colleague in her commercial banking team who had been part of her graduate programme. Despite their comparable performance review ratings and depth of experience, there was unequal progress in terms of pay.

The non-linear relationship between education and career development has been noted in the literature (McDowell, 2008). This was echoed by respondents as they described the more gendered parts of the industry as inaccessible or remote, not due to lack of skill but rather off-putting behaviours and norms (Jane, Sally, Ella and Val). In addition, while working at director level in an investment role Jane (senior in global European bank) spoke of an organizational disregard for her educational achievements. She noted her abilities were not fully utilized or recognized at work, impeding her progress. Krista (senior in global UK bank) commented: "When I passed this exam, I said, 'what is the incentive for me?' to my manager. 'Can we talk about this, a pay rise, promotion?' But I've had nothing, not even, 'we can't promote as we have a pay freeze.' No explanation."

The obstacles participants described to accessing highly paying parts of the sector were based on closed networks and gendered barriers, rather than unmet degrees of attainment. Hilary (senior in global European bank) recognized this difficulty: "At that level it's all about who supports you. Women aren't so good at getting that support … If someone's not banging the drum about you it's hard to do that yourself. As a woman you come across as annoying, too pushy, or too masculine."

Progression to the most senior roles was discussed in terms of the need to have networks or backers and the inevitability of power struggles between those vying for promotion (Jane senior in global European bank). Interviewees referred to hierarchy and political positioning, echoing Acker's (2006) inequality regimes (Ella mid-level HR in global Asian bank and Val mid-level in global Asian bank). The ambitions of respondents were impacted by their willingness to engage in these power struggles, the varied flexibility on offer and the pathways to leadership available to them, as described in the literature (Cassirer and Reskin, 2000; Madden, 2012). Hilary (senior in global European bank) described her career trajectory in this light:

'You need to be noticed. You can get known by drinking and being at the socials, or, by making a lot of money. I got known in the credit crisis, I worked with some of the traders and got known by managing their risk. It wasn't particularly sexy, but it was very effective ... It wasn't my thing to be on golfing weekends, not my scene at all.'

These reflections evidence how typically gendered networking environments may present barriers for women and, in so doing, reproduce existing inequalities. Women's choices are constrained by opportunities and their aspirations are inevitably impacted by what is achievable, or viewed as such (Aisenbrey and Brückner, 2008).

This demonstrates that the translation of investment to outcome is not clear cut, but laden with foundational inequalities and a lack of transparency in how these are rewarded across the diverse range of organizations interviewees worked for. Jacqui (mid-level in global UK bank) described frustrating discussions she had had with management about how to progress within the organization, despite being "more than qualified". Assessment was based around her visibility and profile within the firm, not her achievements and experience. She described how her manager had said:

'"You must have a better strategy and be networking more, you're not visible enough." But it's quite difficult to get that visible. I said: "I'd like to be more visible and I'm more than happy to take the report I write every month [to the senior management meeting], I'm more than happy to deliver it." I was told "the difficulty you've got is they associate your boss as the face of your work" ... I had a chat with one of our women ambassadors, and she said, "that's a very common thing ... they just like dealing with the same person they've always dealt with." So, what do I do?'

The vicious cycle Jacqui found herself in highlights how closed and gendered networks can be, regardless of skill and proficiency.

Participants also described how exposure to different experiences at work and the chance to broaden their skill sets were subject to the whim of managers in enabling these opportunities. This concurs with research findings showing that gender differences in occupation and unobservable characteristics are significant, particularly at the top of the pay spectrum (Blau and Kahn, 2017). Promotion and development were not attributed to education and workplace training, but with reference to other more impactful factors (Jane, Greg, Jacqui and Krista). The hidden complexities both motivating and limiting career trajectories demonstrate the interrelationship between each theoretical perspective in the architectures model.

Favoured character traits and the double bind

A gendering of occupations operates both horizontally and vertically within the banking sector (see Chapters 1 and 4). Interviewees were able to reflect on their experiences of these stereotypes to further illustrate the effect of factors impacting career trajectories beyond their educational investments. These insights demonstrate the depth of normative behaviours, the valuing of roles and the double bind women in the industry face, which is addressed next.

Participants described how credibility and success within post operates within the gendered hierarchies of the workplace. Claire (senior in global UK bank) reflected on how she is perceived within the senior management team: "There's a sense in how they react to me, versus how they react to other senior men in the business. Some do not like to be led by a woman."

The socialization of who is expected to be in a high-paying job is based upon those commonly occupying those roles. This can cast women in senior roles as misfits (Pham et al, 2018: 912).

Alice (senior in global UK bank) described how she wanted to move from retail bank management to a head office role in corporate banking. Her area director responded by telling her: "It's the wrong role for you, you're too nice for that." While her knee-jerk response was to plough ahead with the move anyway, the suggestion that the environment would be too tough illustrates the normative expectation of aggressive masculinized behaviours at work. Conversely, trade union participants were able to reflect on how branch management is now much more feminized and correspondingly less prestigious (Greg and Roy, trade union organizers in the sector). Whether these factors are contingent upon one another is a moot point. What is clear is that the gender hierarchy within retail branch management has been reconstructed and its value has diminished, demonstrating how organizations remain gendered through periods of change (Acker, 1989; Skuratowicz and Hunter, 2004).

The deeply embedded nature of the value associated with women and women's work was noted by Moira (trade union organizer in the sector). She described how female branch staff regularly undervalue themselves in evaluations, frequently commenting, "I'm only part-time ..." (Moira). She concluded that part-time staff often held a lesser perception of their own utility in their performance reviews, because of their limited hours. Regardless of the fact that this wholly negative perception and valuation is not empirically based, the way that these women internalized notions of value shows how pervasive underlying assumptions and inequalities can be (Lerodiakonou and Stavrou, 2015; Chadwick and Flinchbaugh, 2016).

These perceptions of value were accompanied by the identification of favoured character traits. Participants noted how areas like investment, trading and fintech are more heavily gendered and seemingly impervious to change (Sabina, Kate, Jean, Moira, Laila, Ella and Kaye). They identified the varying ways that attributes, such as risk-taking, aggression and confidence, are valued and rewarded in certain parts of the business. Their experiences of the 'double bind' that Acker (2012: 216) describes help illustrate the normative behaviours in certain parts of the industry.

Kaye (senior in global UK bank) noted her experience of working within a high-risk, high-reward environment at the end of the 2000s. She described the organizational expectation to conform to the risk-taking culture and how that ultimately led her to leave: "It was aggressive, the culture was just dog eat dog. The senior guys there, bear in mind they were under huge pressure to deliver, drove this continued pressure to deliver bigger and bigger deals."

The financial crisis prompted recognition of these typically masculine risk-taking cultures inherent within the industry and highlighted their damaging consequences (EHRC, 2009; Walby, 2009). However, despite the association of these behaviours with the consequences of the crisis, masculinized performances are still prevalent in certain parts of the industry (Treasury Committee, 2023a). Participants used terms like "aggressive" to describe the culture of working in asset management, investment, acquisitions, or private equity banking, as compared to more feminized parts of the business like commercial and retail banking (Jane, Sabina, Sally, Ella, Claire and Kaye). Jane (senior in global European bank) referred to the aggressive "slapdash sweary culture" she would expect on a British trading floor.

That said, the lack of diversity and the hard-hitting environment can be experienced in different ways. Claire (senior in global UK bank) described her experience of working in leverage finance: "I think there is this perception by women that this is an aggressive industry to be in. It can be, but that doesn't mean it's not fun or good."

Despite the financial crisis, these behaviours and the increased testosterone associated with them (Sally senior in global UK bank) remain highly rewarded in certain parts of the sector.

Correspondingly, several respondents noted that demonstrating typically male personality traits was viewed negatively (Tali, Sally, Hilary, Jacqui, Jade and Alice). Jacqui (mid-level in senior UK bank) described being asked during interview whether she was "confident enough" to progress to senior management in risk management. Her incredulity and disbelief at this line of questioning was based on her track record of successfully carrying out the role for the previous two years. She gave a further example of an occasion where she was criticized for being "too aggressive" after making what she believed to be a legitimate, measured challenge in a meeting. The common perception of skills, such as women's inferior capacity to negotiate and self-promote, and men's highly competitive risk-taking nature, is widely recognized (Bohnet, 2016; Exley and Kessler, 2019; Treasury Committee, 2023a). This demonstrates the double bind that Acker (2012) describes, as on the one hand her confidence was questioned, while on the other her forceful approach was also deemed inappropriate, or too masculine.

Doing gender at work

The occupational segregation within the sector was also identified by participants in terms of how they experienced gender at work. Women described their experience of being a woman in and around the office and their experiences of discriminatory behaviour.

Interviewees in mid-level and senior roles reflected on the frequent occurrence of being the only woman (Sally, Laila, Hilary, Sophie and Kaye). Val (mid-level in global Asian bank) commented on the judgements made by others with reference to her success at a young age: "You have to defend yourself, they're like, 'you've got there because you're good looking.' You're thinking 'how many times do I have to hear that?' But to them it doesn't matter, it's a male environment! It shouldn't be normal, but it is."

Participants described how they managed working in these gendered environments. For instance, Jane (senior in global European bank) reflected on her own character traits:

'I'm a bit Aspergery ... I'm just oblivious to things other women are sensitive to. It takes me ages to realize people are hitting on me. Once, with a colleague, we were talking about mutual interest and I realized his hand was on my leg. I'm not the most sensitive person.'

She recognized how her lack of perception or concern about behaviours that others may have found off-putting may have, conversely, enabled her progress to seniority in male-dominated areas. This underlines the lack of homogeneity in how women experience masculinized environments and behaviours.

Others described how workplace norms and being the only woman limited their ability to be themselves at work. Kaye (senior in global UK bank) said: "The language changes when you enter the room, they talk differently. My conversations, like gushing about my baby girl, don't happen."

Jacqui (mid-level in global UK bank) described her experience: "I felt excluded from all the banter and chat around the desk. They would talk about blokey things, moan about the wife, talk about football. I love football but don't think I got the chance to say."

Aside from "blokey, lad chat" (Sophie senior in global UK bank) in work, social interactions outside the workplace were described as extensions of these gendered topics and activities, with references made to heavy drinking, golf and sport generally (Roy, Hilary and Jacqui). This illustrates McDowell's (2008, 2010) contention that women are viewed as outsiders in an inherently male industry. These exchanges and activities demonstrate how women may feel excluded, devalued and unable to bring their whole selves to work.

That said, interviewees noted that overt sexism and discriminatory behaviour in the industry has diminished. Some were able to cite a positive shift over their careers. Kaye (senior in global UK bank) recalled the previously commonplace practice of meetings at men-only clubs, while Jane (senior in global European bank) recollected being whistled at on the trading floor and being "groped" at banking events.

Despite progress, others described ongoing discriminatory incidents, reflecting the lack of headway notable in some organizations. Val (mid-level in global Asian bank) described the head of her investment department as "a misogynist", who frequently commented on how her female colleagues were dressed, told sexist jokes and used inappropriate language in the office. Others, as outsiders looking in, recognized the different workplace cultures in certain parts of the sector that women choose not to be part of (Sally senior in global UK bank and Ella mid-level HR in global Asian bank). The shocking sexual allegations prompting the winding down of Odey Asset Management highlight the depths of the problem (Marriage et al, 2023). The impact of these behaviours inevitably contributes to ongoing occupational segregation. These foundational inequalities are now explored in relation to working time and the intersection of work and family life.

Working time, career interruptions and the second shift

The prevalence of the long-hours culture in the finance sector and the effect of normative expectations around maternity leave and parenthood remain critical in understanding the GPG (Hochschild, 2003; England, 2010; Goldin, 2021). The way that interviewees perceive the effect these factors have had on their career paths is therefore insightful.

Working time and the unencumbered worker

Part-time work has been used in Britain to balance the competing demands of work and family life, its availability most prominent in low-pay, low-skill work. The wage penalty associated with this is well understood (Brynin, 2017; Eden, 2017). The significant occupational segregation within banking is one of the drivers of the sector's GPG. Women occupy the majority of clerical part-time roles within finance firms, at the bottom of the pay scale, while men are significantly more prominent in senior roles (see Chapters 1 and 4). The agency interviewees' hold in terms of working time is therefore illustrative in understanding GPGs.

The usage of part-time work to reconcile work and family life is supported by the interview data. Both of the cashiering staff in the interview cohort occupied part-time roles throughout their careers and described how this enabled them to meet their caring responsibilities (Faye cashier and union rep in global UK bank and Belinda cashier in global UK bank). Their career choices were informed by a desire to be around for their children. That said, one was a single parent and so the element of choice was contingent. A further two participants chose to work in the branch network in the early part of their career to meet caring commitments. Once their children had grown up, they felt able to prioritize work and progressed to head office roles (Yasmine mid-level in global UK bank and Alice senior in global UK bank).

Beyond the branch, more senior participants described long working hours, commonly associated with the sector, sometimes with additional requirements of travel and after-hours networking (Tali, Sally, Sophie, Ella and Nia). While these expectations were flagged by those from mid to senior level, interviewees also noted how the increased availability of flexible working had shaped their career choices.

The qualitative data reveals that choice surrounding working time is embedded in an array of hidden complexities. Participants described inconsistency between and within organizations, in terms of the firms' willingness to embrace flexibility. Aside from perceptions of managerial support and seniority, the type of organization was also significant for some. This variability included the job grades being considered, hierarchical variations, the approach of individual line managers, the organization's country of origin and cultural norms (Tali mid-level in global UK bank and Jade senior HR in global investment management firm). For instance, Ella (mid-level HR in global Asian bank) discussed the normative barriers within her firm: "Culturally I think it's not predisposed to flexible working or remote access ... The culture needs long hours, there are certain areas here where you can't go before your boss, they need a lot of face time."

Interviewees described resistance to anything other than "very full-time" work surrounding the most well-paid roles, demonstrating the embedded nature of long hours within the industry (Sophie senior in global UK bank). Participants reflected on the value associated with working time arrangements and the costs they had experienced when choosing roles that supported flexible working and non-standard hours (Sabina, Sally and Ella).

Respondents also recognized that presenteeism was, at times, self-driven by a desire to fit in and do well (Tali, Sophie and Nia). The acknowledgement that this was, at least in part, self-motivated demonstrates the embedded image of the ideal worker. The competing tensions that participants described are illustrative of the ongoing preference for the 'unencumbered worker' in the highest-paying occupations (Acker, 2006). Household responsibilities cannot be present, as the need to fully commit and be flexible to the needs of the job remains paramount. This accords with the favoured masculine character traits and gendered support networks already described.

Presenteeism has been noted for its gendered effects, relating to work–family reconciliation and gender pay inequities (Metcalf and Rolfe, 2009; Rubery and Hebson, 2018: 416). The factors framing how women choose their working time arrangements has shown how this can affect career path trajectories. Women described how their plans and priorities changed as they got older or had families. The importance of work–life balance, alongside expectations around the hours required in certain roles, became a decisive and limiting factor (Sabina, Kate, Hilary, Sophie, Yasmine, Nia, Krista and Kaye). As indicated in Chapter 4, organizations are increasingly recognizing the need for greater flexibility. The variability in how firms facilitate this is explored further in Chapter 7, with reference to the application of workplace policies. The theme of women's career path and care choices is continued here with recognition of how career interruptions and caring requirements frame career trajectories and their ongoing effects.

Maternity leave and care choices

When reflecting on their careers, some participants described the impact of maternity leave and family commitments. Their insights illustrate how care choices were made, the effect of time away from the workplace and the loaded complexities inherent within these decisions. The issues they raised resonate with both economic and sociological explanations of the GPG, with reference to factors such as the lost accumulation of human capital and deeply embedded norms around the workplace and the family. In addition, the continual state of flux in the finance sector has gendered implications contextualizing how careers are shaped. The variable capacity women have to align to these shifts exposes the dynamism in the architectures model and relatedly the limited change in closing the sector's GPG.

Participants described how lost work experience impacted their career development and earnings, despite their returning to work immediately after maternity leave. Krista (senior in global UK bank) outlined her perception of the problem:

'When you come back you have to prove yourself again. When you're in a team you're given a client portfolio and you're given what's left. People have worked with them while you've been off, so you start from scratch and build your client base again. Not only have you lost a year of work experience, but you're working for a year to get back up to where you were, getting less chances to improve yourself. Then women often have another child, so the same scenario starts again.'

The continual change and restructuring in the industry also demonstrate how, alongside human capital choices and investments, other factors routinely impact career development. Hilary (senior in global European bank) discussed the challenges she faced after maternity leave within this context: "You haven't been there to see what's happening and protect yourself, to make sure someone's backing you. And when this stuff happens it's all about backers. The more senior women are, the more quickly they drop away, the support structure isn't there for them."

These comments concerned the impact of organizational change on a group of senior women, previously promoted as part of the drive to improve the firm's gender balance at senior levels. However, when cuts had to be made, these women were in the firing line. She went on: "When it comes down to closing stuff, then who your pals or mates are is important."

The ongoing restructuring in the industry (see Chapters 2 and 3), was discussed as redoubling the impact of time out. While the effect of maternity leave was perceived as detrimental, this was accompanied, in this instance, by the re-emergence of old support networks. A selection process relating to either maternity leave or 'old boys' networks' seems likely to have been discriminatory. The interaction between institutional legal requirements, organizational redundancy policies and sociological explanations, which informed the choices subsequently made, demonstrates the utility of the architectures model in helping illustrate how inequalities persist.

Decisions around the allocation of care were also described with reference to existing foundational inequalities. Participants explained how care decisions were reached based on the earning ability of each partner (Sally, Alice and Kaye), in this way reproducing existing wage inequalities. Kaye (senior in global UK bank) articulated this process:

'My husband works for a private equity firm, if things go well over the next two years … he would get a pay out of a couple of million. So that being the case we've taken an active decision to let his career develop, to prioritize that. I'm steadying the homelife.'

That said, factors beyond the economic rationale as to which partner should take the career break were also discussed during interviews. Reshma (mid-level in global payment firm), despite earning significantly more than her partner, took the full maternity period paid at the statutory minimum without attempting to return to work any earlier. In this instance, a purely human capital analysis fails to consider the crucial relevance of the wider context, invariably impacting her choices in intersectional ways. Gendered cultural and religious family norms were highlighted by Reshma who described, "a huge family network, my kids are raised by my whole family". In addition, the enhanced needs arising from her child's disability further contextualized her decision making.

The experiences interviewees shared highlighted the divergent ways that women and men choose to invest in work and family. The choice to have children is not one usually made by just one person, yet the distinct binary impact of the decision is troubling. This was illustrated by Sally (senior in global UK bank), who described her choice to prioritize building her career before trying for children. Given her substantially higher earnings, the intention was that her husband would be the primary carer. She went on to describe how they were ultimately unable to have children, again demonstrating the contingent choices women make, beyond the simplistic translation of work experience and reward.

There is a choice, albeit gendered, in deciding to have a family. The context and importance of non-economic factors and associated care decisions impact and steer the length of career interruption. The way that both women and men choose is laden with complexity.

The pervasive impact of normative behaviours around care was illustrated by Sally (senior in global UK bank). She recollected a discussion with a male member of her team regarding his concern over the potential effect of taking SPL and interrupting his career: "His reaction was, 'if I take three months off will it be career limiting for me?' I said, 'if it is, your wife's got real problems!'"

In addition, the impact of organizational attitudes and normative expectations around maternity was also evident. To illustrate, Sophie (senior in global UK bank) described her employer's response to her decision to take the full statutory entitlement for maternity leave as positive, suggesting this was unconventional: "They've been really good about it, there was no pressure to come back from maternity leave early at all!"

Expectations and pressure to conform can impact career paths and shape behaviours. This demonstrates how economic rationality and decisions around care are not unencumbered for women or men. The importance of networks to assist career development and enable the job to be done effectively, and the detrimental effect on those networks of taking time out, was flagged by Tali, Sally, Jacqui, Claire, Krista and Kaye. Time out was discussed in terms of lost human capital but also with reference to the impact it has in distancing women from networks, vital for success and progression to more senior roles.

Alongside the effect of caring responsibilities, the literature recognizes how an unequal division of labour within the home contributes to gender pay inequities (Hochschild, 2003). The relevance of this for interviewees is now explored.

Gendered roles within the home

The division of labour for both caring and household work and its impact on working time and the GPG is well recognized (Benard and Correll, 2010; Eden, 2017; Bensidoun and Trancart, 2018). While the family unit and roles within the private sphere have changed, the effect of traditional stereotypes remains relevant. The decisions interviewees made around workplace flexibilities, parenting and household labour helps illustrate the effect of these societal norms and foundational inequalities within the home. Underpinning the architectural framework, the paramount importance of existing inequalities and the interrelationship they have with theoretical explanations at the macro and meso level, helps illuminate how initiatives have impacted and why progress to address the GPG is prone to stalling.

Most interviewees described how, as the mother, they took the lead in parenting. Kate (senior HR in global UK bank) described her belief that women are naturally predisposed to consider the needs of family before career, noting she had done just that. That said, there was no apparent resistance or inherent aversion from interviewees to fathers assuming the lead parenting role, and indeed some families were organized that way (Jane, Sally and Jade). Krista (senior in global UK bank) commented that she would like to see improved paternity rights, to enable men to be more involved. There was also recognition from Claire (senior in global UK bank) that the traditional role of full-time mother was not a natural fit for her:

> 'I know I could never be a stay-at-home parent. I admire anyone that does – I don't know how they do it. Part of my personal identity is caught up in having a professional identity. When I was on maternity leave, I loved it, but I do remember we went to a sing and sign class and I found myself woofing 'twinkle twinkle'. I almost had an out-of-body experience: six months ago I was renegotiating hundreds of millions of dollars, and now I'm woofing 'twinkle twinkle'. What has my life become?!'

The difficulty of combining parenting with work was simply too much for Hilary (senior in global European bank), who saw no way to reconcile the two and so ultimately left her job. However, interviewees also flagged improved opportunities for flexible working (see Chapter 4), demonstrating the progress that has been made and a generational shift. Flexibility had not been available for older participants and, as such, their choices had been more constrained. This cohort had either opted for a traditional approach to balance work and care (Faye, Sue, Belinda and Alice) or, given their earning status, a 'house husband' had taken on the domestic responsibilities (Jane senior in global European bank and Sally senior in global UK bank). For younger women, there was more of a mixture. Sophie, Reshma and Krista utilized full-time work with compressed hours and flexibilities like home working, while Yasmine and Kaye combined part-time working and a more traditional approach. These interviewees all described active parenting roles for the father and a sharing of some responsibilities, though they also acknowledged they took the major share. There were exceptions; Claire (senior in global UK bank) stated: "It's split firmly down the middle." Jade (senior HR in global investment management firm) noted the fortuitous timing of her husband's redundancy, which, given the difficulties they were experiencing with wraparound childcare and long working hours, prompted him to take on primary carer duties full-time. The slowly evolving normative behaviours around parenthood and the role of fathers is evident.

However, the uptake of workplace flexibilities still reveals gendered mentalities. This is demonstrated by the participants who work full-time compressed hours to balance competing demands in a way that their partner does not. The ability to 'have it all' seemingly means that women are still taking most of the parenting load, but now doing so on top of employment demands. It seems that, while greater flexibilities may have opened the potential for women to stay in senior roles, it may not be sufficient to disrupt gendered family norms and may inadvertently further embed them (Grönlund and Magnusson, 2016).

The gendering of roles within the private sphere extends beyond caring responsibilities to encompass the division of household labour. Despite changing social attitudes, women still bear the burden of the 'second shift' at home (Hochschild, 2003; Friedman, 2015). This was explored during interviews. While Belinda and Jacqui stated that they took on the bulk of the work, most did not. Many hired in help (Sophie, Reshma, Alice, Claire Krista and Faye), some described a sharing of responsibilities with their partner (Hilary, Sophie, Yasmine, Jade, Krista and Faye), while others noted that their partners took on most domestic duties (Jane, Sabina, Tali, Sally and Sue). Interestingly, for respondents whose partners assumed the larger proportion of household work, children were either not present or had moved on.

The nature of the sample is relevant here, given these senior women were able to pay for help. It does also suggest that there may be a changing relevance in the burden of household work, at least for high-earning women.[1]

There were interesting reflections from the two younger participants (aged 25–35 and without children), whose partners carried out most household labour tasks because of their long working hours. Tali (mid-level in global UK bank) spoke of her desire to have a more equal share at home and suggested feelings of guilt about their current arrangement. Sabina (mid-level in hedge fund) directly articulated this: "I feel guilty that I should share what needs doing more equally. I should make a bigger effort to deprioritize work and be more available at home to share the chores with him."

The way that these women have invested in the long-hours culture and yet experience guilt demonstrates how normative values concerning domestic labour are internalized. Corresponding comparative discussions with men in similar positions would be helpful to understand their perceptions of these expectations and norms.

The variable ways that career paths are shaped and the effect of caring requirements and normative roles within the home has demonstrated the competing tensions that inform women's decision making. To draw this analysis together, the theoretical approaches that contribute to the architectures of inequality are now used as a scaffold to position these discussions around career paths and care.

Applying the architectures model to the thematic analysis

Over the past 50 years the role of women, both within the public and private spheres, has changed. Nevertheless, the construction of gender and the behaviours associated with traditional masculine and feminine characteristics remain prevalent. Qualitative interview data has shown that inferences made based on gender continue to inform occupational identities within finance. These predetermined patterns and rules, while changeable, operate within and beyond the scope of institutional and organizational structures, implicitly impacting upon them. They are built into the very fabric of society (Criado-Perez, 2019). There is social meaning and value attributed to the skills typically associated with women, and they are of lesser value than those associated with men. This can be seen in the institutional devaluation of women's work and the tendency for devaluing when jobs become progressively feminized (Reskin and Bielby, 2005; England, 2010; Perales, 2013; Rubery and Grimshaw, 2015).

Alongside the gendering of occupations and assumptions of value, these processes and norms can impact career choice and progression (Bensidoun and Trancart, 2018). Occupational positioning may affect the importance placed on promotion prospects in particular roles, compared to others that have flatter career outlooks. Research suggests that this is not because women value promotion less, but is due to the sex segregation that operates in terms of the roles women occupy, and the promotion prospects associated with them (Cassirer and Reskin, 2000). Research has also assessed the effect of performance reviews, which typically do not embody the same career development pathways for men and women (Correll and Simard, 2016). The lack of transparency in how these processes work in the finance sector contributes to the difficulty in challenging them.

This chapter has examined how career paths have been shaped by these behaviours and norms to help explain gendered pay hierarchies. What has become clear are the ways that rational economic choices are further impacted by sociologically constructed workplace values, expectations and culturally situated family norms. The interactions within and between these component parts of the architectures model indicate why the closure of the GPG remains so slow.

Economic explanations

The significance of the economic theoretical approach to the rational choices interviewees made is now explored. The key topics discussed in this chapter – the career path investments and the contingent decisions that frame them – are used to assess the relevance of this component part of the architectures model. This demonstrates the ongoing dynamism in the model and the need to look beyond the economic perspective to fully understand the slow closure of the GPG.

According to the rational economic model, value in the workplace is achieved based on the skills, knowledge and investments of those working within it. Educational attainment, labour force participation and the continuity of work experience are recognized by economic theorists as means to accumulate human capital (Becker, 1985). Within this context, individuals make choices about how they invest their own human capital, impacting upon earnings ability and, consequently, the GPG. Individual preferences, in terms of occupational field, work type, educational investment, labour force experience and hours worked, reflect these choices. This, in turn, determines the value placed upon the individual (Pham et al, 2018).

Theorists suggest that investments are variable; for instance, those with caring responsibilities are subject to interruption. Becker (1985) contended the increased demands women face on their leisure time, due to more intensive household and caring commitments, rendered them less productive at work.

Since the foundational work of Becker (1985), there have been significant increases in both women's participation in the labour force and women's level of educational attainment (OECD, 2017: 274; Quiros et al, 2018: 29). While career breaks for mothers are getting shorter, Polachek (2004) notes the determining impact that any break has on potential earnings. Economic theorists also place significance on the volume of hours worked over the life course. While traditional human capital variables have been amended to keep pace with the increasing level of women's labour force participation, the preference for full-time employment, demonstrated in the legal analysis (Chapters 2 and 3), is also relevant at the organizational level. It seemingly provides the gold standard capable of preventing human capital 'rusting' and against which other contractual arrangements are measured (Rubery and Grimshaw, 2015: 327). Goldin's (2021) Nobel Prize-winning research highlights the impact of long hours and 'greedy work' in understanding the persistence of GPGs at the top of the earnings spectrum.

The relevance of the economic benefit associated with educational investment has shifted. Across all age groups, the proportion of tertiary educated women is now higher for women than for men in almost all OECD countries, including Britain (DfE, 2019b). Across the EU the gap in favour of women has risen from 10% to 14% between 2008 and 2018 (OECD, 2019: 50). Illustrative of how the architecture is constantly being developed, economic theorists now highlight how the choice of subject women study may be of greater importance than the qualification achieved (Chevalier, 2007; Schulze, 2015; DfE, 2019a).

Blau and Kahn (2017: 801) note that education and experience accounted for 27% of the GPG in 1980 in the US context, dropping to 8% in 2010. Their research also highlights a slower decline in progress to eradicate gaps at the top of the earnings distribution; an area where you would expect the translation of educational investment to reward to be most potent. Research shows within the finance sector there is still a qualification gap, albeit declining, as men remain more highly qualified (Healy and Ahamed, 2019). Given the contrary wider educational trends, this suggests that more highly qualified women are less likely to be recruited or promoted. Correspondingly, alongside the development of fintech the impact of women's relatively low level of attainment in STEM subjects is significant and becoming more so (Sorgner et al, 2017; Howcroft and Rubery, 2019).

Interviewees described how the investments they made in and around the workplace to reach seniority have been subject to changing barriers. To illustrate, alongside increases in women's workforce participation and workplace flexibility, there have been seismic shifts in the way finance firms operate. The previously commonplace expectation of a job for life, and the resultant investment this approach required, has changed significantly over the past 50 years (Greg, Roy, Moira and Faye) (Crompton and Birkelund, 2000). The influx of players in the financial services market, beyond Britain's big four banks, the transformation of the branch network and globalization of finance requires different types of investment in work (McDowell, 2008). This fissuring of the workplace means that employees' movement between companies is now commonplace and the incentive to move is high (Olson, 2013; Weil, 2014). Length of tenure as a salary determinant is no longer as relevant as when employees remained with one organization for life.

Participants described the need to move company regularly to maximize their educational investment and returns (Tali, Sally, Alice, Claire and Kaye). Yet the changed workplace continues to reward investments in different gendered ways. Within finance, the premium paid for this movement demonstrates a repositioning of reward and the commodification of the individual and not the job. However, the capacity to go 'job shopping' is not necessarily a 'free' choice (Manning and Swaffield, 2008). This is evidenced by the commute gap for women, marking the way that gendered factors can limit the use of time and the ability to move (Smith, 2019). The expectations and outcomes around investments in work and choices over working have changed, while remaining heavily gendered. This is not because the women interviewed prioritized their families over their careers, or because they were less well-qualified, as economic explanations would suggest. Rather it depended very much on the organizational context and culture in which they were making these decisions and the degree to which they felt they were supported or hindered in their career progress.

When considering the translation of educational attainment and experience into outcomes, the problematic notion of the input/output model is reiterated by the experiences of participants evidenced in this chapter. On the one hand the loss of time and opportunity to develop skills and workplace experience, that participants described, reaffirms the economic theoretical position. However, the interview data revealed a range of limiting factors influencing how career pathways were chosen, including exclusive and inaccessible networks, and the effect of gendered values and assumptions both in the workplace and the home. The impact of maternity leave, factors shaping decisions regarding care responsibilities and flexible working illustrate the practical realities and constraining barriers interviewees experienced.

Shifts in women's educational attainment and workforce participation have corresponded with limited reductions in the large GPGs in the finance sector, seemingly more resistant to progress than other industries. The societal attitudes, norms and values within which gender pay inequity arises and stubbornly persists highlights the fundamental and embedded notions of gender identity both at work and in the home. The interview data has, in this way, evidenced the importance of a multilevel approach to look beyond the model of economic rationality. Choices around maximizing returns on human capital investments are complicated in many ways, blindsided by hidden networks, gendered barriers and the intractable influence of workplace hierarchies.

The resonance of these contradictions of transparency are now examined with reference to the sociological perspectives encompassed by the architectures model.

Sociological explanations

Given the gendered nature of this research, a feminist sociological perspective provides a useful rubric with which to analyse the interview data with reference to the discussions around career trajectories and care.

To understand how gender inequalities are produced and reproduced, sociological explanations consider the norms and values surrounding women and women's work. Notions of power and patriarchy in the workplace and the division of care and household labour in the home are highly relevant themes. Since the inception of the EqPA70, there has been significant change in the sexual division of labour. However, foundational inequalities remain marked, both in the workplace and for domestic and caring responsibilities (Shelton and John, 1996; Sayer, 2005; Friedman, 2015; Eden, 2017). These foundational underlying inequalities are slowly evolving, and the mechanisms that restrict or prompt such movement are at the heart of this enquiry. The phenomenon of the GPG operates within these socially embedded constructs, values and discriminatory behaviours.

Efforts to address inequalities are limited by normative behaviours as those in positions of power define the needs of business and can legitimize resistance to initiatives, for instance, quotas for senior roles. Equally, the cultural frame that suggests that the best person for the job should get the role fails to recognize how gendered the job itself and the process of acquiring it may be (Bohnet, 2016). Gendered management structures may disadvantage the best person if they do not fit the existing mould, thus reproducing existing inequalities.

These theories add weight to Acker's (1990, 2012) notion of gendered hierarchies in the workplace. When considered in the abstract, she suggests the ideal worker is a man. High status roles within finance typically require this unencumbered worker. Commitment to the job is demonstrated by an ability to undertake long hours and the flexibility to meet the demands of commuting, travel and networking. She posits that effectiveness at work is measured against these norms and subsequent rewards are associated with these masculine traits. In this way, the classification of jobs, promotion and wage systems (discussed in Chapter 5) are not neutral but serve to reinforce existing inequalities (Pham et al, 2018). Barriers for women, represented by both the glass ceiling and glass cliff, are synonymous with hierarchies of power. They operate alongside the privileged access and glass cushion afforded to men, when in pursuit of positions of seniority (Eden, 2017).[2] Within banking, research also shows that social relations and common practices are informed by patriarchal assumptions that position women as outsiders, as articulated by interviewees (Wilson, 2014).

These processes and the formation of gender are replicated in the private sphere. Progress towards a more egalitarian sharing of parenting and unpaid household work has apparently stalled since the 1990s (Hochschild, 2003; ONS, 2016). Women's biological capacity to have children continues to inform their status as primary carers. Sociological accounts place the choices associated with these roles, and the motherhood pay penalty incurred as a result, beyond any tangible control mechanism. These normative values instill social pressure to conform to a gender essentialist model of parenting. Hays (1998) suggested the concept of 'intensive mothering' has been reasserted. This creates a paradox in efforts to achieve equality in the workplace, alongside the choice and pressure of balancing work and family life. The tension in these competing expectations can be identified in the guilt experienced by women, as compared to men, in terms of attempting to balance the competing demands of work, caring responsibilities and domestic commitments (Miller, 2012).

These tensions are demonstrated in both the construction and limitations of SPL. Women are required to forgo their leave for men to access this poorly paid provision (BITC, 2018; Kaufman, 2018). The transformative potential of SPL is constrained by this structure, given it reinforces the notion of a singular primary carer to be determined by the mother (Atkinson, 2017). The trend of governance is ever present, informing and contributing to the 'doing of gender' (West and Zimmerman, 1987). Interviewees' experiences of caring requirements, as described in this chapter, highlight that women are not a homogeneous group. Expectations and attitudes concerning the value of women's work and how gender identities are constructed and reproduced within organizations accurately frames the contingent choices they described.

Sociological explanations are pertinent to the initial career choices that interviewees made and their subsequent development, helping to deepen our understanding of inequities within the sector. The interview data helps demonstrate how the movement and interrelationship within and between these explanations insulates the GPG from change. The architectures model provides a means to visualize and understand this lack of progress. The complexity of interwoven factors between each explanatory component helps to address the key research questions of how initiatives have impacted the GPG and why the gender revolution has stalled.

Conclusion

This chapter set out to explore how women approach their career paths, and decisions around family and parenthood. The analysis has shown areas of development and progress, but also the practicalities of evolving barriers and foundational inequalities constraining choice. The ongoing construction and reconstruction of the architectures of inequality in Britain is based upon these foundational principles. The micro-level analysis in this chapter has given voice to the ways this fundamental power imbalance translates for women working in finance.

The application of each thematic lens is useful to fully understand the dynamics and interrelationship within each theoretical approach and the ongoing dynamism in the model.

Within the case study there is a clear divergence in the way that investment and the trade-off with outcomes works across the organizational hierarchy, as demonstrated by the size of GPGs and the typically well-educated status of women at the top of the earnings distribution. Examination of how educational and workplace investments translate to financial reward exposes a lack of visibility in how these decisions are made in different organizations in the sector, as well as for different grades. Informed by foundational inequalities, the data have shown that women do not have the right, power and opportunity to choose freely. Career paths have been shaped by choices laden with normative values and bias.

The persistent and significant GPGs within the finance sector and the shifting relevance of both economic and sociological explanations are enhanced by the application of the architectures of inequality model. The developments that have been evidenced here, such as greater flexibility in reconciling work and family life, are positioned within this dynamic framework. Alongside progress, participants also described the variable and non-linear nature of change. Much like the contradictions of transparency discussed throughout the research, this chapter has shown how improvements in one area have been counterbalanced by resistance and lack of change elsewhere. For instance, the type of work carried out may mark a degree of resistance to embracing diversity, demonstrating an alternative perspective to that of Dobbin (2009). Understanding the continual movement of changing investments and choices around work and family, has revealed how ongoing tensions frustrate change.

The degrees to which legislation and workplace policies are implemented, diluted or obscured is discussed next in Chapter 7, helping to indicate where future change efforts should be focussed.

Notes

[1] The gendered nature of hired help was not discussed, though this too may reinforce traditional gender norms and intersectional inequities. Paid domestic roles are still deemed women's work, typically low paid, vulnerable and outside the scope of social protection systems.

[2] Eden (2017: 116) describes the glass cliff experience women can have when trying to breach the glass ceiling, typically offered roles where others have failed. This contrasts with the more supportive glass cushion promotions afforded to men.

7

Organizational Norms, HRM and the Gap Between Policy and Practice

Introduction

During the first evidence session of the new parliamentary inquiry into 'Sexism in the City', experts acknowledged that a lot is being said about gender inequity; however, not so much is being done (Treasury Committee, 2023a). Attention here is given to the mechanisms and initiatives designed to support organizational change and the gaps participants experienced between policy and practice. This chapter provides the third and final part of the qualitative stream of analysis. The application of organizational policies builds on the topics career paths, care, and contingent choices, articulated in Chapter 6, to further contextualize interviewees' decision making.

First, the barriers to progression and working time choices are explored by looking at policies designed to address the lack of women in senior roles and the availability of flexible working. This demonstrates how far organizations go beyond statutory compliance. Interviewees described their perceptions of these organizational approaches and the effect of organizational cultures on change efforts. This reveals how workplace norms and behaviours can both enable and obstruct policies targeting change.

Second, the impact of organized labour and group litigation to challenge policy and build momentum for change is then identified. Various forms of collective resistance have raised the awareness and visibility of pay inequities and given impetus to the drive for change (Deakin et al, 2015). However, the limited reality of this potential for interviewees, described in Chapter 6, is acknowledged.

Organizational explanations are then considered to situate these findings within the architectures model. The interview data is examined considering Dobbin's (2009) contention that HRM professionals have been the instigators of equality and diversity policies. While organizations have signed up to institutionally sanctioned change processes, such as the WiFC, these are too frequently 'empty shells' (Hoque and Noon, 2004). This demonstrates the resonance of these explanations to interviewees, highlighting the limitations of Dobbin's (2009) approach and demonstrating the need to examine the lived reality of organizational policies.

By framing this analysis as a component part of the architectures model, the limited effect that organizational initiatives have had for the women interviewed is more readily understood. The degree to which organizational structures and practices impact policy demonstrates the importance of addressing the issue of accountability, alongside the continual movement and counterbalancing tensions in the theoretical architectures framework. While organizations are willing to recognize and focus resource on some of the causative aspects of the GPG, the complexity of the inequality regimes in operation remain largely invisible to them (Acker, 2006). Understanding the variety of ways in which the problem is obscured from view suggests where sustained and renewed interventions need to occur, as will be discussed in Chapter 8.

Progression and flexible working policies

The sectoral variation in pay gaps highlights the importance of understanding the relationship between both institutional and organizational policy and practice. This indicates the need to consider the differential role of organizations and their macro-level responses to statutory institutional regulations. The financial imperatives for organizations to address GPGs are well established (McKinsey, 2018; WEF, 2018; Eswaran, 2019). However, despite these motivating factors, there is variability in how finance firms approach the problem, suggesting the pursuance of equality is subject to competing pressures (Davies et al, 2015; Makortoff, 2019).

Most organizations, according to the accompanying narratives (see Chapter 4), attribute their GPG to occupational segregation. Understanding routes to promotion and barriers to seniority is therefore vital. In Chapter 5 we saw how the lack of transparency around pay remains obstructive. The ability to balance work and family life was raised as a key theme in Chapter 6. To further contextualize the opportunities and barriers women face, this chapter now assesses the practical application of policies designed to support women's progression and flexibility at work. The interview data reveals layers of complexity in their availability and usage. This demonstrates how the somewhat myopic organizational perception of the problem acts to insulate the GPG from change.

Promotion: mentoring, networking and shortlists

Occupational segregation within the finance sector has prompted firms to implement mentoring and networking programmes to help women reach senior roles. However, divergence in the application and extent of these schemes reflects how organizational approaches are subject to barriers within the architectures.

The drive to improve the problem of the lack of senior women was reflected on by Hilary (senior in global European bank). She described her experience of being part of a women's leadership programme. While she acknowledged the programme was successful, in terms of enabling her and her seven female colleagues to reach senior positions, a subsequent period of organizational restructuring led to foundational gendered inequalities resurfacing. During this period, all eight of these women, previously supported, left the business in a highly gendered raft of redundancies. She felt that while male management networks were happy to support them to a point, the extent of this was limited:

'They worked so hard to get people like me put in those positions but, when it came down to it, management said, "we've got to get rid of staff", and then it was the women [who had been developed through the leadership programmes] that went. Nobody sat down and said, "there's a problem here, look at who you're choosing."'

Participants also voiced frustration with policy efforts such as 50/50 shortlists. Sophie, Sue and Yasmin described the demoralizing effect of being invited to interviews purely to make up the numbers, their experiences evidencing a tokenistic application of the policy. "They're very good at putting out things which look good and talk the talk, but when it comes down to it, not much has changed" (Jacqui mid-level in global UK bank).

While good practice awards and policies were described as commonplace, participants viewed this as window dressing, an assessment supported by the evidence of ongoing inequities.

Limitations in the scope of initiatives were also recognized. Tali (mid-level in global UK bank) described how organizational efforts to support women to reach senior levels were seemingly targeted at those already in senior management positions. She described the frustration she felt given her own ambitions to reach a senior level, concluding: "At the moment I have no visibility on how to get there." While initiatives may look good on paper, they were all out of reach for her. The limited focus on enabling transition from mid-level roles, as opposed to more senior progression points, has been flagged in the 'Sexism in the city' parliamentary inquiry, echoing these assertions (Treasury Committee, 2023a). Another participant described frustration with a women's networking day she had attended. Despite the group coming up with useful and valid suggestions for change, Sophie (senior in global UK bank) explained how these were subsequently not acted upon. This led her to surmise that the networking scheme was merely a "talking shop".

Conversely Jacqui (mid-level in global UK bank) noted her firm's reluctance to go as far as others in their efforts to support women: "Are we being as radical as some other organizations? No. Putting shortlists together for interview candidates? Absolutely not."

These experiences confirm the 'empty shell' hypothesis, evidencing a tick-box approach to equality (Hoque and Noon, 2004; Healy et al, 2011). Participants described their own organization's limitations with a resigned acceptance of the "glacial" and "slow" speed of change to address the gender imbalance (Jane, Roy, Sally, Ella and Nia).

Participants noted how the accessibility and application of policies was impacted by inertia or apathy at various points in the management pipeline. This illustrates the ways that progress may be obstructed, contributing to the intransigence of pay inequalities.

Alongside the variable applicability of these organizational approaches to promotion, participants also cited how improvements to flexibility were applied within firms.

Flexibility and the long-hours culture

While interviews were carried out pre-COVID-19, when homeworking became the norm, the availability of flexible working was already described as a much-improved landscape. The types of policies firms have in place and their usage was considered by interviewees with reference to job type, seniority and resistance along the management chain.

Participants discussed the numerous forms of flexible working arrangements they were engaged in, including: compressed; term-time only; part-time; working from home; and use of parental leave (Faye, Sophie, Sue, Yasmine, Belinda, Jacqui, Alice, Claire and Kaye). Interestingly, job-share was only identified in terms of its absence (Jade senior HR in global investment management firm). The degree of choice around flexible working appears to impact in different ways across the pay spectrum and in different parts of the industry. Despite efforts to embed flexibility becoming more widespread, a common theme was the variable way flexibility requirements were understood across occupational hierarchies (Greg, Sabina, Faye and Yasmine). While higher status participants in retail, commercial and corporate banking acknowledged that a range of working-time patterns was increasingly available, this was not the perception of those lower down the pay scale. Faye (cashier and union rep in global UK bank) described her experience of this disconnect: "We have low-level managers who don't know it [flexible working policy] exists, or how to implement it. If a member asks for flexi-working they say 'no', as it's easier to brush them off than try to make it work." The part-time hours that these staff can access are seemingly inflexible.

Pay gaps are typically lower at the bottom of the income scale. In banking, women are prominent working in these lower status, lower pay, and often part-time roles (see Chapter 4). Of the participants who were currently working, or had previously worked in lower status jobs, they all acknowledged their choice in doing so was motivated by the need to prioritize family, resonating with economic explanations (Faye, Sue and Belinda).

At the mid and top end of the pay spectrum, most participants described a much-improved approach to flexibility from their managers. They mentioned the growth of connectivity and technical ability to work from home, alongside restrictions on office space, as helping support this change of organizational mindset. The various forms of flexible working were not identified in terms of any perceived detriment to their career trajectories, but rather they were largely seen as a positive development. Participants did not make a connection between their choice of alternative flexible working patterns and any negative impacts on pay in the longer term.

That said, the impact of the organizational response to part-time work was cited as crucial in determining some participants' choice of hours. Interviewees reflected on the lack of reduction in workload when moving to part-time hours. Yasmine (mid-level in commercial in global UK bank) explained that this resulted in her choice to work three, not four, days a week. Despite her preference for the latter, she believed appropriate cover for her job would only be provided if she worked for three days and so decided to take the accompanying financial detriment and work less. Equally, Krista (senior in corporate banking for global UK bank) decided to go back to full-time hours, given the continued expectations and lack of reduction in her work when she had been part-time. This lack of adjustment to account for 'off' days and the need for a better understanding of flexibility was also raised by Sophie, Claire and Kaye who were working compressed hours. This suggests that the use of flexibility is significant for those on both full- and part-time contracts, somewhat undermining the relevance of the economic approach. Any flexibility associated with hours was described as having an impact, diminishing the importance of overall investment of time. This demonstrates how the organizational aspect is seemingly more pressing and highlights the interrelationship between economic and organizational explanations. Understanding how these decisions operate for both employees and organizations is vital to ensure that the drive to improve flexibility does not further embed pay inequities (Bian and Wang, 2019).

Following on from the way cultural practices affect issues like pay secrecy and promotion, the deeply ingrained expectation of presenteeism further contributes to reinforcing gender divisions (Metcalf and Rolfe, 2009; Treasury Committee, 2010; Atkinson, 2011). Despite pressure to address the problem (EHRC, 2009), post-financial crisis research suggests that working hours have actually increased (Healy and Ahamed, 2019: 322). Expectations of working long hours, including frequent weekends, and working through or cancelling holidays, was described as normal for some interviewees (Sally, Val and Claire). Others recalled periods during their career when they had worked in this way (Sophie, Sue, Jacqui and Jade).

Participants reflected on the horizontal occupational segregation and the typical jobs associated with these expectations. In so doing, they noted that resistance to addressing the long-hours culture and embracing flexible working in certain parts of the business was legitimized by the requirements of certain roles (Sally senior in global UK bank). They were most notably discussed by those working currently, or previously, in higher paying and typically more male-dominated occupations, such as asset management, investment and leverage finance (Val, Jade and Claire). The ability for the typically higher earning parts of the sector to decouple from the push for flexibility is, in this way, legitimized by the apparent needs of the work environment. For instance, participants spoke about traders needing to record calls, or home computer systems not having the capacity for more technical roles (Ella mid-level HR in global Asian bank and Jade senior HR in global investment management firm). As technological innovations grow, it will be interesting to see whether this persists, or if the growing ability to work flexibly, as demanded by the pandemic, generates wholesale change in the way the sector works (Howcroft and Rubery, 2019; Treasury Committee, 2023a).

The long-hours culture prevalent in the sector is further marked by vertical occupational segregation. Kate (senior HR global UK bank) and Kaye (senior in global UK bank) described how, from middle management upwards, the ability to have a reasonable work–life balance was increasingly eroded. Yasmine (mid-level in global UK bank) noted:

'That's one of the reasons why I've chosen not to pursue my career beyond the level I'm at. There's an expectation if you progress beyond a certain level that, regardless of what's going on with you, at whatever time of evening or weekend, that you will just drop things.'

In this way, profitability and diversity are positioned as diametrically opposed, with the benefits afforded by flexibility viewed as a secondary concern (Davies et al, 2015).

That said, interviewees noted the significant improvement in policies to address flexibility at work (Sophie, Sue, Yasmine, Jacqui, Jade, Nia, Allice, Claire, Krista and Kaye). The growth of flexible working initiatives, beyond statutory requirements, shows how the drive for diversity and inclusion is achieving some traction. Krista (senior in global UK bank) described this change:

'In 2015–16 it was not common to work flexibly. I had lots of young male peers who didn't understand it at all. It makes you feel quite isolated. This team is different, but also the bank has changed in the last three to five years. There's a better understanding from them that people have their lives. It's more mature I would say.'

Participants acknowledged the importance of the growth of flexibility, in enabling them to maintain a career in the industry alongside their caring commitments (Sophie, Sue, Yasmine, Alice, Claire, Krista and Kaye).

Respondents noted how this change also increased their ability to move jobs, given they were able to secure new flexible working arrangements. Krista (senior in global UK bank) described how she felt less tied to her employer. "They've relied on it [flexibility] a lot; they think people will just stay. For females my age they think, you get that and you won't leave. But other banks get flexibility as well now."

This change was directly articulated by Sophie (senior in global UK bank), who described how flexible working was part of her opening discussion with a new firm. Given the higher pay awards achieved through changing firm, the progress organizations have made in improving and embedding flexibility is critical in helping women capitalize on these potential increases.

That said, much remains to be done. The improved access to flexible working was identified as not operationally viable for those in lower grades. Participants noted that it was often much easier for mid to senior levels to be able to work flexibly (Greg, Roy, Sabina, Faye and Yasmine). These findings support research that has identified policy gaps in access to flexible working at the lower end of the pay distribution in the financial sector (Healy and Ahamed, 2019: 321).

Tali, Faye and Claire also noted how the organizational drive to embed flexibility can be lost along the management chain. Sally (senior in global UK bank) described how the escalation policy in an individual's right to request flexible working had been changed at her organization to address this.[1] The need to be organizationally alert to resistance from middle management was accompanied by the importance of accountability and the tone from the top, critical components to driving change. The variability in management values informs and shapes the organizational culture and this can hinder organizational policy attempts to achieve greater gender equality.

The cultural expectations within firms and interviewees' ability to challenge them, through collective opposition, provides another avenue to explore how policies are utilized and shaped, which we turn to now.

Organizational reluctance and declining unionization

There is seemingly a growing acceptance of a range of policies to improve diversity. However, the degree to which firms, and the different levels of strata within them, embrace requirements is mixed. Interviewees reflected on how international banks perceive British equality requirements, building on the organization-type analysis in Chapter 4. This exposes an aspect of organizational reluctance to see and target the GPG, highlighting the need to look beyond the role of HRM (Dobbin, 2009). The competing tensions frustrating change are then further reflected on, with reference to the importance of collective campaigning, despite declining levels of unionization in the sector.

Cross-national perspectives and the organizational environment

The rebuttal of equality initiatives and suggestions of 'diversity fatigue' in certain parts of the sector, demonstrates the variability in motivation to address the problem (Makortoff, 2019; PWC, 2019; Treasury Committee, 2023a). Assessment of normative perspectives from foreign banks on the British regulatory context highlights how this reluctance can work. Some interviews were conducted with women working for Japanese, German or French banks. These interviewees all highlighted the gap between the culture of their firm and British equality requirements. These gaps are now considered with reference to workplace flexibility, the GPRR and maternity leave.

First, with reference to flexibility, Ella (mid-level HR in global Asian bank) described the management mindset at her firm. She directly attributed their reluctance to implement workplace flexibilities to the prevalence of alternative cultural norms. "In Japan it's not even something [referring to flexible working]. Women are only just thinking about going back to work after having kids there. It's a very masculine environment, they're hamstrung by that."

Jane (senior in global European bank) acknowledged this cultural disconnect, suggesting the mindset at her organization was more rooted in the country it is from, as opposed to the country it is in. She described this with reference to women's role in the workplace and the home: "It's very traditional here. In Germany, most schools send kids home at lunchtime, as mum's at home. It will change, but very slowly. It definitely won't be at the front."

The interviews revealed how organizational approaches are shaped by these cultural and normative practice, which undermine British policy attempts to reduce gender inequalities. The scope and direction of policy, and ultimately its usage, is impacted by these normative cultural aspects. The emergence and proliferation of large global organizations within the finance sector mean alternative institutional frameworks are indirectly relevant. Those working in global organizations reflected on the, at times, unmatched nature of regulatory requirements, initiatives and attitudes across their different locales. Jade (senior HR in global investment management firm) noted alternative perceptions of flexible working: "General attitudes to agile working are different depending on the location of the manager. So, in France for example, they're not in the same place. We have a home working policy, but there [in France] working from home is considered skiving."

In terms of implementing new policy, decisions around how to position the organizational approach were acknowledged. Ella (mid-level in global Asian bank) described how policy development is a process, with some companies more likely to be leading the way, while others follow or lag behind: "We need to rewrite our [flexible working] policy, so we will go out and look at what others do. But we'll wait until there's a steer elsewhere, culturally we're cautious. If other banks go ten out of ten, we'll go seven or eight" (Ella).

This adds a further level of nuance to Dobbin's (2009) argument. There is clearly variability between organizations and their willingness to engage in equality practices. However, for global firms, improvements in one locale will inevitably drive pressure elsewhere. For example, the EU Pay Transparency Directive, which came into force in June 2023, will inevitably result in increased pressure on transparency. Firms may help drive innovation through adopting best practice approaches across jurisdictions.

For firms that are more reluctant, interviewees perceived the importance of benchmarking across the finance sector as vital for helping start the conversation to catalyze equality initiatives (Jane, Ella and Jade). This also highlights the relevance of institutional theory by demonstrating how similar processes and resistance can be among firms (DiMaggio and Powell, 1983). While organizations may resemble one another, one of the difficulties of reaching a critical mass of acceptance to change is illustrated by the cross-national variability of global finance firms. This analysis of normative expectations and values within the sector, both in terms of hours worked and flexibilities, has evidenced how gender divisions are reinforced at the meso level in multiple and intersecting ways.

There are numerous sites of tension for legislation in its translation into organizational policy and working lives. Understanding context is vital to the perceived importance and impact of statutory and voluntarist approaches. The perception of British legal requirements, when viewed in the world of global finance, highlighted these interesting dimensions during interviews. The divergence of legal approaches in different national jurisdictions globally, flags the need to understand how organizations respond to their positioning within the British legislative framework. For example, Jade (senior HR in global investment firm), acknowledged the positive impact of the GPRR within her firm: "We are a global company and this [GPRR] has shifted the conversation in other locations. My view is the UK has really helped here. It's changed the conversation entirely. It has shifted it up a big notch."

Equally, organizational reluctance to British legislation was also raised. Ella (mid-level HR in global Asian bank) attributed her employer's response as indicative of the firm's country of origin: "One of the reasons Asian organizations are loath to invest here is the regulatory requirements. Compared to Thailand they're huge, and off-putting."

Further reflections highlighted the impact of different maternity entitlements in global companies. Hilary (senior in corporate banking in global European bank) described her experience of maternity leave while working with a largely American team:

'Lots of my managers were American, so six months sounded like an insane luxury as they get 12 weeks, whereas here it's sort of the minimum … There was a huge amount of pressure to go back early. My manager would say, "I don't know anybody who takes this long." He actually said I was coming back at some point when I wasn't. It was very unpleasant.'

The interview data demonstrates how the push and pull of cross-national perspectives from foreign banks can impact the implementation of British equality requirements.

The role and remit of trade unions and collectivism

Institutional perspectives on gender pay inequality recognize the positive role trade unions can have as institutional structures that are involved in wage setting, campaigning, and enforcing legislation (ILO, 2016). Despite limited and declining influence, interviews confirmed that unions retain the potential to drive policy implementation and change within the sector.

The scope of existing collective bargaining arrangements is limited to the lower end of the organizational hierarchy. Union membership is typically concentrated in clerical grades in retail banking (Greg, Roy and Moira) (see Chapter 5). The huge restructuring within the industry, resulting from technological innovations and the financial crisis (see Chapters 2 and 3), resulted in significant numbers of jobs both lost and outsourced. Participants reported how those taking the voluntary redundancy packages on offer contributed to declining levels of union membership, given the age of those more likely to take them and the typical union member profile (Greg, Roy and Moira). Membership within the industry had fallen to just over 10% in 2021 (Bishop, 2022).

For those at the lower end of the earnings distribution, changes in the sector have been accompanied by an erosion of terms and conditions as a further means of organizational cost saving (Roy trade union organizer in the sector). For example, final salary pension schemes have been closed and sickness benefits have diminished. Given the declining number of members, unions described resource constraints resulting in a focus on recruitment, as opposed to campaigning and organizing in the sector (Greg, Roy and Moira).

The individual reluctance to challenge pay decisions, as described by interviewees in Chapter 5, has been mirrored by a reluctance to challenge collectively. Since 1997, there has been a trend away from industrial action, and a move towards less militant unions within banking and finance (Prosser, 2011; Gall, 2017: 164 and 114). This was confirmed during interview. Faye (cashier and union rep in global UK bank) commented: "Nobody every strikes or objects. You believe when you start that your manager will look after you." The impact of this was considered by Roy (trade union organizer in the sector):

'The problem is there's no recent history of industrial militancy. There was a time when we would take action, and members felt part of that collective opposition. The last significant industrial dispute was patchy at best, and it was 15 years ago. That infects people's thinking about what is achievable from a collective point of view.'

This reduced industrial muscle and climate of acceptance can perhaps be partially understood with reference to the reality of the pay process itself and the deeply ingrained fear of repercussions when challenging management. The collective bargaining agreements, which cover pay negotiations for the lower grades, are conducted for the whole pay pot, as PRP systems are in place. Unions have a limited role in how that is then distributed, and do not have a role in negotiating bonuses (see Chapter 5). In addition, there is an organizational expectation of gratefulness to have a job, given the huge churn in jobs the sector has experienced post-financial crisis, cost pressures arising from low interest rates, and uncertainty as technological innovations change the shape of work (Crow, 2019). Reasserting a collective voice, when resources are stretched and numbers are declining, is inevitably challenging. This wider context illustrates the limitations of institutional explanations in the context of this deep-rooted form of voluntarist governance in the collective space, a principle foundational in the architectures of inequality.

At the same time, cause for a potentially more positive outcome can be drawn from interview discussions that described a campaign that unions are running with a view to litigating on pension inequities. The state clawback pension scheme, operated by two of the big four banks, requires employees to pay back 1/80th of their state pension per year of service, regardless of their earnings: this has a disproportionate impact on low-paid part-time workers. Given the make-up of the industry, these are typically women. The policy only affects those on the final salary scheme, which has since been closed to new starters. Those affected have formed a campaign group. Unions are now involved and campaigning to change the policy by preparing a legal challenge on the basis of indirect discrimination (Jones, 2019). Such claims have precedent, for example *Bilka* discussed in Chapter 4. Faye (cashier and union rep in global UK bank) described how the policy affects her:

'So, for cashier level like me, I've never progressed. I had kids, then elderly parents. My husband was the one with the career. I've given

35 years of my life, now I'm going to get 35 eightieths of state pension reduced off my bank pension. Obviously, mine is a much smaller pension pot than mid-level management, inevitably a man. Their pension pot is much bigger, but still has the same ★ years' worth of money deducted.'

Sue (mid-level in global UK bank) described how she found out about the clawback scheme in her early 50s:

'I can categorically say that I was not aware of the scheme. I will lose an amount based on my service and I didn't know. This targets those finishing at lower grades, they'll lose out and they're predominantly women, clerical part-time workers. The only saving grace for me is now I've gone up [previously cashier, now working in head office on management track] so in money terms it doesn't mean as much.'

This confirms the potent and disruptive potential that both litigation and unions still hold, as suggested by Deakin et al (2015). Despite declining levels of union membership, unions retain a capacity to help focus on inequalities within the sector and drive change. It strikes a chord with calls by the Fawcett Society to recognize the wider issue of lost pension rights beyond the finance sector, alongside other amendments to equal pay legislation to counter some of the difficulties experienced by claimants (Bazeley and Rosenblatt, 2019). It also suggests how, in reality, recourse to the law and the ability to challenge organizational policy may be limited to those with support.

Correspondingly, where employees are not part of a trade union, the lack of support, and not just in a financial sense, is undoubtedly a barrier to pursuing redress for pay inequities individually or collectively. The heavy weight of sectoral, occupational and normative cultural context, described in this chapter, underlines why. The capacity to address unequal pay, barriers to progression, or the variable application of workplace policy is seemingly limited at the macro, meso, and micro levels. The interview data has shown how the potential for union opposition is subject to variability and limitations in the same way as other institutional explanations. The organizational trends outlined are now discussed with reference to the architectures model.

Applying the architectures model to the thematic analysis

Drawing on perspectives from interviewees at the micro level has allowed us to examine how actions, at the macro level of regulation and at the meso level of the organization, intersect to perpetuate gender inequalities. The application of each theoretical explanation within the architectures model is useful to fully understand these dynamics and demonstrates how limitations in institutional and organizational initiatives slow progress.

To draw together this qualitative stream of analysis (Chapters 5–7) focus is now given to organizational perspectives, building on the topics discussed. This assessment demonstrates how examination of organizational explanations and the effectiveness of workplace policy enhances our understanding of the GPG trajectory.

Organizational explanations

The development of policies to improve equality and diversity in the workplace has been enhanced by the professionalization and growth of HRM (Dobbin, 2009). However, despite the proliferation of policies, progress in reducing the GPG has been partial and slow, prompting research to explore where progress has been achieved, and where it has not (Dobbin and Kalev, 2016). The importance of accountability, leadership from top and middle management, mandating diversity as a key strategic priority, and holding managers to account have been recognized as crucial in driving the culture shift that is needed (Bohnet, 2016; HM Treasury, 2016; PWC, 2019; Treasury Committee, 2023a). The impact and effectiveness of policies alongside organizational practice and normative behaviour have therefore been considered.

The large GPGs within finance are attributed to the occupational segregation within the industry, both horizontally and vertically (Benson et al, 2018). Women are prominent in junior lower quartile roles, and men occupy the majority of jobs in the top quartile of organizations. In addition, there is an uneven distribution of men and women in particular parts of the sector, with men occupying the higher paid roles in areas like trading and investment banking. This polarization of roles and the lack of women in the top organizational echelons is a characteristic of GPGs within the sector. To understand how these organizational and occupational trends contribute, this chapter has considered recruitment and promotion practices. The GEO (2018b) has designated initiatives to address gendered organizational hierarchies (for example shortlists) (Acker, 2006) as effective, and promising (such as networking and mentoring) (see Chapter 4). Despite the prominence of these initiatives in accompanying narratives, the maintenance of existing hierarchies has been facilitated by unequal power relations and foundational inequalities at the firm level. The interview data has shown how these features of the architectures model restrict change (Reskin and Maroto, 2011).

Normative cultural and gendered behaviours, often used in sociological explanations for the GPG and discussed in Chapter 6, are a key component contributing to the architectures of inequality in Britain. They demonstrate the need to look beyond the argument of Dobbin (2009), to identify the obstacles that efforts to address gender equality face at the meso level. Resonant with the arguments of Acker (2009), the interview data exposes how foundational gender differences and the doing of gender in organizations are central to organizational explanations (Martin, 2003).

This chapter has also evidenced cross-national variability in measures pursued and implemented at the firm level, demonstrating the tensions and barriers within and between the theoretical components of the architectures model. For instance, the effect of the employing organization's country of origin demonstrates an alternative perspective to that of Dobbin (2009). The pervasive and intersecting ways that attitudes and inequalities operate also have an external perspective. While there is a growing literature on the business benefits of improved diversity, an alternative approach to the embedded nature of attitudes and norms is uncovered by Solal and Snellman (2019). They identify the gender penalty on market value that companies with good measures of diversity can achieve, resulting not from poor firm performance but the negative perception of investors given assumptions about organizational priorities. Their research finds that market value diminishes as investors assume that a preference for social aims corresponds with a deprioritization of shareholder gain. This demonstrates the multiple ways that gendered values impact and restrict change, undermining efforts to address GPGs.

The priority afforded to equality by governments and the law has been restricted by economic needs since the outset (see Chapter 2). However, this chapter has shown how, despite a move to regulatory compliance, institutional structures and workplace policy can be rendered immune as organizations act as a filter to dilute and obscure requirements. These restrictive mechanisms have been further enhanced by the declining influence of trade unions in the sector.

Conclusion

Organizations have a pivotal role as an explanatory factor for the GPG, as the gap between policy and practice explored in this chapter has shown (Jewell et al, 2020). The increased focus on gender pay inequities, partly as a result of the GPRRs, has resulted in the implementation of initiatives to offset the problem (Dobbin, 2009). The assessment given here, of promotion and flexibility policies, has revealed both progress and resistance. On the one hand the potential for change has been evidenced as interviewees flagged improvements, such as workplace flexibility. However, the interview data also shows how organizational reluctance can temper both institutional requirements and policy initiatives.

Organizational practices towards pay equity operate and develop alongside sectoral trends. Workplace cultures, pay and reward processes, and the management of people are all critical catalysts around which the substantial inequalities associated with the finance sector have been reconfigured. The attention paid to these inequalities can be diverted if and when organizations deem necessary. Just as the architectural framework surrounding GPGs is continually redrawn, the natural consequence of reorganization within the finance sector is, seemingly, the redefinition of the inequality within it.

The provision and accessibility of equality policies is marked by key factors: occupational difference; a focus on particular points in the pay spectrum; individual management discretion; and organizational culture. The pace and direction of approaches pursued highlights the role of organizations and those working within them. Employers need to understand if and how efforts are being implemented across the management chain, how they are perceived by those they are intended to support, and how cross-national perspectives may be limiting their effect. There is evidence of decoupling from best practice requirements, with a marked variability in certain higher paying parts of the industry. This illustrates Bohnet's (2016) assertion that organizations themselves are biased, impacting the effectiveness of initiatives.

This series of chapters has evidenced how the GPG needs to be examined in the broader sectoral context, in relation to regulatory change and from the perspective of workers. This multilevel examination of actors and domains within the architectures is critical in bringing contradictions and impediments sharply into view. Mutually constituting aspects – such as a lack of transparency around pay and reward, policy that fails to walk the talk, a lack of collectivism, and the difficulties of reconciling work and family life – present opportunities for bold actions. However, while there is an increased focus on the GPG in the finance sector, change remains limited by how organizations perceive the problem. Suddaby (2010: 18) describes organizations as interpretive mechanisms that translate broader social systems. Despite the shift in laissez faire governance, evident in the implementation of the GPRRs, institutional requirements can be rendered immune as organizations dilute and obscure them. This is further enhanced by the declining influence of trade unions in the sector. These findings underline the importance of this phase of the research. The architectures model captures this sense of movement by recognizing how, regardless of the increased focus on inequities, ongoing inequalities still breathe through the building. The analysis has shown how the fragility of equality gains can easily be destabilized and is subject to the continual momentum and ongoing reconstruction of the architectures of inequality.

Note

1   The Flexible Working Regulations 2014 include the right to make a flexible working request, subject to having 26 weeks' continuous employment.

8

Contradictions of Transparency

Introduction

This research set out to understand how the GPRR and broader legal and organizational initiatives designed to combat gender pay inequities have impacted Britain's GPG. Despite the well-established moral, legal and financial imperatives, the GPG remains a stubborn phenomenon. Ongoing persistent inequalities in the face of progressively broadened approaches designed to target inequities require the need for fresh theoretical consideration. This has been achieved through this interdisciplinary empirical study of gender pay inequity within Britain's finance sector.

Key findings from this multilevel analysis are presented in this chapter as follows.

First, the various data streams are woven together. Interrogation of the largely untapped reporting data, legal and organizational policy evaluation, and qualitative insights from women in finance underline the multiple mechanisms and key actors that have impacted the GPG trajectory. These macro-, meso- and micro-level elements of the research design provide the scaffold upon which the architectures of inequality model is assembled. This approach affords a rich picture of the complexity of the problem and the trends and barriers that obstruct progress.

Second, application of the architectures model provides useful insights to understand ongoing gender pay inequity. The evidence of foundational inequalities and common architectural trends is used to demonstrate the utility of this new conceptual approach, helping to indicate where change efforts should be focussed. This multilevel research design has shown that, while the GPRR have increased the visibility of GPGs, organizations are myopic in their focus. The approach exposes where tensions need to be resolved, areas that are critical for policy to address and policy blind spots that remain unrecognized.

Finally, when summing up the impacts of the GPRR this book has shown both positive and unintended consequences. Organizational compliance with the regulations means we are now able to monitor firms and assess areas of progress. The data can show where problems arise and be used to drive interventions. However, at the 'Sexism in the City' inquiry, experts reiterated the importance of moving beyond virtue-signalling. Fiona Mackenzie, CEO of The Other Half, urged firms to use this knowledge to "Give the scaffolding ... for real action" (Treasury Committee, 2023a). With our increased knowledge and familiarity with GPGs there is also evidence of both complacency and contempt. Reports into ongoing inequity within the finance sector suggests some firms merely 'dust down' reporting requirements once a year, while 20% of men in the city think diversity has gone too far (Treasury Committee, 2023a). This push-and-pull dynamic, as initiatives are extended and foundational trends reassert, demonstrates the ongoing movement within and between each theoretical dimension of the architectures model. These shifting goalposts demonstrate the non-linear nature of change and help to account for ongoing gender pay inequities (Rubery and Grimshaw, 2015). With that in mind, and to draw together the insights achieved in this research, the threats and opportunities in the current equality landscape are outlined.

The architectures of inequality blueprint

The trend for broadening institutional and organizational measures has been accompanied by slowly declining GPGs, which have been prone to stalling over time (Hochschild, 2003). This continual modification of initiatives has been assessed at the macro, meso, and micro levels.

Macro-level evolution of the institutional legal framework

The phased assessment of legal development highlighted the importance of key actors in the changing regulatory landscape, establishing how shifting parameters determine the shape, speed, direction, and application of legal initiatives (Chapters 2–3). While the law is slow moving, by situating the legislative approach to equality within its socio-legal context, the impact of wider social structures and normative values is clear.

Since the inception of equal pay law, the needs of business, and government reluctance to impose 'bureaucratic' requirements, have been a persistent central theme. The remit and effectiveness of legal arrangements has been limited as the issue of accountability remains at the behest of individual employers, despite successive reforms. That said, there has been an increasing use of both voluntarist and statutory approaches, demonstrating a shift from the preference for laissez faire governance towards greater institutional compliance.

However, despite the introduction of the GPRR, difficulties related to a lack of transparency endure. Hidden complexities in terms of knowledge, access, cost, and the claimant-driven requirement for legal redress, remain obstructive, despite the progressive broadening of legislative equality measures. Foundational inequalities continue to be an inherent part of the legal character, present in both the construction and application of law.

Meso-level organizational response to the legal framework

The macro-level case study examination has shown how legal requirements are applied in the finance sector (Chapter 4). This demonstrated the interaction between institutional and organizational perspectives and how sector wide trends, alongside workplace policies and norms, contribute to ongoing inequities. The GPRR data evidences slow progress, significant and ongoing occupational segregation and organization-type trends associated with the intractability of the GPG. Beyond the quantitative statistical findings, ongoing light-touch governance and transparency barriers were identified. Identification of these implicit trends demonstrates the importance of visualizing the problem beyond the institutional dimension.

The data showed evidence of organizational progress, but also indicated where firms are less willing to make change. This demonstrates that, while the GPRR are a useful monitoring tool, the underlying inequalities that informed their construction ultimately limit their effectiveness. Despite the increased transparency afforded by the Regulations, there are several ways in which conditions become more hidden, for example in relation to pay secrecy. Gender pay inequality within the finance sector is a long-standing problem, yet, despite the costs of failing to address it, improvement remains marginal.

Notwithstanding these limitations, there has been an organizational willingness to report (despite the lack of compulsion from 2019–20) and focus on inequities in the sector has sharpened, prompting larger relative declines (Healy and Ahamed, 2019). Better data monitoring could be used to drive further improvements. This suggests that the organizational element of the architectures currently retains the greatest potential to effect change.

Micro-level experiences of inequities within the workplace

To fully understand the impact of legal and organizational initiatives qualitative interviews explored the lived realities of pay systems, career paths and workplace policies (Chapters 5–7). The insights and experiences of women working for a range of finance firms operating in Britain enabled the resonance of institutional, organizational, economic and sociological explanations accounting for the GPG to be ascertained. The controversy around the causes and remedies of gaps, embraced in the research design, was used to consider the relevance of these competing explanations at the micro level.

Women working in finance described the practical realities of both statutory and voluntarist institutional approaches targeting gender pay inequities. A lack of transparency was described in terms of how legal requirements, organizationally self-determined policies, pay processes and opportunities for progression were filtered and diluted, making them impenetrable. The empirical evidence showed how, despite ongoing modifications to the law and workplace policy, foundational inequalities and an overriding lack of transparency continue to curb their efficacy.

Interviewees described how the rational economic choices they had made were implicitly affected by networks, power struggles and preferred character traits at the firm level, demonstrating Ackers (2006) inequality regimes. This demonstrates the multiple ways that embedded stereotypes and values continue to inform and shape organizational approaches and expectations around working time, underlining the importance of sociological explanations.

The dynamic nature of the architectures model was evident in the ongoing reconstruction and extension of approaches targeting inequities. The salience of organizational explanations was examined, demonstrating the importance of HRM innovations alongside limiting path-dependent sectoral norms. The qualitative data exposed the similarity between organizations and the policies they offer, and those to which they are blind and seemingly not willing to consider. Qualitative insights confirmed how, despite the move from laissez faire governance to compliance, the influence of factors, such as management cultures and cross-national perspectives on British equality requirements, have restricted the pursuit of equality.

While the GPRR oblige firms to report, contradictions of transparency at the macro, meso and micro levels demonstrate how significant aspects of the problem remain hidden. The progressive depth afforded through the application of alternative theoretical explanations evidenced the interrelationship between these approaches. The interpretation of fieldwork interviews, in this way, demonstrates the necessity and utility of the architectures model, supporting the conclusions the research offers. The model helps to pinpoint the pervasive and restrictive effect of common architectural features and, in so doing, better understand the nature of change and resistance.

Architectural insights and policymaking

The empirical evidence presented has demonstrated how discrimination can occur hidden in plain sight, adding to the opacity of the problem. Astoundingly, four in ten people still do not know they have the right to equal pay (Bazeley and Rosenblatt, 2019). Legal policy efforts can remain marginalized as their application at the meso level is constrained according to the architectural features of transparency and governance, and the restrictive effect of foundational inequalities. This is despite the economic gains potentially realized by progressing more stringent and transparent approaches, alongside the benefits both for business and the whole family unit. As an analytical tool, the architectures of inequality model helps elucidate the tensions slowing the change progress. These tensions and the ongoing movement in the model are now outlined, recommendations arising from these insights suggested, before offering a cautionary summation on where the path of progress may lead next.

Dynamism in the architectures

The movement within and between each component part of the architecture demonstrates the difficulty in combating the GPG. In trying to visualize where efforts to shift the dial need to be focused, understanding the dynamism within the model is useful. By mapping the interrelationship between the theoretical explanations, their relative importance can be ascertained and the most likely potential for improvement located. The model is predicated on Marginson's (2019: 298) assertion: 'The drive for universal explanation overrides real world complexity ... the task of research is [therefore] to determine which explanations (s) is (are) primary, not to impose an exclusive straight jacket on the material.'

Throughout the research, the application of each theoretical lens has showed how momentum for progress towards eradicating GPGs is not necessarily continual or indeed linear. Each explanation has revealed a constant reconfiguring, as the problem has evolved. The pay gap is in a continual battle to remain relevant, prioritized and declining. As Rubery and Grimshaw (2015) contend, shifting goalposts are inevitable. Understanding and visualizing these interactions and movement is helpful to suggest which approach currently offers the most potent potential for improvement.

The macro-level institutional analysis showed the declining scale of the public sector and influence of organized labour in Britain, alongside the ongoing preference for free market governance (Gallie, 2007a). Within this context, the difficulties that potential claimants encounter, related to aspects like knowledge, access and cost, to assert their legal entitlements, further undermine the law's capacity to eradicate the GPG. The unintended consequences of Brexit and the economic fallout from the pandemic will further erode the likelihood of imminent future legal developments. Given the economic climate, Acker's (2012: 221) pessimistic post–financial crisis assessment of the ramifications for gendered inequities is again relevant. While the GPRR are a useful monitoring tool, providing impetus to sustain momentum, their limitations are evident. The ongoing failure of government to embrace the imperatives for more wholesale change and implement necessary ammendments is unlikely to alter in the near future. Correspondingly, the willingness of organizations to report in 2019–20, despite suspension, and the increased understanding of business and reputational benefits achieved through positive development, suggest the organizational avenue is a more promising one for change. The fundamental role organizations have, in terms of applying and building on statutory requirements, underlines this potential.

The constant shifting within the architectures also serves to highlight policy implications and the need for future research arising from this enquiry.

Policy implications and future research

In the current context of economic uncertainty, legislative developments such as improving the GPRR, progressing with ethnicity and disability reporting, or a more comprehensive approach to greater transparency, while necessary, seem highly unlikely (CRED, 2021). The historical trajectory of policy trends suggests risk for gender equality measures. The policy implications and shifting conceptualization of equality, arising from this analysis, are useful and can be ascertained by again referring to the key actors (government, courts, unions, social movements and business).

Firstly, in terms of the role of government, the risk of decoupling from the EU's policy agenda has materialized as the passing of the EU's Pay Transparency Directive and erosion of equal pay protections demonstrates (Wigand, 2021; BBC, 2023). Alongside reporting GPGs, this instrument provides: greater pay information for job seekers, gives employees the right to request pay information, bans potential employers from requesting salary history information, and shifts the default burden of proof in discrimination claims to the employer. Research from the US demonstrates the positive impact that a legislative approach to banning pay secrecy and sharing of salary history can have, as noted in Chapter 7 (Kim, 2015). Given the contradictions of transparency highlighted throughout this research, concrete measures such as these are vital.

The evolving influence of key actors, as described, indicates a reconceptualization of equality is imminent. The positive potential afforded by contestation in the courts and various forms of collective opposition, as provided by unions or feminist activists, remains critical in the change process. Case law developments concerning worker status (*Uber v Aslam* (2021)) and wider recognition of intersectionality by government evidence this progress (GEO, 2020b). It is also worth acknowledging that inequalities within the existing framework have not yet been resolved. The pending equal pay case against Dundee City Council, concerning gender disparity in the roles eligible for bonus, demonstrates the ongoing need to fight for equal pay (Livingston, 2021). Recognition of the "markedly overcomplicated" nature of equal pay cases is set to continue (*Asda v Brierley* [2021]: para. 6). Within a Phase V conceptualization, the layering of change will continue as the pursuit of long-standing rights remains a challenge.

Within this context, the failure of the Equal Pay (Information and Claims) Bill to make it passed the second reading is concerning (Creasy, 2020). The continued deferral of the Employment Bill, with its promise to safeguard workers' rights post-Brexit and the suggestion that tribunal fees may be reintroduced, implies that the typical deference to the needs of business within Britain will continue (Ames, 2020; Partington, 2021). Women's absence in policymaking throughout the COVID-19 crisis reiterates the unequal architectural foundations of policy measures. Policymakers should confront this tendency and take measures to ensure diversity in decision making, ensuring these risks do not perpetually resurface. This lack of consideration for women's concerns also signals the potential for regression (Madgavkar et al, 2020; Topping, 2021; BBC, 2023). The UK's GPG at a national level is larger than the EU average of 14.1% (European Commission, 2020). To ensure no future slippage, Britain should go further than the EU Pay Transparency Directive and 'build back better' from the current crisis. This could secure potential economic gains that have yet to be realized, by treating women more fairly for their contribution to the economy. The consequences of failure to address this imperative will remain significant in terms of legal judgements, lost incomes and ongoing persistent GPGs.

Given the current economic difficulties and trends outlined, an increased reliance on cross-party collective pressure and ongoing campaigning for regulatory change within a Phase V conceptualization is likely. Finding ways to embrace the potential of collective opposition and further target the role of the organization is therefore critical (Moore, 2018). The development and facilitation of wage and bonus sharing, via secure templates, could assist the confidential communication within organizations of pay arrangements, helping to leverage change and bypass organizational aversion to pay audits. Women could use this information to enter pay discussions and negotiations in an informed manner, equipping them with the tools to challenge inequities.

At this juncture, it is also useful to consider where further research could develop this enquiry. Greater clarity on the problem of gender pay inequity would benefit from an intersectional assessment of GPGs in finance. While the current parliamentary inquiry again remains focussed solely on gender, a better understanding of how overlapping identities impact gaps is a critical blind spot (Bridge Group, 2023; Treasury Committee, 2023a). A rich area for future enquiry, such a focus may be supported by the increasing willingness of organizations to report ethnicity gaps, noted in Chapter 4, and the emerging requirement for an accompanying action plan when they do (CRED, 2021).

COVID-19 required a shift to homeworking and, in so doing, highlighted the adaptability of organizations to meet this need. The importance and development of improved flexibility at work, alongside the barriers to these changes in certain high-paying parts of the sector, would benefit now from further investigation. There is a clear disparity in how firms are positioning the 'new normal' (Moore, 2021). As the 'Sexism in the City' inquiry has noted, it seems some finance sector firms are failing to capitalize on these benefits by insisting on a full return to the office (Treasury Committee, 2023a). Understanding how change has been enabled, and what the longer-term implications may be, would be a useful enquiry that could catalyze future change. This prompts discussion of potential developments and risks to the equality agenda, to which we turn now.

Brexit, COVID-19 and the new digital world of work

Despite the GPRR and the resultant increased awareness of GPGs, gender equality in pay remains 'nice to have', rather than critical, despite the evidence suggesting otherwise. Previous economic crises have depositioned the priority afforded to equality efforts, despite the economic benefit potentially unlocked through positive progress (Acker, 2012: 221; Guerrina and Masselot, 2018; Criado-Perez, 2019). The uncertainties associated with Brexit and the pandemic also represent significant periods of crisis. Past recessions have legitimized organizations prioritizing their competitive edge, and the link between high performance work practices and gender gaps has been established (Davies et al, 2015). The consequences of Brexit will mean a lack of recourse to the ECJ, compliance with legal developments, and best practice in the EU (BBC, 2023). The EU has provided an important input in the positive development of equality practices. On the one hand, the wider climate of uncertainty created by the pandemic may excuse the failure to meet equality targets, as seen in the suspension of the GPRR. Ongoing at the time of writing, former cabinet secretary Helen Macnamara gave evidence at the UK's Covid Inquiry (2023) describing how women became "invisible overnight" as a "macho culture" took hold of government. The lack of diversity and women's voices, in both Brexit and COVID-19 planning committees, evidences a systemic disregard for their concerns (Guerrina and Masselot, 2018; Macleavy, 2018; Fuhrman and Rhodes, 2020; Queisser et al, 2020; Wenham, 2020).

On the other hand, the level of protest around Black Lives Matter and against gender inequalities and violence reached unprecedented public visibility during 2020–21, building on the #metoo and #timesup social movements. Potentially, this suggests that normative social values around equality are changing in a way that governments and organizations cannot ignore and have been forced to be seen to act on. In particular, significant legal cases on equal pay and the status of gig workers have also received high-profile attention. These will have repercussions beyond the sectors immediately affected by these rulings.

Previous modifications within the architectures model, and the analysis of resistance and change, have shown how existing structures can replicate. Analysis showed how equality goals have remained peripheral to organizational restructuring since the 1980s up until and beyond the current period. The narrative surrounding inequities, the preference for voluntary targeting and the self-determination of organizational priorities underline this positioning of the gender agenda. The pandemic has accelerated changes to the world of work and digital working, ably demonstrated by the move to homeworking. While this has the potential to address the well-established need for greater flexibility, the findings of this empirical analysis loom large. In particular, for those whose work already required long hours, issues such as presenteeism may translate into expectations of hyper-connectivity in a digital workplace. Research by Deutsche Bank suggested that, post pandemic, its employees choosing to work from home could pay a 5% premium for the privilege, with the money generated being used to supplement the low incomes of those who cannot (Harper, 2020). This suggests a double-edged sword where on the one hand change can be seen as enabling access and flexibility. Conversely, some of the unintended consequences of these developments may contribute to the reformulation of gendered organizations.

At the same time, efforts to address women's representation at senior levels may be inadvertently enhanced by COVID-19. The model of what successful leadership looks like has been challenged by female-led government during the pandemic. Research by Garikipati and Kambhampati (2020) assessed how best to understand the marked success women have had, highlighting the importance of decisive and clear communication styles and their approach to the question of risk. The reality of this success, shifting normative masculinized cultures of leadership alongside the emergence of alternative ways of working, has been demonstrated during the pandemic, as Brexit unfolded. However, despite the potential benefit to business, experience has also shown that women have suffered more and are potentially more vulnerable to future job losses (Conaghan, 2020; Landivar et al, 2020; Verdin and O'Reilly, 2021).

The emerging digital divide and ensuing inequality are increasingly apparent in the finance sector, with the shift to online banking and the digitalization of money (Lloyds, 2020; Hall, 2022). Job losses resulting from branch closures continue apace, with women more likely to be affected (Dunkley, 2017: 268). An unintended consequence of this may prompt a reduction in the GPG, given the prominence of women working in these lower-paid branch roles. The shift may also provide a boost for the fintech industry as customers seek digital services. The implications of this may have detrimental impacts on equality progress arising due to: the lack of women currently working in the sector; well-reported problems of a 'leaky pipeline' causing those that do join to leave; and the gender gap in STEM qualifications (Krieger-Boden and Sorgner, 2018; Quiros et al, 2018; Rubery, 2018b: 98; Howcroft and Rubery, 2019: 221). Without engaging in too much crystal ball gazing, these shifts highlight the continual momentum of forces impacting each theoretical dimension in the architectures model.

Conclusion

Gender pay inequity is a long-standing and intractable problem. The architectures of inequality model provides a blueprint to scrutinize how efforts designed to tackle it have impacted. Embracing conceptual controversy, this comprehensive examination has shown how initiatives are limited by embedded architectural features and foundations. The development of both institutional and organizational efforts have been counterbalanced by underlying inequalities, governance trends and a lack of transparency, slowing progress. While the architectures are constantly being adapted, some modifications remain seemingly out of reach.

Institutionally, the impenetrability and remoteness of the law weakens its effectiveness. A lack of knowledge, the claimant-centred approach, cost, timescale, impact, and the gendered limitations in the law itself, enable inequities to remain hidden in plain sight. Improved approaches to transparency have enabled us to look through, rather than at, the problem.

These difficulties are compounded within organizations as requirements are translated according to a logic determined by the apparent needs of the sector and individual firm. The pursuit of equality and diversity, while increasingly recognized, remains peripheral to more pressing economic challenges and can therefore be disregarded. Hidden pay, performance, and progression systems, defined as necessary, are difficult to challenge. Historic and embedded inequalities are preserved as women do not have access to the tools needed to leverage equality.

All the while, women's voices remain marginal and the potential to shift the dial on gender pay inequity seems remote. The characteristics of both the institutional and organizational architectures reflect policy efforts that are fundamentally compromised by foundational inequalities and the contradictions of transparency. Britain needs to move beyond the perfunctory transparency of the GPRR and keep pace with EU developments. Embracing the economic imperative and addressing systemic foundational obstructions would enable the 'doing of gender' to be done better (Martin, 2003). The common architectural features do more than show where and how policy fails; they indicate how the very fabric of policy efforts to offset the problem are flawed. Greater transparency is a necessary precursor in addressing the GPG (Conley and Torbus, 2019: 145). The evidence has shown that more open and accessible means by which to understand pay, the value of work and the mechanisms that define it, are critical (Wrohlich, 2017; Dromey and Rankin, 2018; Conley and Torbus, 2019). Speaking from within the industry, experts also acknowledge, "sunlight is the best disinfectant" (Treasury Committee, 2023b). To invest in greater equality requires resolving the pervasive cultures of secrecy and contradictions of transparency at the heart of the architectures model.

APPENDIX 1

Case Digests

Full case reference and summary outline of the cases referred to in the research.

Abdulla v Birmingham City Council [2012] UKSC 47
A landmark ruling following the claims of 174 women who worked for Birmingham City Council. Their claims for equal value extended the time limit for equal pay cases to six years and led to a settlement in excess of £750 million.

Ahmed v BBC [2020] 1 WLUK 16
The case concerned an equal pay claim brought by Samira Ahmed against the BBC, citing Jeremy Vine as a comparator. Like work was established, there were no grounds for a market forces defence and the claim was upheld.

Asda Stores Ltd v Brierley [2021] UKSC 10
The Supreme Court upheld the judgement that shopfloor workers could use the terms and conditions of employees working in distribution centres as a valid comparison, for the purposes of equal pay. While the establishments were separate, it was held that the respondent applied common terms and conditions. The case involves thousands of workers and is ongoing, with the next stage due to establish the equal value test and consider whether ASDA can rely on a material factor defence.

Audit Commission v Haq [2012] EWCA Civ 1621
The case appealed against an Employment Appeal Tribunal (EAT) decision involving indirect discrimination and pay protection. The appointment of men, whose pay had been the subject of protection, onto higher rates of pay was found to be indirectly discriminatory with no objective justification. In giving the lead judgement, Mummery LJ noted the difficulty of equal pay claims, given their high cost, unpredictable and complex nature.

Bahl v Law Society [2004] EWCA Civ 1070
The case concerned a sex and race discrimination claim during which the Court of Appeal insisted that each claim be dealt with and proven separately.

Bilka–Kaufhaus GmbH v Karin Weber von Hartz [1986] 2 CMLR 701 (ECJ) Case 170/84

A fundamental case on part-time work, which outlined the three-part test for the indirect discrimination material factor defence. The claimant was refused benefits under an occupational pension scheme given her part-time status. While indirectly discriminatory, as disproportionally affecting predominately female staff, the company could claim the intention to limit part-time workers was objectively justified, but this would be up to the national court to decide. The test for objective justification was established: it must be objective and genuine to the need of the enterprise, suitable for obtaining the objective pursued, and necessary.

British Coal Corp v Smith [1996] 3 All ER 97

A multiparty litigation case involving female canteen workers and cleaners who cited male surface mineworkers as comparators. The claim was upheld as separate wage structures were not found to be a 'genuine material factor' defence. The women were not limited to choosing a comparator from their own establishment; the broadly similar terms and conditions were sufficient to enable the claim.

Capita Customer Management Ltd v Mr M Ali [2018] 4 WLUK 83

The EAT decided that offering enhanced maternity pay and only statutory shared parental pay was not discriminatory. It stated that maternity leave is for the health and wellbeing of the mother and so cannot serve as a comparator for SPL.

Chandler v American Airlines Inc (5 July 2011, ET)

The case concerned restrictions on working hours. The tribunal found that women are still more likely than men to be primary child carers and so held that the restrictions were indirectly discriminatory.

Cooper v House of Fraser (Stores) Ltd [2012] EqLR 991 (ET)

The provision, criterion and practice of full-time working was found to put women at a disadvantage in *Cooper* and, as such, indirect discrimination was established.

The case did not support the reasoning of Lady Smith in *Hacking*. The tribunal questioned the EAT's reasoning, finding that women still have the main burden of care.

Dekker v Stichting Vormingscentrum Voor Jonge Volwassen Plus [1992] ICR 325 (ECJ) Case 177/88

Referred to the ECJ by the Dutch court, the case considered the principle of equal treatment with reference to pregnant women. As only women could be dismissed on grounds of pregnancy, this was held to be direct discrimination with no need for a hypothetical comparator.

Defrenne v Sabena [1976] 2 CMLR 98 (ECJ) Case 43/75

Female cabin crew claimants challenged the requirement for female staff to retire at 40. The ToR57 was found to have horizontal direct effect and, as such, could be enforced regardless of whether Member States had domestic legislation to that effect.

While the original inclusion in the Treaty was based on economic grounds and competitive advantage, this case asserted the importance of the social aim.

Dietz v Stichting [1997] 1 CMLR 199 (ECJ) Case 435/93

The case was brought by part-time workers who had been denied access to an occupational pension scheme. It was found they were able to rely on Article 119 of ToR57 and could claim retroactively.

Douglas Harvey Barber v Guardian Royal Exchange Assurance Group [1991] 1 QB 344

The case highlighted an age condition in an occupational pension scheme, which upon redundancy treated men and women differently, as women were able to claim from a younger age. Referred to the ECJ, the case had implications for how pension schemes were considered as 'pay'. Ultimately the court found the equal pay provision should also apply to occupational pension schemes.

Dugdale v Kraft Foods Ltd [1977] ICR 48

The case considered claimants doing slightly different work, by virtue of a night shift requirement. It was held that where work is broadly similar then pay should be equal, except with the addition of a nightwork payment.

Dixon v Rees [1994] ICR 39 and ***Hopkins v Shepherd and Partners*** [1994] ICR 39

These two appeals were brought regarding dismissals of pregnant women. The first was dismissed as the employer did not want to lose her replacement. The second was also dismissed for reasons not related to the pregnancy but for business convenience. The EAT found that, in both cases, there was no evidence that a man would not have been treated in the same way. While Dekker and Webb were considered, with regard to the need for a male comparator, it was found that it was still open to the tribunal to consider how a man would have been treated.

EC v UK [1982] ECR 2601 (ECJ) Case 61/81

The European Commission brought the case against the UK, which had failed to implement Directive 75/117 concerning equal value. The EqVA83 was passed soon after.

Electrolux v Hutchinson [1977] ICR 252

The case considered what is 'like work' and whether contractual differences have any practical difference. The contractual requirement for overtime, night and Sunday working for male employees was found to be of no practical difference. The EAT held that there must be a 'genuine material difference' with the opportunity to transfer from one grade to the other. The employer's appeal was dismissed and the claim was upheld.

Enderby v Frenchay [1991] 1 CMLR 626
Speech therapists brought an equal value pay claim against male comparators working in pharmacy and clinical psychology. The separate Whitley Council collective bargaining agreements covering the different groups of staff were found not to be discriminatory in themselves, though the resulting pay systems were. The case took over ten years to resolve.

Garland v British Rail Engineering Ltd [1983] 2 AC 751
The case concerned a discounted travel benefit that male employees retained the right to after retirement for themselves and their families, whereas women only retained the right for themselves. Reference was made to the ECJ to see whether Article 119 of the ToR57 applied. The court held that it did.

Glasgow City Council v Fox Cross Claimants [2014] CSIH 27
The case reversed the ET judgement and held that the respondents were associated employers. As a result, the female claimants whose employment had transferred were able to compare their pay with men still working for Glasgow City Council.

GMB v Allen [2008] EWCA Civ 810
The case was brought against the GMB trade union concerning the role the union previously had in collectively negotiating discriminatory pay protection agreements, favouring male members. The tribunal's indirect discrimination finding was upheld, but GMB's actions in persuading female claimants to accept the agreement were found to be a proportionate means of achieving a legitimate aim.

Hacking & Paterson v Wilson [2010] 5 WLUK 723
The case concerned a request to return to work from maternity leave on a part-time basis. Lady Smith determined that society had changed. While this alone did not strike out the claim, she stated a woman's decision to work part-time, following maternity leave, 'is a matter of choice rather than necessity' (para. 28). However, subsequent cases have not supported Lady Smith's reasoning.

Handels-OG Kontorfunktionaerernes Forbund I Danmark (acting for Herz) v Dansk Arbejdsgiverforening (acting for Aldi Marked K/S) [1991] IRLR 31 (ECJ) Case 179/88
The *Herz* judgement was given on the same day and reiterated the *Dekker* approach that treating women differently as a result of pregnancy is discrimination. The case itself concerned sick leave that was taken after maternity leave had expired. As a result, it was found that the dismissal was fair.

Handley v H. Mono Ltd [1979] ICR 147
The case concerned the lower pay rate given to part-time employees, finding a material difference based on something other than sex. It was stressed that women who worked 40 hours per week would be paid at the same rate as men.

Hayes v Malleable Working Men's Club and Institute [1985] ICR 703
The case found that the SDA75 could be applied for pregnant workers in analogous circumstances. The *Turley* case was not followed, although the minority *Turley* judgement, comparing pregnancy to the case of a sick man, was applied.

HBJ Claimants v Glasgow City Council [2017] CSIH 56
The case concerned a job evaluation scheme that was used to implement the SSA regrading agreement to bring staff and manual workers under one pay scheme. The scheme used had not been subject to peer review, did not follow the EOC advice and was held to be invalid.

Hewage v Grampian Health Board [2012] UKSC 37
The case concerned a constructive dismissal and sex and race discrimination claim. While the claimant was not required to split the race and sex elements of the discrimination claim, the court did not go as far as overturning the *Bahl* approach.

Iske v P&O European Ferries (Dover) Ltd [1997] IRLR 401
The case found that no comparator was needed with a sick man for a pregnancy discrimination claim. The EAT referred to *Dekker* and *Webb* and found the claimant had suffered unlawful discrimination. As a pregnant female seafarer, she was not offered shore-based work, as per company policy.

Jenkins v Kingsgate [1981] 1 WLR 1485
The court held that the difference in pay for part-time and full-time employees was legitimate as motivated by the company's desire to reduce absenteeism and ensure full use of their machinery. The equal pay claim was therefore not upheld.

Lawrence v Regent Office Care Ltd [2003] ICR 1092 (ECJ)
The comparison for equal pay was not upheld as there was no one body responsible for the inequality and therefore in a position to restore equal pay.

Macarthys v Smith [1980] 2 CMLR 205
The case considered whether the fact that the claimant was not employed contemporaneously with the comparator could be held as a defence against an equal pay claim. The claimant had been paid £10 less per week and employed four months after the male comparator. The case was referred to the ECJ, which found that, as there was only a short gap between the claimant and comparator's employment, equal pay could be required. The case also considered the question of part-time work, but found it was up to the national court to decide whether the difference was justified.

Macken v BNP Paribas London Branch [2019] 2208142/2017 and 2205586/2018 (ET) (unreported)
The tribunal upheld the allegations of sexual discrimination and victimization. A senior employee at BNP Paribas, the claimant was subject to underpayment

in relation to a male colleague and mistreatment amounting to victimization in the workplace.

Magorrian v Eastern Health and Social Services Board [1998] All ER (EC) 38
The exclusion of part-time nurses from certain occupational pension rights was found to be indirect discrimination. The claim also considered back pay, previously limited to two years. It was held that national laws of this kind should not be applied. This ultimately extended the right to compensation in equal pay cases.

Middlesbrough Borough Council v Surtees [2008] EWCA Civ 885
The case concerned a council pay protection scheme that had been implemented to protect typically male workers after regrading. Female claimants highlighted their lack of protection from the red circling arrangements, adding to the historical pay inequities revealed by the job evaluation scheme.

North Yorkshire CC v Ratcliffe [1995] ICR 833
This equal value case concerning compulsory competitive tendering was brought by a group of female catering assistants. While they had established equal value with male comparators when the service was put out to tender, they were not afforded equal treatment with men carrying out equivalent work. The women were dismissed as redundant and re-employed on lower rates of pay than those of their equal value male employees. The case was an important catalyst for the Single Status agreement in local government.

O'Reilly v BBC 2200423 (19 November 2010 ET)
The former *Countryfile* presenter claimed sex and age discrimination. While the tribunal acknowledged and accepted intersectional discrimination as a possibility, the claim was ultimately progressed under the characteristic of age.

Pimlico Plumbers Ltd v Smith [2018] UKSC 29
The case concerned the employment status of the claimant. The Supreme Court dismissed the appeal finding that he was a 'limb b' worker and, as such, could pursue his claims for unlawful deductions, holiday pay and disability discrimination in the tribunal.

R (on the application of Essex CC) v Secretary of State for Education [2012] EWHC 1460
The case concerned a decision to reduce funding for schools and nurseries. The case confirmed that the Public Sector Equality Duty is a rigorous and important requirement.

R (on the application of UNISON) v Lord Chancellor [2017] UKSC 51
The case held that fees for employment tribunals are unlawful because they impede access to justice and defy the rule of law.

Redcar and Cleveland Borough Council v Bainbridge [2008] EWCA Civ 885
The case was brought by female catering and care employees who compared their terms and conditions and the absence of bonuses and allowances,

with those paid to male refuse employees. While separate collective bargaining agreements had led to these differences in pay, this was not a valid material factor defence. The pay protection afforded when the Green Book of local government terms and conditions was implemented meant that previous indirect discrimination, while recognized, had continued.

Roberts v Hopwood [1925] AC 578

The local council was not required to increase the wages of female employees to bring them in line with male employees. It was held that the law did not require equal pay.

Snell v Network Rail [2016] 8 WLUK 348

The case considered an employer's policy to give enhanced shared parental pay to mothers and primary adopters, but not to partners and secondary adopters. The tribunal held that the policy amounted to sex discrimination.

Tantum v Travers Smith Braithwaite Service [2013] 5 WLUK 437

Upon conclusion of the case, the tribunal also required the employer to implement diversity training for all their staff.

Turley v Allders Department Stores [1980] ICR 66

A claim of pregnancy discrimination and less favourable treatment was not upheld given the impossibility of finding a pregnant male comparator. The minority judgement of Smith J introduced the idea of a sick man as a potential comparator, though this was not accepted.

Uber BV v Aslam [2018] EWCA Civ 2748

The case appealed to the Supreme Court to establish where Uber driver workers can be categorized as 'limb b', a third category of employment status potentially establishing the right to minimum wage.

Uber v Aslam [2021] UKSC 5

The case confirmed that Uber drivers are to be considered workers and not independent contractors. The judgement is significant, not just for the drivers and their subsequent entitlement to minimum wage and holiday pay, but for the wider question of worker status in the gig economy.

Van Gend en Loos v Nederlandse Administraie der Belashingen [1963] ECR 1 (ECJ) Case 26/62

A landmark ECJ case, this held that articles that are clear, precise and unconditional, so as not to require further measures of implementation, are directly applicable and can be relied upon within Member States.

Walker v Co-operative Group Ltd [2020] EWCA Civ 1075

Equal value claim with the Co-operative Group asserting a material factor defence, citing various factors unrelated to gender. Despite the EAT upholding Walker's claim that the material factor defence had expired, the Court of Appeal overturned this finding. Walker was also held liable for Co-op's costs of £20,000.

Webb v EMO Air Cargo UK Ltd [1995] 1 WLR 1454

The case considered pregnancy, sex discrimination and unfair dismissal. It was found that no comparator was needed to establish discrimination of a pregnant woman. The case was referred to the ECJ, which confirmed that discrimination by virtue of pregnancy was sex discrimination. In the instance of *Webb*, she was employed to cover another's leave and then stayed when she returned, having had a baby. Shortly thereafter she discovered that she too was pregnant. The company dismissed her as a result. The claim of direct discrimination was not upheld, but indirect discrimination was.

APPENDIX 2

Construction of the Sample Dataset

Organizational pay reports are given a SIC code, which identifies the relevant business activity of the organization. For organizations with a company number, this is automatically populated with the SIC code held at Companies House. The GPRR note that the accuracy of this data is reliant on organizations keeping their Companies House record up to date. Where employers have entered multiple SIC codes, the pay reports use the first displayed code to classify.

When constructing the sample dataset, I initially planned to conduct a full finance sector analysis, with categorization of different types of finance and banking firms. Under the category 'Financial and Insurance activities', 441 company reports are included on the pay data reporting website for 2017–18. Given the focus on inequities within finance and banking, insurance firms were excluded. The search was subsequently refined to financial activities, with a resulting dataset of 206 companies.

Comparison of these organizations highlighted difficulties due to the overlapping nature of SIC code categories. For instance, numerous large banking organizations listed themselves under 'Professional, scientific and technical' codes and so were not included. A further complication was identified as not all companies provide a SIC code, and some list different functions in different areas. To ensure the target population was reliable, transparent and replicable I simplified the process of selecting organizations for analysis.

The following SIC codes were used to populate the sample dataset: Central Banking 64110; Banks 64191; Building Societies 64192. (A full breakdown of the SIC list is available at: https://www.gov.uk/government/publications/standard-industrial-classification-of-economic-activities-sic.)

This was not intended to create an exhaustive list of Britain's financial institutions, for the reasons described, but is transparent, replicable and comparable. This robust definition ensures the validity of the research and, as stated, is able to provide indicative trends for the wider sector.

APPENDIX 3

Full Details of the Sample Dataset

The following breakdown of mean pay and bonus gaps relates to Figure 4.2 and pay reports for 2022–23. It gives the full list of firms and has been sorted smallest to largest. The firms listed at the bottom with no accompanying gaps did not report in the 2022–23 reporting window. The manually coded variables of age and organization type are shown.

Employer	Age	Type	2022–23 Mean GPG %	2022–23 Mean bonus gap %
C. Hoare & CO.	Pre-1970	Private/asset/wealth management	8	17
Clearbank Ltd	Post-2007	Credit/payment/clearing	12.1	23
Starling Bank Ltd	Post-2007	Smaller UK	12.3	33.2
Lloyds Bank Corporate Markets Plc	Pre-1970	Private/asset/wealth management	13.8	28.5
Triodos Bank UK Ltd	1970–2007	Global	16.9	0
Monzo Bank Ltd	Post-2007	Smaller UK	18	56
Metro Bank Plc	Post-2007	Smaller UK	18.4	31
Aldermore Bank Plc	Post-2007	Global	21.8	92.3
Hampshire Trust Bank Plc	1970–2007	Smaller UK	22	47
Julian Hodge Bank Ltd	1970–2007	Smaller UK	22.8	47
SMBC Bank International Plc	Pre-1970	Global	24.1	44.7
Barclays Bank UK Plc	Pre-1970	Global	25	57.5
The Co-operative Bank Plc	Pre-1970	Smaller UK	25	40.4

Employer	Age	Type	2022–23 Mean GPG %	2022–23 Mean bonus gap %
Zopa Bank Ltd	1970–2007	Smaller UK	25.5	33
Investec Bank Plc	1970–2007	Private/asset/wealth management	25.6	64.4
Yorkshire Building Society	Pre-1970	Building Society	25.7	38.7
Credit Agricole CIB	Pre-1970	Global	25.9	49.2
Bank of China (UK) Ltd	Pre-1970	Global	26.2	23.4
Skipton Building Society	Pre-1970	Building Society	26.6	51.8
Principality Building Society	Pre-1970	Building Society	26.8	30.7
RCI Bank UK Ltd	1970–2007	Credit/payment/clearing	26.9	19.7
Atom Bank Plc	Post-2007	Smaller UK	27.6	49
Newcastle Building Society	Pre-1970	Building Society	28.4	42
Santander UK Plc	Pre-1970	Global	28.5	55.2
Clydesdale Bank Plc	Pre-1970	Smaller UK	28.5	47.8
AIB Group (UK) Plc	Pre-1970	Global	28.6	-5.4
National Westminster Bank Plc	Pre-1970	Global	28.7	52.5
ICBC Standard Bank Plc	1970–2007	Global	28.9	49.1
Standard Chartered Bank	Pre-1970	Private/asset/wealth management	29	49.3
Handelsbanken Plc	Pre-1970	Global	29.2	100
Vanquis Bank Ltd	1970–2007	Credit/payment/clearing	29.3	49.2
TSB Bank Plc	Pre-1970	Smaller UK	29.5	47.4
Schroder & Co Ltd	Pre-1970	Private/asset/wealth management	29.8	54.8
Nationwide Building Society	Pre-1970	Building Society	30	43.7
Coventry Building Society	Pre-1970	Building Society	30.1	39.2
Bank of Ireland (UK) Plc	Pre-1970	Global	30.5	0
HSBC UK Bank Plc	Pre-1970	Global	31.1	53
Lloyds Bank Plc	Pre-1970	Global	31.4	56.5

Employer	Age	Type	2022–23 Mean GPG %	2022–23 Mean bonus gap %
Leeds Building Society	Pre-1970	Building Society	32.1	43.5
Cynergy Bank Ltd	Pre-1970	Global	33.5	37.2
Cumberland Building Society	Pre-1970	Building Society	34	74
RBC Europe Ltd	Pre-1970	Private/asset/wealth management	34	53
United Trust Bank Ltd	Pre-1970	Smaller UK	34	82
Sainsbury's Bank Plc	1970–2007	Smaller UK	34.3	83.1
EFG Private Bank Ltd	Pre-1970	Private/asset/wealth management	34.8	62.8
Secure Trust Bank Plc	Pre-1970	Smaller UK	36	65.1
Shawbrook Bank Ltd	Post-2007	Smaller UK	36.5	56.5
Mizuho International Plc	Pre-1970	Global	37.8	59.3
Nottingham Building Society	Pre-1970	Building Society	38	59.2
Credit Suisse International	Pre-1970	Global	39	59.3
West Bromwich Building Society	Pre-1970	Building Society	39.1	75.8
Joh Berenberg, Gossler & Co. KG – London Branch	Pre-1970	Private/asset/wealth management	41.7	59.6
Barclays Plc	Pre-1970	Global	42.4	67.7
Onesavings Bank Plc	Pre-1970	Smaller UK	42.6	73.2
Barclays Bank Plc	Pre-1970	Global	42.9	67.5
HSBC Bank Plc	Pre-1970	Global	43.2	54.4
J.P. Morgan Securities Plc	Pre-1970	Private/asset/wealth management	49.3	63.1
Goldman Sachs Asset Management Int	Pre-1970	Private/asset/wealth management	51.3	69.2
Brown Shipley & Co Ltd	Pre-1970	Private/asset/wealth management	60.3	66.5
First Rate Exchange Services Holdings Ltd	1970–2007	Credit/payment/clearing		
First Rate Exchange Services Ltd	1970–2007	Credit/payment/clearing		

Employer	Age	Type	2022–23 Mean GPG %	2022–23 Mean bonus gap %
The Royal Bank of Scotland Plc	Pre-1970	Global		
Al Rayan Bank Plc	1970–2007	Global		
HSBC Private Bank (UK) Ltd	Pre-1970	Private/asset/wealth management		
Bank of America Merrill Lynch Int Ltd	Pre-1970	Private/asset/wealth management		
J.P. Morgan Ltd	Pre-1970	Private/asset/wealth management		
Blackrock Asset Management Ltd	1970–2007	Private/asset/wealth management		
Couts & Company	Pre-1970	Private/asset/wealth management		
Virgin Money Ltd	1970–2007	Smaller UK		

APPENDIX 4

Participant Recruitment

Over the course of the research, 80 contacts were made and, ultimately, 26 interviews were carried out. Due to the hard-to-reach nature of intended participants, these contacts were not targeted at particular organizations or parts of the sector. Trade union networks assisted in the recruitment of HRM contacts, which then translated into interviews. Academics in the University of Sussex Business School and the researcher's personal networks led to further respondent-driven contacts and the majority of participants. The recruitment process was challenging and driven solely by respondent willingness to participate.

Once a potential participant was identified, they were then contacted via email. The email included: a broad outline of the research; a request to take part; reassurances around confidentiality and anonymity; a participant information sheet; and a consent form. No incentives were offered for taking part in the research.

The sequence of interviews was driven by respondent availability and took place between January and July 2019.

The 26 interviews that were conducted included:

- Four HRM management participants, two of whom were very senior and two mid-level.
- Four trade unionists, three of whom were employed directly by unions (two male, one female) – two from smaller banking staff associations and one larger general union – alongside one lay rep, who was employed by a bank but given facility time to undertake a union role.
- Ten participants in management grades, two of whom were at managing director or global head level.
- Seven mid-level roles.
- Two junior cashier level roles, one of whom undertook union duties.

Aside from the two trade union participants, all participants were women. They ranged from those relatively new to the sector (three years' experience), to those with careers spanning 30 plus years. Nineteen participants were British, alongside five European, one Asian and one Australasian. Their age range was spread fairly evenly from 25 to 60. Over four fifths of the sample were educated to degree level and two fifths had master's or post-doctoral qualifications. In addition, just over a third of the women interviewed did not have children, while the majority had one or more, ranging from infant to adult.

Fourteen interviews were carried out face to face, with the remaining conducted either by Skype or phone. Interviews typically lasted around one hour. A list of similar questions was drawn up for trade unions, management and employees, respectively. Topics were then developed dependent on experiences, with cues being taken from participants. The intention for this loose structure and responsive interview technique was to give voice and ownership, enabling interviewees to exert some control over the process (Skinner, 2012: 13). The researcher was able to guide the conversation around broad themes, while participants retained an ability to tell their stories.

Despite the focus on gender pay inequalities in the banking sector, it has remained largely resilient to change. To understand how and why this has occurred, the lived reality of this resilience is illustrative. We all play a part in the different discourses of our social reality, and so it is vital to understand how women define their own experiences. Interviewing as a method enables the researcher to capture individual experiences, hear the individual narratives that accompany them and highlight the constraints of the workplace (Seidman, 2013: 19).

References

Ablan, J. (2019) 'Pimco defends its culture in gender and race discrimination suit: Asset manager cites working mothers in its senior legal team in court filing', *Financial Times*, 17 November.

Acker, J. (1989) *Doing Comparable Worth: Gender, Class, and Pay Equity*. Philadelphia: Temple University Press.

Acker, J. (1990) 'Hierarchies, jobs, bodies: A theory of gendered organizations', *Gender & Society*, 4 (2): 139–58.

Acker, J. (1991) 'Thinking about wages: The gendered wage gap in Swedish Banks', *Gender and Society*, 5 (3): 390–407.

Acker, J. (2006) 'Inequality regimes gender, class, and race in organizations', *Gender and Society*, 20 (4): 441–64.

Acker, J. (2009) 'From glass ceiling to inequality regimes', *Sociologie du Travail*, 51 (2): 199–217.

Acker, J. (2012) 'Gendered organizations and intersectionality: Problems and possibilities', *Equality, Diversity and Inclusion: An International Journal*, 31 (3): 214–24.

Adams, C.A. and Harte, G. (1998) 'The changing portrayal of the employment of women in British banks' and retail companies' corporate annual reports', *Accounting, Organizations and Society*, 23 (8): 781–812.

Adams, L., Luanaigh, A.N., Thomson, D. and Rossiter, H. (2018) *Measuring and Reporting on Disability and Ethnicity Pay Gaps*. London: EHRC. Available at: https://www.equalityhumanrights.com/sites/default/files/measuring-and-reporting-on-ethnicity-and-disability-pay-gaps.pdf (Accessed: 20 November 2023).

Adzuna (2022) *Show Me the Money: Salary Transparency in 2022*. London: Adzuna.

Aharoni, Y. (2011) 'Fifty years of case research in international business: The power of outliers and black swans', in Piekkari, R. and Welch, C. (eds) *Rethinking the Case Study in International Business and Management Research*. Cheltenham: Edward Elgar Publishing, pp. 41–54.

Aisenbrey, S. and Bruckner, H. (2008) 'Occupational aspirations and the gender gap in wages', *European Sociological Review*, 24 (5): 633–49.

Albertyn, C., Fredman, S. and Fudge, J. (2014) 'Introduction: Elusive equalities – sex, gender and women', *International Journal of Law in Context*, 10 (4): 421–26.

Alston, P. (2018) *Statement on Visit to the United Kingdom: Special Rapporteur on Extreme Poverty and Human Rights*. London: United Nations. Available at: https://www.ohchr.org/EN/NewsEvents/Pages/DisplayNews.aspx?NewsID=23881&LangID=E (Accessed: 20 November 2023).

Ames, J. (2020) 'Ministers plan to bring back work tribunal fees', *The Times*, 15 June.

Andrew, K. (2017) *The Gender Pay Gap: A Briefing*. London: Institute of Economic Affairs. Available at: https://iea.org.uk/publications/the-gender-pay-gap-a-briefing/ (Accessed: 20 November 2023).

Annesley, C. and Scheele, A. (2011) 'Gender, capitalism and economic crisis: Impact and responses', *Journal of Contemporary European Studies*, 19 (3): 335–47.

Ardanaz-Badia, A. and Rawling, J. (2018) *Understanding the Gender Pay Gap in the UK*. Newport: ONS. Available at: https://www.ons.gov.uk/employmentandlabourmarket/peopleinwork/earningsandworkinghours/articles/understandingthegenderpaygapintheuk/2018-01-17 (Accessed: 20 November 2023).

Arndt, P. and Wrohlich, K. (2019) *Gender Quotas in a European Comparison: Tough Sanctions Most Effective*. Berlin: German Institute for Economic Research. Doi:10.18723/diw_dwr:2019-38-1

Atkinson, C., Beck, V., Brewis, J., Davies, A. and Duberley, J. (2021) 'Menopause and the workplace: New directions in HRM research and HR practice', *Human Resource Management Journal*, 31 (1): 49–64. Doi:10.1111/1748-8583.12294

Atkinson, J. (2011) 'Gendered organizations and women's career progression in the UK financial services sector', *Journal of Social Welfare and Family Law*, 33 (3): 243–54.

Atkinson, J. (2017) 'Shared parental leave in the UK: Can it advance gender equality by changing fathers into co-parents?', *International Journal of Law in Context*, 13: 356–68.

Babcock, L. and Laschever, S. (2003) *Women Don't Ask: Negotiation and the Gender Divide*. Princeton: Princeton University Press.

Barnard, C. and Hepple, B. (2000) 'Substantive equality', *Cambridge Law Journal*, 59 (3): 562–85.

Basit, T. (2003) 'Manual or electronic? The role of coding in qualitative data analysis', *Educational Research,* 45 (2): 143–54.

Bauld, L., Judge, K. and Paterson, I. (2017) 'New directions for the British welfare state', in Gilbert, N. and Van Voorhis, R. (eds) *Changing Patterns of Social Protection*. Abingdon: Routledge.

Bazeley, A. and Rosenblatt, G. (2019) *Why Women Need a Right to Know: Shining a Light on Pay Discrimination*. London: The Fawcett Society. Available at: https://www.fawcettsociety.org.uk/Handlers/Download.ashx?IDMF=cd8d56a1-52cb-43f2-bd2d-ba272ff802a6 (Accessed: 20 November 2023).

BBC (2019) 'Glasgow equal pay women shocked by legal fees on payouts', *BBC*. Available at: https://www.bbc.co.uk/news/uk-scotland-49985113 (Accessed: 20 November 2023).

BBC (2022) 'Birmingham City Council workers balloted over equal pay delay claims', *BBC*, 8 August. Available at: https://www.bbc.co.uk/news/uk-england-birmingham-62466431 (Accessed: 20 November 2023).

BBC (2023) 'Brexit: EU-derived equal pay protections to be retained', *BBC*. Available at: https://www.bbc.co.uk/news/uk-politics-66656661 (Accessed: 20 November 2023).

BBC Sounds (2023) 'Anne-Marie Imafidon on fighting for diversity and equality in science', *BBC*, 14 June. Available at: https://www.bbc.co.uk/programmes/m001mt3h (Accessed: 20 November 2023).

Becker, G.S. (1985) 'Human capital, effort, and the sexual division of labor', *Journal of Labor Economics*, 3 (1): S33–S58.

BEIS (2011) *Women on Boards: The Davies Review*. London: The Stationery Office. Available at: https://ftsewomenleaders.com/2011-2015-the-davies-review/ (Accessed: 20 November 2023).

BEIS (2017) *Hampton-Alexander Review. FTSE Women Leaders: Improving Gender Balance in FTSE Leadership*. London: The Stationery Office. Available at: https://assets.publishing.service.gov.uk/government/uploads/system/uploads/attachment_data/file/658126/Hampton_Alexander_Review_report_FINAL_8.11.17.pdf (Accessed: 20 November 2023).

BEIS (2018a) *Gender Pay Gap Reporting*. London: The Stationery Office. Available at: https://publications.parliament.uk/pa/cm201719/cmselect/cmbeis/928/92802.htm (Accessed: 20 November 2023).

BEIS (2018b) *Trade Union Membership: Statistical Bulletin*. London: The Stationery Office. Available at: https://assets.publishing.service.gov.uk/government/uploads/system/uploads/attachment_data/file/805268/trade-union-membership-2018-statistical-bulletin.pdf (Accessed: 20 November 2023).

BEIS (2020) *Third of FTSE 100 Board Members Now Women, but Business Secretary Says More Needs to be Done*. London: The Stationery Office. Available at: https://www.gov.uk/government/news/third-of-ftse-100-board-members-now-women-but-business-secretary-says-more-needs-to-be-done (Accessed: 20 November 2023).

BEIS (2022) *Trade Union Membership Statistics 2021. Tables*. London: The Stationery Office.

Bell, M. (2011a) 'Achieving the objectives of the Part-Time Work Directive? Revisiting the Part-Time Workers Regulations', *Industrial Law Journal*, 40 (3): 254–79.

Bell, M. (2011b) 'British developments in non-discrimination law: The Equality Act', in Schulze, R. (ed.) *Non-Discrimination in European Private Law*. Tubingen: Mohr Siebeck, pp. 209–31.

Benard, S. and Correll, S.J. (2010) 'Normative discrimination and the motherhood penalty', *Gender & Society*, 24 (5): 616–46.

Bennedsen, M., Simintzi, E., Tsoutsoura, M. and Wolfenzon, D. (2019) *Do Firms Respond to Gender Pay Gap Transparency? NBER Working Paper Series*. Cambridge: National Bureau of Economic Research. Available at: https://papers.ssrn.com/sol3/papers.cfm?abstract_id=3315240 (Accessed: 20 November 2023).

Bensidoun, I. and Trancart, D. (2018) 'Career choices and the gender pay gap: The role of work preferences and attitudes', *Population,* 73 (1): 35–59.

Benson, C., Friis Hamre, E. and Wright, W. (2018) *Understanding the Gender Pay Gap in Banking and Finance: Analysis of Gender Pay Gap Data and Female Representation in UK Financial Services*. London: New Financial. Available at: https://newfinancial.org/report-understanding-the-gender-pay-gap-in-banking-and-finance/ (Accessed: 20 November 2023).

Beveridge, F. and Velluti, S. (2008) *Gender and the Open Method of Coordination: Perspectives on Law, Governance and Equality in the EU*. Abingdon: Ashgate Publishing.

Bian, X. and Wang, J. (2019) 'Women's career interruptions: An integrative review', *European Journal of Training and Development*, 43 (9): 1–20.

Bird, C. (1990) 'High finance, small change: Women's increased representation in bank management', in Reskin, B. and Roos, P. (eds) *Job Queues, Gender Queues – Explaining Women's Inroads into Male Occupations*. Philadelphia: Temple University Press, pp. 145–66.

BIS (2015) *Improving the Gender Balance on British Boards*. London: The Stationery Office. Available at: https://assets.publishing.service.gov.uk/government/uploads/system/uploads/attachment_data/file/482059/BIS-15-585-women-on-boards-davies-review-5-year-summary-october-2015.pdf (Accessed: 20 November 2023).

Bishop, I. (2022) *Trade Union Membership 2021. Statistical Bulletin*. London: Department for Business, Energy & Industrial Strategy.

BITC (2018) *Equal Lives: Parenthood and Caring in the Workplace*. London: Business in the Community. Available at: https://www.bitc.org.uk/report/equal-lives-parenthood-and-caring-in-the-workplace/ (Accessed: 20 November 2023).

Blau, F.D. and Kahn, L.M. (2017) 'The gender wage gap: Extent, trends, and explanations', *Journal of Economic Literature*, 55 (3): 789–865.

Bohnet, I. (2016) *What Works: Gender Equality by Design*. London: Harvard University Press.

Brannen, J. and Lewis, S. (2000) 'Workplace programmes and policies in the United Kingdom', in Haas, L., Hwang, P. and Russell, G. (eds) *Organizational Change & Gender Equity*. London: Sage, pp. 99–116.

Bridge Group (2023) *Shaping our Economy: Senior Roles in Financial Services and Socio-Economic Diversity*. London: Progress Together.

Britton, D.M. and Logan, L. (2008) 'Gendered organizations: Progress and prospects', *Sociology Compass*, 2 (1): 107–21.

Brooks, L. (2018) 'Glasgow: Thousands of women to strike over pay discrimination', *The Guardian*, 15 October.

Browne, J. (2004) 'Resolving gender pay inequality? Rationales, enforcement and policy', *Journal of Social Policy*, 33 (4): 553–71.

Brussevich, M., Dabla-Norris, E., Kamunge, C., Karnane, P., Khalid, S. and Kochhar, K. (2018) *Gender, Technology, and the Future of Work: IDEAS Working Paper Series*. St Louis: International Monetary Fund. Available at: https://www.imf.org/en/Publications/Staff-Discussion-Notes/Iss ues/2018/10/09/Gender-Technology-and-the-Future-of-Work-46236 (Accessed: 20 November 2023).

Brynin, M. (2017) *The Gender Pay Gap*. Colchester: University of Essex: Institute for Social and Economic Research.

Buckler, S. and Dolowitz, D. (2000) 'Theorizing the third way: New Labour and social justice', *Journal of Political Ideologies*, 5 (3): 301–20.

Burchell, B., Hardy, V., Rubery, J. and Smith, M. (2014) *A New Method to Understand Occupational Gender Segregation in European Labour Markets*. Luxembourg: Publications Office of the European Union. Available at: https://www.diversite-europe.eu/sites/default/files/cck-files-offic ial-documents/150119_segregation_report_web_en.pdf (Accessed: 20 November 2023).

Burri, S. and Prechal, S. (2013) *EU Gender Equality Law*. Luxembourg: Publications Office of the European Union. Doi: 10.2838/84769. Available at: https://op.europa.eu/en/publication-detail/-/publication/c7a08f35-e9e8-47f8-8c8b-b8375646d22c (Accessed: 20 November 2023).

Busby, N. (2001) 'The Part-Time Workers (Prevention of Less Favourable Treatment) Regulations 2000: Righting a wrong or out of proportion?', *The Journal of Business Law*, July: 344–56.

Butler, S. (2018) 'Tesco faces £4bn equal pay bill as claimant numbers swell to 1,000', *The Guardian*, 11 July.

Butler, S. (2021) 'Supreme Court rules against Asda workers' equal pay case', *The Guardian*, 26 March.

Cabinet Office (2011) *Red Tape Challenge*. London: The Stationery Office. Available at: https://www.gov.uk/government/news/red-tape-challenge (Accessed: 20 November 2023).

Caruso, L. (2018) Digital innovation and the fourth industrial revolution: Epochal social changes? *AI & Society*, 33 (3): 379–92.

Cassirer, N. and Reskin, B. (2000) 'High hopes: Organizational position, employment experiences, and women's and men's promotion aspirations', *Work and Occupations*, 27 (4): 438–63.

Chadwick, C. and Flinchbaugh, C. (2016) 'The effects of part-time workers on establishment financial performance', *Journal of Management*, 42 (6): 1635–62.

Chevalier, A. (2007) 'Education, occupation and career expectations: Determinants of the gender pay gap for UK graduates', *Oxford Bulletin of Economics and Statistics*, 69 (6): 819–42.

Chinwala, Y., Haymoz, M. and Barrow, J. (2020) *HM Treasury Women in Finance Charter: Annual Review 2019*. London: New Financial. Available at: https://assets.publishing.service.gov.uk/government/uploads/system/uploads/attachment_data/file/894197/HM_Treasury_Women_in_Finance_Charter_-_Annual_Review_2019.pdf (Accessed: 20 November 2023).

Chinwala, Y., Barrow, J. and Singhal, S. (2022) *HM Treasury Women in Finance Charter: Annual Review 2021*. London: New Financial. Available at: https://newfinancial.org/report-hm-treasury-women-in-finance-charter-annual-review-2021/ (Accessed: 20 November 2023).

Clarke, H., Sanders, D., Steward, M. and Whiteley, P. (2011) 'Valence politics and electoral choice in Britain, 2010', *Journal of Elections, Public Opinion & Parties*, 21 (2): 237–53.

Clarke, N. (2023) 'BBC boss: Eight equal pay cases currently open is an "achievement"'. *Independent*, 14 June.

Clarke, S. and Cominetti, N. (2019) *Setting the Record Straight: How Record Employment Has Changed the UK*. London: Resolution Foundation.

Colebrook, C., Snelling, C. and Longlands, S. (2018) *The State of Pay: Demystifying the Gender Pay Gap*. London: Institute of Public Policy Research. Available at: https://www.ippr.org/files/2018-05/state-of-pay-may18.pdf (Accessed: 20 November 2023).

Colella, A., Paetzold, R., L., Zardkoohi, A. and Wesson, M.J. (2007) 'Exposing pay secrecy', *The Academy of Management Review*, 32 (1): 55–71.

Conaghan, J. (2020) 'Covid-19 and inequalities at work: A gender lens', *Futures of Work*, 13. Available at: https://futuresofwork.co.uk/2020/05/07/covid-19-and-inequalities-at-work-a-gender-lens/ (Accessed: 15 June 2023).

Conley, H. (2014) 'Trade unions, equal pay and the law in the UK', *Economic and Industrial Democracy*, 35 (2): 309–23.

Conley, H. and Page, M. (2018) 'The good, the not so good and the ugly: Gender equality, equal pay and austerity in English local government', *Work, Employment and Society*, 32 (4): 789–805.

Conley, H. and Torbus, U. (2019) 'Transparency and the gender pay gap', in Conley, H., Gottardi, D., Healy, G., Mikolajczyk, B. and Peruzzi, M. (eds) *The Gender Pay Gap and Social Partnership in Europe: Findings from 'Close the Deal, Fill the Gap'*. Abingdon: Routledge, pp. 145–66.

Conley, H., Healy, G., Martin, P. and Warren, S. (2019) 'Decentralisation and the gender pay gap in the UK context', in Conley, H., Gottardi, D., Healy, G., Mikolajczyk, B. and Peruzzi, M. (eds) *The Gender Pay Gap and Social Partnership in Europe: Findings from 'Close the Deal, Fill the Gap'*. Abingdon: Routledge, pp. 90–113.

Correll, S.J. and Simard, C. (2016) 'Research: Vague feedback is holding women back' *Harvard Business Review*. Available at: https://hbr.org/2016/04/research-vague-feedback-is-holding-women-back (Accessed: 20 November 2023).

Covid Inquiry (2023) 'Transcript of module 2 public hearing on 1 November 2023 UK Covid-19 Inquiry archives', *UK Covid-19 Inquiry*. Available at: https://covid19.public-inquiry.uk/documents/transcript-of-module-2-public-hearing-on-1-november-2023/ (Accessed: 20 November 2023).

Creasy, S. (2020) 'Equal Pay (Information and Claims) Bill', UK Parliament. Available at: https://bills.parliament.uk/bills/2793. (Accessed: 20 November 2023).

CRED (2021) *The Report of the Commission on Race and Ethnic Disparities*. London: The Stationery Office. Available at: https://www.gov.uk/government/publications/the-report-of-the-commission-on-race-and-ethnic-disparities (Accessed: 20 November 2023).

Crenshaw, K. (1989) 'Demarginalizing the intersection of race and sex: A Black Feminist critique of anti-discrimination doctrine, feminist theory and antiracist politics', *University of Chicago Legal Forum*, (1): 139–67.

Cressey, P. and Scott, P. (1992) 'Employment, technology and industrial relations in the UK clearing banks: Is the honeymoon over?', *New Technology, Work, and Employment*, 7 (2): 83–96.

Criado-Perez, C. (2019) *Invisible Women: Data Bias in a World Designed for Men*. New York: Vintage Publishing.

Croft, J. (2019) 'Women fight for equal pay at supermarkets', *Financial Times*, 16 June.

Crompton, R. (1989) 'Women in banking: Continuity and change since the Second World War', *Work Employment & Society*, 3 (2): 141–56.

Crompton, R. and Birkelund, G.E. (2000) 'Employment and caring in British and Norwegian banking: An exploration through individual careers', *Work, Employment & Society*, 14 (2): 331–52.

Crow, D. (2019) 'HSBC to axe up to 10,000 jobs in cost-cutting drive', *Financial Times*, 6 October.

Daniel, E. (1999) 'Provision of electronic banking in the UK and the Republic of Ireland', *International Journal of Bank Marketing*, 17 (2): 72–83.

Datta Gupta, N. (2018) 'Maternity leave versus early childcare – What are the long-term consequence for children?', *IZA World of Labor Newsletter,* 438. Doi: 10.15185/izawol.438

Davies, M. (2008) 'Feminism and the flat law theory', *Feminist Legal Studies,* 16 (3): 281–304.

Davies, R. and Richardson, P. (2010) 'Evolution of the UK banking system', *Bank of England Quarterly Bulletin,* 50 (Q4): 321–32.

Davies, R., McNabb, R. and Whitfield, K. (2015) 'Do high-performance work practices exacerbate or mitigate the gender pay gap?', *Cambridge Journal of Economics,* 39 (2): 537–64.

De Ramon, S., Francis, W. and Milonas, K. (2017) *An Overview of the UK Banking Sector Since the Basel Accord: Insights from a New Regulatory Database.* London: Bank of England. Available at: https://www.bankofengland. co.uk/working-paper/2017/an-overview-of-the-uk-banking-sector-since-the-basel-accord-insights-from-a-new-regulatory-database (Accessed: 20 November 2023).

Deakin, S., Fraser Butlin, S., Mclaughlin, C. and Polanska, A. (2015) 'Are litigation and collective bargaining complements or substitutes for achieving gender equality? A study of the British Equal Pay Act', *Cambridge Journal of Economics,* 39 (2): 381–403.

Department of Children, Disability, Integration and Youth (2022) *Minister O'Gorman Announces Introduction of Gender Pay Gap Reporting in 2022.* Dublin: Government Publications Office. Available: https://www.gov.ie/ en/press-release/aa331-minister-ogorman-announces-introduction-of-gen der-pay-gap-reporting-in-2022/ (Accessed: 20 November 2023).

DfE (2019a) *Participation Rates in Higher Education: Academic Years 2006/ 2007 – 2017/2018.* London: The Stationery Office. Available at: https:// assets.publishing.service.gov.uk/government/uploads/system/uploads/atta chment_data/file/843542/Publication_HEIPR1718.pdf (Accessed: 20 November 2023).

DfE (2019b) *Education and Training Statistics for the United Kingdom 2019.* London: The Stationery Office. Available at: https://assets.publishing.serv ice.gov.uk/government/uploads/system/uploads/attachment_data/file/ 847318/UKETS_2019_Main_text.pdf (Accessed: 20 November 2023).

Di Torella, E.C. (2007) 'New Labour, New Dads – The Impact of family friendly legislation on fathers', *Industrial Law Journal,* 36 (3): 318–28.

Diamond, P. (2013) 'The progressive dilemmas of British social democracy: Political economy after New Labour', *The British Journal of Politics and International Relations,* 15 (1): 89–106.

Dickens, L. (2005) 'Walking the talk? Equality and diversity in employment', in Bach, S. (ed.) *Managing Human Resources: Personnel Management in Transition.* Hoboken: John Wiley & Sons, pp. 178–207.

Dickens, L. (2007) 'The road is long: Thirty years of equality legislation in Britain', *British Journal of Industrial Relations,* 45 (3): 463–94.

Dickens, L. (2014) 'The coalition government's reforms to employment tribunals and statutory employment rights-echoes of the past', *Industrial Relations Journal,* 45 (3): 234–49.

DiMaggio, P.J. and Powell, W.W. (1983) 'The iron cage revisited: Institutional isomorphism and collective rationality in organizational fields', *American Sociological Review,* 48 (2): 147–60.

Dobbin, F. (2009) *Inventing Equal Opportunity.* Princeton: Princeton University Press.

Dobbin, F. and Kalev, A. (2016) 'Why diversity programs fail', *Harvard Business Review,* 94 (7): 52–61.

Dobbin, F., Sutton, J.R., Meyer, J.W. and Scott, R. (1993) 'Equal opportunity law and the construction of internal labor markets', *American Journal of Sociology,* 99 (2): 396–427.

Doward, J (2016) 'Equality watchdog's human rights fight "under threat" after cuts', *The Guardian,* 20 November.

Dray, S. (2021) *Mandatory Ethnicity Pay Gap Reporting.* London: The Stationery Office. Available at: https://lordslibrary.parliament.uk/mandat ory-ethnicity-pay-gap-reporting/ (Accessed: 20 November 2023).

Dromey, J. and Rankin, L. (2018) *The Fair Pay Report: How Pay Transparency Can Help Tackle Inequalities. Women and the Economy.* London: The Institute for Public Policy Research. Available at: http://www.ippr.org/research/publications/the-fair-pay-report (Accessed: 20 November 2023).

Duggan, M. (2010) *Equality Act 2010: A Guide to the New Law.* London: The Law Society.

Dunkley, E. (2017) 'HSBC signals end to UK branch closure programme', *Financial Times,* 24 January. Available at: https://www.ft.com/content/76232cac-e19b-11e6-8405-9e5580d6e5fb (Accessed: 20 November 2023).

Dunstan, R. (2021) *Reform of Shared Parental Leave Needs to be a Priority for Ministers.* London: Maternity Action.

Durbin, S., Page, M. and Walby, S. (2017) 'Gender equality and "austerity": Vulnerabilities, resistance and change', *Gender, Work & Organization,* 24 (1): 1–6.

Eden, C. (2017) *Gender, Education and Work: Inequalities and Intersectionality.* London: Taylor & Francis Ltd.

EHRC (2009) *Financial Services Inquiry: Sex Discrimination and Gender Pay Gap Report of the Equality and Human Rights Commission.* Manchester: EHRC. Available at: https://www.equalityhumanrights.com/sites/default/files/financial_services_inquiry_report_0.pdf (Accessed: 20 November 2023).

EHRC (2018) *Closing the Gap: Enforcing the Gender Pay Gap Regulations.* London: EHRC.

EHRC (2019) *Our Litigation and Enforcement Policy: 2019–22*. London: EHRC. Available at: https://www.equalityhumanrights.com/sites/default/files/our-litigation-and-enforcement-policy-2019-2022_0.docx (Accessed: 20 November 2023).

England, P. (2010) 'The gender revolution', *Gender & Society*, 24 (10): 149–66.

Eswaran, V. (2019) *The Business Case for Diversity in the Workplace Is Now Overwhelming*. Geneva: WEF. Available at: https://www.weforum.org/agenda/2019/04/business-case-for-diversity-in-the-workplace/ (Accessed: 20 November 2023).

European Commission (2019) *Human Capital: Digital Inclusion and Skills. Digital Economy and Society Index Report*. Brussels: Publications Office of the European Union.

European Commission (2020) *The Gender Pay Gap Situation in the EU*. Luxembourg: Publications Office for the European Union. Available at: https://ec.europa.eu/info/policies/justice-and-fundamental-rights/gender-equality/equal-pay/gender-pay-gap-situation-eu_en (Accessed: 20 November 2023).

European Union Agency for Fundamental Rights (2019) *Subgroup on Equality Data*. Vienna: Publications Office of the European Union. Available at: https://fra.europa.eu/en/project/2019/subgroup-equality-data (Accessed: 20 November 2023).

Exley, C.L. and Kessler, J.B. (2019) *The Gender Gap in Self-Promotion*. Cambridge, MA: National Bureau of Economic Research. Doi: 10.3386/w26345

Fagan, C. and Rubery, J. (2017) 'Advancing gender equality through European employment policy: The impact of the UK's EU membership and the risks of Brexit', *Social Policy and Society*, 17 (2): 1–21.

Fairbairn, C. (2018) *CBI Comments on Gender Pay Gap Reporting Deadline – April 2018*. London: CBI. Available at: https://www.cbi.org.uk/media-centre/articles/cbi-comments-on-gender-pay-gap-reporting-deadline-april-2018/ (Accessed: 20 November 2023).

Fawcett Society (2018a) *Sex Discrimination Law Review*. London: Fawcett Society. Available at: https://www.fawcettsociety.org.uk/sex-discrimination-law-review-final-report (Accessed: 20 November 2023).

Fawcett Society (2018b) *1 in 3 Women and Men in Work Do Not Know that Pay Discrimination Is Illegal*. London: Fawcett Society. Available at: https://www.fawcettsociety.org.uk/Handlers/Download.ashx?IDMF=a3baddd3-1d15-4ddc-abd8-eb1b972e008b (Accessed: 20 November 2023).

Fawcett Society (2020) *Fawcett's Equal Pay Bill: Just 3 in 10 Women Say Their Bosses Would Tell Them the Truth on Equal Pay*. London: Fawcett Society. Available at: https://www.fawcettsociety.org.uk/news/fawcetts-equal-pay-bill (Accessed: 20 November 2023).

Feast, P. and Hand, J. (2015) 'Enigmas of the Equality Act 2010 – "Three uneasy pieces"', *Cogent Social Sciences*, 1 (1): 1–9. Doi: 10.1080/23311886.2015.1123085

Fitzpatrick, B. (1987) 'The Sex Discrimination Act 1986', *Modern Law Review*, 50 (7): 934–51.

Francis-Devine, B. (2020) *How Much Less Were Women Paid in 2019?* London: The Stationery Office. Available at: https://commonslibrary.parliament. uk/how-much-less-were-women-paid-in-2019/#:~:text=The%20high est%20earners%20have%20a,highest%20paid%2010%25%20of%20men (Accessed: 20 November 2023).

Francis-Devine, B. and Pyper, D. (2020) *The Gender Pay Gap. Briefing Paper*. London: The Stationery Office. Available at: https://commonslibrary.par liament.uk/research-briefings/sn07068/ (Accessed: 20 November 2023).

Franklin, J. and Miller, J. (2023) 'Goldman Sachs to pay $215mn to settle gender discrimination lawsuit', *Financial Times*, 9 May.

Franzoni, J.M. and Sanchez-Ancochea, D. (2016) *The Quest for Universal Social Policy in the South: Actors, Ideas and Architectures*. Cambridge: Cambridge University Press.

Fredman, S. (2011) 'The public sector equality duty', *Industrial Law Journal*, 40 (4): 405–27.

Friedman, S. (2015) 'Still a "stalled revolution"? Work/family experiences, hegemonic masculinity, and moving toward gender equality', *Sociology Compass*, 9 (2): 140–55.

Fuhrman, S. and Rhodes, F. (2020) *The Absence of Women in COVID-19 Response*. London: CARE International. Available at: https://insights.carein ternational.org.uk/publications/why-we-need-women-in-covid-19-respo nse-teams-and-plans (Accessed: 20 November 2023).

Fullerton, J. (2021) 'Female banker sues BNP Paribas for £3.4m in "stigma" pay after winning discrimination case', *The Telegraph*, 14 March.

Gall, G. (2017) *Employment Relations in Financial Services: An Exploration of the Employee Experience After the Financial Crash*. London: Palgrave Macmillan.

Gallie, D. (2007a) 'Production regimes, employment regimes, and the quality of work', in Gallie, D. (ed.) *Employment Regimes and the Quality of Work*. Oxford: Oxford University Press, pp. 1–34.

Gallie, D. (2007b) 'Welfare regimes, employment systems and job preference orientations', *European Sociological Review*, 23 (3): 279–93.

Garikipati, S. and Kambhampati, U. (2020) 'Leading the fight against the pandemic: Does gender "really" matter?', *SSRN*. Doi:10.2139/ssrn.3617953

GEO (2012) *Equality Act 2010: Employment Tribunals' Power to Make Wider Recommendations in Discrimination Cases and Obtaining Information Procedure. Government Response to the Consultation*. London: The Stationery Office. Available at: https://assets.publishing.service.gov.uk/government/uploads/ system/uploads/attachment_data/file/136235/consultation-response.pdf (Accessed: 20 November 2023).

GEO (2013) *Review of the Public Sector Equality Duty: Report of the Independent Steering Group.* London: The Stationery Office. Available at: https://www. gov.uk/government/publications/the-independent-steering-groups-rep ort-of-the-public-sector-equality-duty-psed-review-and-government-response (Accessed: 20 November 2023).

GEO (2015) *Think, Act, Report.* London: The Stationery Office. Available at: https://www.gov.uk/government/publications/think-act-report/think-act-report (Accessed: 20 November 2023).

GEO (2018a) *100% of UK Employers Publish Gender Pay Gap Data.* London: The Stationery Office. Available at: https://www.gov.uk/gov ernment/news/100-of-uk-employers-publish-gender-pay-gap-data (Accessed: 20 November 2023).

GEO (2018b) *Reducing the Gender Pay Gap and Improving Gender Equality in Organisations: Evidence-Based Actions for Employers.* London: The Stationery Office. Available at: https://gender-pay-gap.service.gov.uk/actions-to-close-the-gap (Accessed: 20 November 2023).

GEO (2019a) *Eight Ways to Understand Your Organisation's Gender Pay Gap.* London: The Stationery Office. https://www.gov.uk/government/news/ new-guidance-to-help-employers-close-gender-pay-gap (Accessed: 20 November 2023).

GEO (2019b) *Four Steps to Developing a Gender Pay Gap Action Plan.* London: The Stationery Office. Available at: https://gender-pay-gap. service.gov.uk/public/assets/pdf/action-plan-guidance.pdf (Accessed: 20 November 2023).

GEO (2020a) *Employers Do Not Have to Report Gender Pay Gaps.* London: The Stationery Office. Available at: https://www.gov.uk/government/news/ employers-do-not-have-to-report-gender-pay-gaps?utm_source=c47d4 416-b6ed-44c5-9f99-b1d52d58ae7c&utm_medium=email&utm_c ampaign=govuk-notifications&utm_content=immediate (Accessed: 20 November 2023).

GEO (2020b) *'Fight for Fairness' Speech to Set Out Government's New Approach to Equality.* London: The Stationery Office. Available at: https://www.gov. uk/government/news/fight-for-fairness-speech-to-set-out-governments-new-approach-to-equality (Accessed: 20 November 2023).

GEO (2021) *Changes to the Enforcement of Gender Pay Gap Regulations Due to the Impact of Covid-19 (Coronavirus).* London: The Stationery Office. Available at: https://www.gov.uk/guidance/gender-pay-gap-reporting-changes-to-enforcement (Accessed: 20 November 2023).

GEO (2022) *Government Launches Pay Transparency Pilot to Break Down Barriers for Women.* London: The Stationery Office.

Goldin, C. (2021) *Career and Family: Women's Century Long Journey Toward Equity,* Maine: Princeton University Press.

Goodwin, M. and Heath, O. (2016) *Brexit Vote Explained: Poverty, Low Skills and Lack of Opportunities*. London: Joseph Rowntree Foundation. Available at: https://www.jrf.org.uk/report/brexit-vote-explained-poverty-low-ski lls-and-lack-opportunities (Accessed: 20 November 2023).

Gracie, C. (2019) *Equal: How We Fix the Gender Pay Gap*. London: Virago.

Grönlund, A. and Magnusson, C. (2016) 'Family-friendly policies and women's wages – is there a trade-off? Skill investments, occupational segregation and the gender pay gap in Germany, Sweden and the UK', *European Societies*, 18 (1): 91–113.

Guerrina, R. and Masselot, A. (2018) 'Walking into the footprint of EU law: Unpacking the gendered consequences of Brexit', *Social Policy & Society*, 17 (2): 319–30.

Hall, M. (2022) 'Is Britain ready to go cashless?', *RSA*. Available at: https://www.thersa.org/blog/2022/03/is-britain-ready-to-go-cashless (Accessed: 20 November 2023).

Hampton, S.P. (2021) *Hampton-Alexander Review FTSE Women Leaders: Improving Gender Balance – 5 Year Summary Report*. London: KPMG.

Harkness, S. (1996) 'The gender earnings gap: Evidence from the UK', *Fiscal Studies*, 17 (2): 1–36.

Harkness, S. (2004) 'Women and work: Changes in employment and earnings since the 1970s', *Semantic Scholar*. Available at: https://www.sema nticscholar.org/paper/Women-and-work-%3A-changes-in-employment-and-earnings-Harkness/00e351b4821726245762da9d67c600b3ab1336ea (Accessed: 20 November 2023).

Harper, J. (2020) 'Deutsche Bank research: Tax home workers "to help those who cannot"', *BBC*, 11 November. Available at: https://www.bbc.co.uk/news/business-54876526 (Accessed: 20 November 2023).

Hays, S. (1998) *The Cultural Contradictions of Motherhood*. London: Yale University Press.

Healy, G. and Ahamed, M. (2019) 'Gender pay gap, voluntary interventions and recession: The case of the British financial services sector', *British Journal of Industrial Relations*, 57 (2): 302–27.

Healy, G., Kirton, G. and Noon, M. (2011) 'Inequalities, intersectionality and equality and diversity initiatives: The conundrums and challenges of researching equality, inequalities and diversity', in Healy, G., Kirton, G. and Noon, M. (eds) *Equality, Inequalities and Diversity: Contemporary Challenges and Strategies*. Basingstoke: Palgrave Macmillan, pp. 1–17.

Healy, G., Broadbent, K. and Strachan, G. (2018) 'Inequality regimes and the gendered professional context', in Broadbent, K., Strachan, G. and Healy, G. (eds) *Gender and the Professions: International and Contemporary Perspectives*. Milton: Routledge, pp. 1–24.

Heery, E. (2006) 'Equality bargaining: Where, who, why?', *Gender, Work & Organization*, 13 (6): 522–42.

Hendy QC, L.J. (2020) *The Gaps in the Government's Coronavirus Income Protection Plans*. Liverpool: IER.

Hepple, B.A. (2000) *Equality: A New Framework: Report of the Independent Review of the Enforcement of U.K. Anti-Discrimination Legislation*. Oxford: Hart Publishing.

Hepple, B.A. (2011) *Equality: The New Legal Framework*. Oxford: Hart Publishing.

Hickman, T. (2013) 'Too hot, too cold or just right? The development of the public sector equality duties in administrative law', *Public Law*, 2: 325–44.

HM Treasury (2016) *Women in Finance Charter: A Pledge for Gender Balance Across Financial Services*. London: The Stationery Office. Available at: https://www.gov.uk/government/publications/women-in-finance-char ter (Accessed: 20 November 2023).

HM Treasury (2017) *Almost Half of UK Financial Services Staff Now Covered by Ground Breaking Women in Finance Charter*. London: The Stationery Office. Available at: https://www.gov.uk/government/news/almost-half-of-uk-financial-services-staff-now-covered-by-ground-breaking-women-in-fina nce-charter (Accessed: 20 November 2023).

Hobolt, S.B. (2016) 'The Brexit vote: A divided nation, a divided continent', *Journal of European Public Policy*, 23 (9): 1259–77.

HoC (2019a) *Gender Pay Gap Reporting: Government Response to the Committee's Thirteenth Report. Sixteenth Special Report of Session 2017–19*. London: The Stationery Office. Available at: https://publications.parliam ent.uk/pa/cm201719/cmselect/cmbeis/1895/1895.pdf (Accessed: 20 November 2023).

HoC (2019b) *Oral Evidence: Women in Finance*. London: The Stationery Office. Available at: http://data.parliament.uk/writtenevidence/commit teeevidence.svc/evidencedocument/treasury-committee/women-in-fina nce/oral/103031.pdf (Accessed: 20 November 2023).

Hochschild, A.R. (2003) *The Second Shift*. New York: Penguin Books.

Hofman, J., Nightingale, M., Bruckmayer, M. and Sanjurjo, P. (2020) *Equal Pay for Equal Work: Binding Pay-Transparency Measures*. Luxembourg: Publications Office for the European Union. Available at: https://www.europarl.europa.eu/RegData/etudes/STUD/2020/642 379/IPOL_STU(2020)642379_EN.pdf (Accessed: 20 November 2023).

Hoque, K. and Noon, M. (2004) 'Equal opportunities policy and practice in Britain: Evaluating the "empty shell" hypothesis', *Work, Employment & Society*, 18 (3): 481–506.

Howcroft, D. and Rubery, J. (2019) '"Bias in, bias out": Gender equality and the future of work debate', *Labour & Industry: A Journal of the Social and Economic Relations of Work*, 29 (2): 213–27.

Hunter, R.C., McGlynn, C., Rackley, E. and Hale, B. (2010) *Feminist Judgments: From Theory to Practice*. Oxford: Hart Publishing.

Hutton, G. (2022) *Financial Services: Contribution to the UK Economy*. London: The Stationery Office.

ICB (2011) *Final Report: Recommendations*. London: Independent Commission on Banking. Available at: https://www.gov.uk/government/news/independent-commission-on-banking-final-report (Accessed: 20 November 2023).

ILO (2016) *Global Wage Report 2016/17: Wage Inequality in the Workplace*. Geneva: ILO.

Jackson, B. (2018) 'Learning from New Labour', *The Political Quarterly*, 89 (1): 3–4.

Jenkins, J. (2013) *Women in the Labour Market: 2013*. Newport: ONS.

Jewell, S.L., Razzu, G. and Singleton, C. (2020) 'Who works for whom and the UK gender pay gap', *British Journal of Industrial Relations*, 58 (1): 50–81.

Joyce, S., Stuart, M. and Forde, C. (2022) 'Theorising labour unrest and trade unionism in the platform economy', *New Technology, Work and Employment*, 38 (1): 1–20.

Jones, R. (2019) 'Ex-HSBC staff voice anger over bank's pension clawback', *The Guardian*, 30 March.

Kaufman, G. (2018) 'Barriers to equality: Why British fathers do not use parental leave', *Community, Work & Family*, 21 (3): 310–25.

Kentish, B. (2018) 'BBC gender pay gap: 170 female employees demand apology over salary differences and "culture of discrimination"', *Independent*, 30 January.

Kilpatrick, C. (2003) 'Has New Labour reconfigured employment legislation?', *Industrial Law Journal*, 32 (3): 135–63.

Kim, M. (2015) 'Pay secrecy and the gender wage gap in the United States', *Industrial Relations: A Journal of Economy and Society*, 54 (4): 648–67.

Klarsfeld, A., Ng, E. and Tatli, A. (2012) 'Social regulation and diversity management: A comparative study of France, Canada and the UK', *European Journal of Industrial Relations*, 18 (4): 309–27.

Korotana, M.S. (2016) 'The Financial Services (Banking Reform) Act 2013: Smart regulatory regime?', *Statute Law Review*, 37 (3): 195–211.

Koskinen Sandberg, P. (2017) 'Intertwining gender inequalities and gender-neutral legitimacy in job evaluation and performance-related pay', *Gender, Work & Organization*, 24 (2): 156–70.

Krieger-Boden, C. and Sorgner, A. (2018) 'Labor market opportunities for women in the digital age', *Economics*, 12 (28): 1–8A.

Labour Party (1964) *The New Britain*. London: Labour Party. Available at: http://labour-party.org.uk/manifestos/1964/1964-labour-manifesto.shtml (Accessed: 20 November 2023).

Labour Party (1966) *You Know Labour Government Works: Time for Decision*. London: Labour Party. Available at: http://www.labour-party.org.uk/manifestos/1966/1966-labour-manifesto.shtml (Accessed: 20 November 2023).

Lambie-Mumford, H. and Green, M. (2017) 'Austerity, welfare reform and the rising use of food banks by children in England and Wales', *Area*, 49 (3): 273–9.

Landivar, L.C., Ruppanner, L., Scarborough, W.J. and Collins, C. (2020) 'COVID-19 and the gender gap in work hours', *Gender, Work, and Organization*, 28 (S1): 101–12.

Leigh Day (2023) *Next Staff Secure Significant Victory in Equal Pay Battle*. London: Leigh Day Solicitors.

Lerodiakonou, C. and Stavrou, E. (2015) 'Part time work, productivity and institutional policies', *Journal of Organizational Effectiveness: People and Performance*, 2 (2): 176–200.

Liff, S. and Ward, K. (2001) 'Distorted views through the glass ceiling: The construction of women's understandings of promotion and senior management positions', *Gender, Work & Organization*, 8 (1): 19–36.

Livingston, E. (2021) 'Care workers and cleaners of Dundee in fight for equal pay', *The Guardian*, 20 February.

Lloyds Bank (2020) *Lloyds Bank UK Consumer Digital Index 2020*. London: Lloyds Bank. Available at: https://www.lloydsbank.com/banking-with-us/whats-happening/consumer-digital-index.html (Accessed: 20 November 2023).

Machin, S. and Puhani, P.A. (2003) 'Subject of degree and the gender wage differential: Evidence from the UK and Germany', *Economics letters*, 79 (3): 393–400.

Mackay, F., Monro, S. and Waylen, G. (2009) 'The feminist potential of sociological institutionalism', *Politics & Gender*, 5 (2): 253–62.

Macleavy, J. (2018) 'Women, equality and the UK's EU referendum: Locating the gender politics of Brexit in relation to the neoliberalising state', *Space and Polity*, 22 (2): 205–23.

Macpherson, S.W. (1999) *The Stephen Lawrence Inquiry*. London: The Stationery Office.

Madden, J.F. (2012) 'Performance-support bias and the gender pay gap among stockbrokers', *Gender & Society*, 26 (3): 488–518.

Madgavkar, A., White, O., Krishnan, M., Mahajan, D. and Azcue, X. (2020) *COVID-19 and Gender Equality: Countering the Regressive Effects*. London: McKinsey Global Institute. Available at: https://www.mckinsey.com/featured-insights/future-of-work/covid-19-and-gender-equality-countering-the-regressive-effects (Accessed: 20 November 2023).

Makortoff, K. (2019) '"Depressing" gender pay gap widens in fund management firms', *The Guardian*, 2 October.

Mandl, I., Curtarelli, M., Riso, S., Vargas Llave, O. and Gerogainnis, E. (2015) *New Forms of Employment, Research Report*. Luxembourg: Eurofound.

Manning, A. and Petrongolo, B. (2008) 'The part-time pay penalty for women in Britain', *The Economic Journal*, 118 (526): F28–F51.

Manning, A. and Swaffield, J. (2008) 'The gender gap in early-career wage growth', *The Economic Journal*, 118 (530): 983–1024.

Marginson, S. (2019) 'Limitations of human capital theory', *Studies in Higher Education*, 44 (2): 287–301.

Marriage, M. (2018) 'Men only: Inside the charity fundraiser where hostesses are put on show', *Financial Times*, 23 January.

Marriage, M., Cundy, A. and Caruana Galizia, P. (2023) 'How Crispin Odey evaded sexual assault allegations for decades', *Financial Times*, 8 June.

Martin, P.Y. (2003) '"Said and done" versus "saying and doing": Gendering practices, practicing gender at work', *Gender & Society*, 17 (3): 342–66.

Masselot, A. (2015) 'The EU childcare strategy in times of austerity', *Journal of Social Welfare and Family Law*, 37 (3): 345–55.

McBride, A. (2000) *Regulations Introduce New Rights for Part-Time Workers*. Dublin: Eurofound.

McDowell, L. (1998) 'Elites in the City of London: Some methodological considerations', *Environment and Planning A*, 30 (12): 2133–46.

McDowell, L. (2008) *Capital Culture: Gender at Work in the City*. Hoboken: Wiley.

McDowell, L. (2010) 'Capital culture revisited: Sex, testosterone and the City', *International Journal of Urban and Regional Research*, 34 (3): 652–8.

McDowell, L. and Court, G. (1994a) 'Gender divisions of labour in the post-Fordist economy: The maintenance of occupational sex segregation in the financial services sector', *Environment and Planning A*, 26 (9): 1397–418.

McDowell, L. and Court, G. (1994b) 'Missing subjects: Gender, power, and sexuality in merchant banking', *Economic Geography*, 70 (3): 229–51.

McKinsey (2016) *The Power of Parity: Advancing Women's Equality in the United Kingdom*. London: McKinsey Global Institute. Available at: https://www.mckinsey.com/featured-insights/gender-equality/the-power-of-parity-advancing-womens-equality-in-the-united-kingdom (Accessed: 20 November 2023).

McKinsey (2018) *Delivering Through Diversity: Why Diversity Matters*. London: McKinsey Global Institute. Available at: https://www.employdiversitynetwork.com/resources-1/2018/3/16/a-mckinsey-report-delivering-through-diversity (Accessed: 20 November 2023).

McLaughlin, C. and Deakin, S. (2011) *Equality Law and the Limits of the 'Business Case' for Addressing Gender Inequalities*. Cambridge: University of Cambridge.

Meager, N. (2019) 'Self-employment: independent "enterprise", or precarious low-skilled work? The case of the UK', in Conen, W. and Schipper, J. (eds) *Self-Employment as Precarious Work: A European Perspective*. Cheltenham: Elgaronline.

Menéndez-Viso, A. (2009) 'Black and white transparency: Contradictions of a moral metaphor', *Ethics and Information Technology*, 11 (2): 155–62.

Metcalf, H. and Rolfe, H. (2009) *Employment and Earnings in the Finance Sector: A Gender Analysis*. Manchester: EHRC.

Miller, T. (2012) 'Balancing caring and paid work in the UK: Narrating "choices" as first-time parents', *International Review of Sociology*, 22 (1): 39–52.

Millns, S. (1992) 'Pregnancy discrimination: The gulf between British and European community perspectives', *Journal of Contemporary Legal and Social Policy Issues*, 14 (2): 187–200.

Milner, S. (2019) 'Gender pay gap reporting regulations: Advancing gender equality policy in tough economic times', *British Politics*, 14 (2): 121–40.

Moon, J., Richardson, J.J. and Smart, P. (1986) 'The privatisation of British Telecom: A case study of the extended process of legislation', *European Journal of Political Research*, 14 (3): 339–55.

Moore, J. (2021) 'Has Goldman Sachs signalled the work-from-home counter-revolution?', *Independent*, 26 February.

Moore, M. (2018) 'BBC staff share their pay details to fight gender gap', *The Times*, 17 July.

Moss, P. and Koslowski, A. (2021) 'Making time to care: parental leave today and tomorrow', *IOE Blog*, 14 September. Available from: https://blogs.ucl.ac.uk/ioe/2021/09/14/making-time-to-care-parental-leave-today-and-tomorrow/ (Accessed: 20 November 2023).

Murray, J., Rieger, P. and Gorry, H. (2019) *Employers' Understanding of the Gender Pay Gap & Actions to Tackle it: Research Report on the 2018 Survey*. London: The Stationery Office.

Niederle, M. and Vesterlund, L. (2007) 'Do women shy away from competition? Do men compete too much?', *Quarterly Journal of Economics*, cxxii (3): 1067–102.

Norman, J. (2020) 'Gender and Covid-19: The immediate impact the crisis is having on women', *LSE COVID-19 blog*, 23 April. Available at: https://blogs.lse.ac.uk/politicsandpolicy/gender-and-covid19/ (Accessed: 20 November 2023).

O'Leary, K.E. (1992) 'Creating partnership: using feminist techniques to enhance the attorney–client relationship', *The Legal Studies Forum*, 16 (2): 207–38.

O'Reilly, J. (1992) 'Banking on flexibility: A comparison of the use of flexible employment strategies in the retail banking sector in Britain and France', *The International Journal of Human Resource Management*, 3 (1): 35–58.

O'Reilly, J. (2006) 'Framing comparisons: Gendering perspectives on cross-national comparative research on work and welfare', *Work, Employment and Society*, 20 (4): 731–50.

O'Reilly, J., Smith, M., Deakin, S. and Burchell, B. (2015) 'Equal pay as a moving target: International perspectives on forty-years of addressing the gender pay gap', *Cambridge Journal of Economics*, 39 (2): 299–317.

O'Reilly, J., Froud, J., Johal, S., Williams, K., Warhurst, C., Morgan, G., Grey, C., et al (2016) 'Brexit: Understanding the socio-economic origins and consequences', *Socio-Economic Review*, 14 (4): 807–54.

OECD (2017) *Going Digital: The Future of Work for Women*. Paris: OECD Publishing. Doi: 10.1787/9789264281318-26-en

OECD (2019) *Education at a Glance: OECD Indicators*. Paris: OECD Publishing. Doi: 10.1787/f8d7880d-en

Olsen, W., Gash, V., Kim, S. and Zhang, M. (2018) *The Gender Pay Gap in the UK: Evidence from the UKHLS*. London: The Stationery Office.

Olson, J. (2013) 'Human capital models and the gender pay gap', *Sex Roles*, 68 (3): 186–97.

ONS (2016) *Women Shoulder the Responsibility of 'Unpaid Work'*. London: ONS. Available at: https://www.ons.gov.uk/employmentandlabourmarket/peopl einwork/earningsandworkinghours/articles/womenshouldertheresponsibil ityofunpaidwork/2016-11-10 (Accessed: 20 November 2023).

Oswick, C. and Noon, M. (2014) 'Discourses of diversity, equality and inclusion: Trenchant formulations or transient fashions?', *British Journal of Management*, 25 (1): 23–39.

Özbilgin, M. and Tatli, A. (2011) 'Mapping out the field of equality and diversity: Rise of individualism and voluntarism', *Human Relations (New York)*, 64 (9): 1229–53.

Özbilgin, M.F. and Woodward, D. (2004) ' "Belonging" and "otherness": Sex equality in banking in Turkey and Britain', *Gender, Work & Organization*, 11 (6): 668–88.

Parise, T. and Shenai, V. (2018) 'The value effect of financial reform on U.K. banks and insurance companies', *International Journal of Financial Studies*, 6 (3): 1–28.

Parker, J. (2001) *EOC Urges New Action on Equal Pay*. Dublin: Publications Office of the European Union. Available at: https://www.eurofound.eur opa.eu/publications/article/2001/eoc-urges-new-action-on-equal-pay (Accessed: 20 November 2023).

Parker, J. (2020) *Ethnic Diversity Enriching Business Leadership: An Update Report from the Parker Review*. London: EY UK. Available at: https://ass ets.ey.com/content/dam/ey-sites/ey-com/en_uk/news/2020/02/ey-par ker-review-2020-report-final.pdf (Accessed: 20 November 2023).

Partington, R. (2021) ' "Deafening silence": UK government blasted over delays to employment reforms', *The Guardian*, 18 February.

Paul, K. (2020) 'Hundreds of Amazon warehouse workers to call in sick in coronavirus protest', *The Guardian*, 21 April.

Penner, A.M., Petersen, T., Hermansen, A.S., Rainey, A., Boza, I., Elvira, M.M., et al (2023) 'Within-job gender pay inequality in 15 countries', *Nature Human Behaviour*, 7 (2): 184–9.

Perales, F. (2013) 'Occupational sex-segregation, specialized human capital and wages: Evidence from Britain', *Work, Employment & Society*, 27 (4): 600–20.

Perfect, D. (2011) *Gender Pay Gaps*. Manchester: EHRC. Available at: https://www.equalityhumanrights.com/sites/default/files/briefing-paper-2-gender-pay-gap_0.pdf (Accessed: 20 November 2023).

Però, D. (2020) 'Indie unions, organizing and labour renewal: Learning from precarious migrant workers', *Work, Employment and Society*, 34 (5): 900–18.

Perraudin, F. (2014) 'Labour calls for transparency on gender pay gap across UK', *The Guardian*, 16 December.

Perry, B. (2011) 'Case study research', in May, T. (ed.) *Social Research: Issues, Methods and Process*. Maidenhead: Open University Press, pp. 219–42.

Pfefer, E.D. (2020) *The Silence of Transparency: A Critical Analysis of the Relationship between the Organisational Salary Environment and the Gender and Gender/ Ethnic Pay Gain in UK Higher Education*. London: Queen Mary University of London.

Pham, X., Fitzpatrick, L. and Wagner, R. (2018) 'The US gender pay gap: The way forward', *International Journal of Sociology and Social Policy*, 38 (9/10): 907–20.

Polachek, S. (2004) 'How the human capital model explains why the gender wage gap narrowed', *IDEAS Working Paper Series from RePEc*.

Prescott, K. (2021) 'Asda workers win key appeal in equal pay fight', *BBC*, 26 March. Available at: https://www.bbc.co.uk/news/business-56534988 (Accessed: 20 November 2023).

Prosser, T. (2011) *UK: The Representativeness of Trade Unions and Employer Associations in the Banking Sector*. Dublin: Publications Office of the European Union.

PWC (2019) *Time to Get Serious: If Diversity Is a Business Imperative, Treat It Like One*. London: PwC.

PWC (2022) *Gender Pay Gap and Diversity in Financial Services. What's Changing? Updated Year 4 Gender Pay Gap Reporting 2020/21*. London: PwC.

PWC (2023) *Mandatory UK Gender Pay Gap Reporting. Beyond the Gender Pay Gap: Embracing Broader Diversity, Equity and Inclusion Reporting to Create Meaningful Change. Year 6 Gender Pay Gap Reporting 2022/23*. London: PwC.

Pyper, D. (2018) *The Public Sector Equality Duty and Equality Impact Assessments*. (Research Briefing Number 06591). London: The Stationery Office.

Pyper, D. (2020) *The Public Sector Equality Duty and Equality Impact Assessments* (Research Briefing Number 06591). London: The Stationery Office.

Pyper, D., McGuinness, F. and Brown, J. (2017) *Employment Tribunal Fees* (Research Briefing Number 7081) London: The Stationery Office.

Queisser, M., Adema, W. and Clarke, C. (2020) *COVID-19, Employment and Women in OECD Countries*. London: VoxEU. Available at: https://voxeu.org/article/covid-19-employment-and-women-oecd-countries (Accessed: 20 November 2023).

Quiros, C.T., Morales, E.G., Pastor, R.R., Carmona, A.F., Ibanex, M.S. and Herrera, U.M. (2018) *Women in the Digital Age. Digital Agenda for Europe.* Luxembourg: Publications Office of the European Union.

Rankin, J. (2022) 'EU agrees "landmark" 40% quota for women on corporate boards', *The Guardian*, 7 June.

Rees, T. (2005) 'Reflections on the uneven development of gender mainstreaming in Europe', *International Feminist Journal of Politics*, 7 (4): 555–74.

Reskin, B. and Bielby, D. (2005) 'A sociological perspective on gender and career outcomes', *The Journal of Economic Perspectives*, 19 (1): 71–86.

Reskin, B. and Maroto, M. (2011) 'What trends? Whose choices? Comment on England', *Gender & Society*, 25 (1): 81–7.

Riddell, S. and Watson, N. (2011) 'Equality and human rights in Britain: Principles and challenges', *Social Policy & Society*, 10 (2): 193–203.

Roach, G. (2021) *Just 13 FTSE 100 Firms Report Ethnicity Pay Gap.* London: IR Magazine. Available at: https://irmagazine.com/case-studies/just-13-ftse-100-firms-report-ethnicity-pay-gap (Accessed: 20 November 2023).

Rubery, J. (2003) *The Organization of Employment: An International Perspective*, Basingstoke: Palgrave Macmillan.

Rubery, J. (2015) 'Austerity and the future for gender equality in Europe', *ILR Review*, 68 (4): 715–41.

Rubery, J (2018a) 'Joan Acker and doing comparable worth', *Gender, Work & Organization*, 26 (12): 1786–93.

Rubery, J. (2018b) 'A gender lens on the future of work', *Journal of International Affairs*, 72 (1): 91–106.

Rubery, J. and Grimshaw, D. (2015) 'The 40-year pursuit of equal pay: A case of constantly moving goalposts', *Cambridge Journal of Economics*, 39 (2): 319–43.

Rubery, J. and Hebson, G. (2018) 'Applying a gender lens to employment relations: Revitalisation, resistance and risks', *Journal of Industrial Relations*, 60 (3): 414–36

Rubery, J., Grimshaw, D. and Figueiredo, H. (2005) 'How to close the gender pay gap in Europe: Towards the gender mainstreaming of pay policy', *Industrial Relations Journal*, 36 (3): 184–213.

Ruddick, G. (2018) 'Trust is broken at BBC over equal pay, Carrie Gracie tells MPs', *The Guardian*, 31 January.

Ruddin, L.P. (2006) 'You can generalize stupid! Social scientists, Bent Flyvbjerg, and case study methodology', *Qualitative Inquiry*, 12 (4): 797–812.

Saldaña, J. (2015) *The Coding Manual for Qualitative Researchers*. California: Sage Publications.

Sanders, A., Annesley, C. and Gains, F. (2019) 'What did the coalition government do for women? An analysis of gender equality policy agendas in the UK 2010–2015', *British Politics*, 14 (2): 162–80.

Sayer, L.C. (2005) 'Gender, time and inequality: Trends in women's and men's paid work, unpaid work and free time', *Social Forces*, 84 (1): 285–303.

Scholar, S.M. (2009) *Chair of the UK Statistics Authority letter to GEO*. London: UK Statistics Authority. Available at: https://osr.statisticsauthor ity.gov.uk/wp-content/uploads/2015/11/letter-from-sir-michael-scholar-to-harriet-harman-qc-mp-11062009-and-ma-note-42009_tcm97-26239. pdf (Accessed: 20 November 2023).

Schulze, U. (2015) 'The gender wage gap among PhDs in the UK', *Cambridge Journal of Economics*, 39 (2): 599–629.

Scott, L. (2019) 'Surprised that women are still struggling for equal pay? You shouldn't be', *The Guardian*, 17 November.

Scully, P. and Miliband, E. (2021) *Paternity Leave: Written Questions, Answers and Statements*. London: The Stationery Office.

Sealy, R., Vinnicombe, S. and Singh, V. (2008) *The Female FTSE Report 2008: A Decade of Delay*. Bedford: Cranfield University.

Seddon-Daines, O., Barrow, J. and Chinwala, Y. (2019) *HM Treasury Women in Finance Charter: Annual Review 2018*. London: New Financial. Available at: https://www.gov.uk/government/publications/new-financial-women-in-finance-annual-review-march-2018 (Accessed: 20 November 2023).

Seidman, I. (2013) *Interviewing as Qualitative Research: A Guide for Researchers in Education and the Social Sciences*, 4th edn. New York: Teachers College Press.

Seierstad, C. (2011) 'The use of quotas in the most equal region: politics and corporate boards in the Scandinavian countries', in Healy, G., Kirton, G. and Noon, M. (eds) *Equality, Inequalities and Diversity: Contemporary Challenges and Strategies*. Basingstoke: Palgrave Macmillan, pp. 171–94.

Shaw, J. (2005) 'Mainstreaming equality and diversity in European Union law and policy', *Current Legal Problems*, 58 (1): 255–312.

Sheerin, C. and Garavan, T. (2021) 'Female leaders as "Superwomen": Post-global crisis media framing of women and leadership in investment banking in UK print media 2014–16', *Critical Perspectives on Accounting*, 76: 1–21. Doi:10.1016/j.cpa.2021.102307

Shelton, B.A. and John, D. (1996) 'The division of household labor', *Annual Review of Sociology*, 22 (1): 299–322.

Skinner, J. (2012) *The Interview: An Ethnographic Approach*. London: Berg.

Skuratowicz, E. and Hunter, L.W. (2004) 'Where do women's jobs come from? Job resegregation in an American bank', *Work and Occupations*, 31 (1): 73–110.

Smeaton, D. and Marsh, A. (2006) 'Maternity and paternity rights and benefits: survey of parents 2005', *Employment Relations Research Series*. London: Policy Studies Institute.

Smith, R. (2019) *Gender Pay Gap in the UK: 2019*. London: ONS.

Solal, I. and Snellman, K. (2019) 'Women don't mean business? Gender penalty in board composition', *Organization Science*, 30 (6): 1270–88.

Sorgner, A., Bode, E. and Krieger-Boden, C. (2017) *The Effects of Digitalization on Gender Equality in the G20 Economies*. Kiel: Kiel Institute for the World Economy. Available at: https://www.econstor.eu/handle/10419/170571 (Accessed: 20 November 2023).

Squires, J. (2005) 'Is mainstreaming transformative? Theorizing mainstreaming in the context of diversity and deliberation', *Social Politics: International Studies in Gender, State and Society*, 12 (3): 366–88.

Staton, B. (2020) 'The upstart unions taking on the gig economy and outsourcing', *Financial Times*, 19 January.

Streeck, W. and Thelen, K.A. (2005) *Beyond Continuity: Institutional Change in Advanced Political Economies*. Oxford: Oxford University Press.

Suddaby, R. (2010) 'Challenges for institutional theory', *Journal of Management Inquiry*, 19 (1): 14–20.

Suddaby, R. and Greenwood, R. (2005) 'Rhetorical strategies of legitimacy', *Administrative Science Quarterly*, 50 (1): 35–67.

Summer, H. (2020) 'UK society regressing back to 1950s for many women, warn experts', *The Guardian*, 18 June.

Szalay, E. (2019) 'Tribunal exposes gender gap in banking culture and pay', *Financial Times*, 20 September.

Taylor, M. (2017) *Good Work: The Taylor Review of Modern Working Practices*. London: The Stationery Office.

Taylor-Gooby, P. (2013) *The Double Crisis of the Welfare State and What We Can Do About It*. Basingstoke: Palgrave Macmillan.

Tetlow, G. (2018) 'Two-thirds of UK gender pay gap remains unexplained', *Financial Times*, 17 January.

Topping, A. (2021) 'EHRC urged to investigate ministers for "equality failures" in Covid response', *The Guardian*, 15 February.

Toyin Ajibade, A., Aiyenitaju, O. and Olatunji, D.A. (2021) 'The work–family balance of British working women during the COVID-19 pandemic', *Journal of Work-Applied Management*, 13 (2): 241–60.

Traynor, I. and Goodley, S. (2012) 'Brussels leaves 40% quota for women at mercy of member states', *The Guardian*, 14 November.

Treasury Committee (2010) *Women in the City*. London: The Stationery Office.

Treasury Committee (2018) *Women in Finance*. London: The Stationery Office.

Treasury Committee (2023a) *Oral Evidence (17 October). Sexism in the City: HC 1746*. London: The Stationery Office. Available at: https://committees.parliament.uk/event/19517/formal-meeting-oral-evidence-session/ (Accessed: 20 November 2023).

Treasury Committee (2023b) *Oral Evidence (15 November). Sexism in the City: HC 1746*. London: The Stationery Office. Available at: https://committees.parliament.uk/event/19699/formal-meeting-oral-evidence-session/ (Accessed: 20 November 2023).

TUC (2015) *Two in Five New Fathers Won't Qualify for Shared Parental Leave, Says TUC*. London: TUC. Available at: https://www.tuc.org.uk/workplace-issues/work-life-balance/employment-rights/two-five-new-fathers-won%E2%80%99t-qualify-shared (Accessed: 20 November 2023).

TUC (2021) *The TUC, CBI and EHRC Issue Joint Call for Mandatory Ethnicity Pay Gap Reporting*. London: TUC. Available at: https://www.tuc.org.uk/news/tuc-cbi-and-ehrc-issue-joint-call-mandatory-ethnicity-pay-gap-reporting (Accessed: 20 November 2023).

TUC (2023) *1 in 2 Families Struggle Financially When Dads Take Paternity Leave – TUC poll*. London: TUC. Available: https://www.tuc.org.uk/news/1-2-families-struggle-financially-when-dads-take-paternity-leave-tuc-poll (Accessed: 20 November 2023).

Verdin, R. and O'Reilly, J. (2020) 'What future for gender equality policy in the UK after Brexit?', *Northern Ireland Legal Quarterly*, 71 (1): 1–15.

Verdin, R. and O'Reilly, J. (2021) *A Gender Agenda for the Future of Work in a Digital Age of Pandemics: Jobs, Skills and Contracts*. Dusseldorf: Institute of Economic and Social Research (WSI). Available at: https://www.boeckler.de/de/faust-detail.htm?sync_id=HBS-007927 (Accessed: 20 November 2023).

Wadham, J. (2012) *Blackstone's Guide to the Equality Act 2010*. Oxford: Oxford University Press.

Walby, S. (2009) *Gender and the Financial Crisis*. Lancaster: UNESCO. Available at: http://www.lancs.ac.uk/fass/doc_library/sociology/Gender_and_financial_crisis_Sylvia_Walby.pdf (Accessed: 20 November 2023).

Ware, D. (2012) *Legislative Proposals to Promote Equal Pay*. London: The Stationery Office.

Warraich, E. (2023) *Make Ethnicity Pay Gap Reporting Mandatory – TUC*. London: BBC. Available: https://www.bbc.co.uk/news/uk-politics-65315793 (Accessed: 20 November 2023).

Watkins, D. and Burton, M. (2013) *Research Methods in Law*. Hoboken: Taylor and Francis.

Watkins, J. (2000) 'Is a step-by-step approach to change a viable option for the UK retail banking sector?', *Journal of Business Research*, 47 (1): 65–74.

Webber, A. (2023) 'Thousands yet to publish as gender pay gap deadline looms', *Personnel Today*, 29 March. Available at: https://www.personneltoday.com/hr/gender-pay-gap-as-deadline-2022-23/ (Accessed: 20 November 2023).

WEF (2018) *The Global Gender Gap Report: Insight Report*, 13th edn. Geneva: World Economic Forum. Available at: https://www.wefo rum.org/reports/the-global-gender-gap-report-2018 (Accessed: 20 November 2023).

Weil, D. (2014) *The Fissured Workplace: Why Work Became So Bad for So Many and What Can Be Done to Improve It.* London: Harvard University Press.

Wenham, C. (2020) 'Women have been largely ignored in the COVID-19 response. This must change', *LSE COVID-19 blog*, 12 May. Available at: https://blogs.lse.ac.uk/covid19/2020/05/12/women-have-been-largely-ignored-in-the-covid-19-response-this-must-change/ (Accessed: 20 November 2023).

West, C. and Zimmerman, D.H. (1987) 'Doing gender', *Gender & Society*, 1 (2): 125–51.

White, N. (2022) *Gender Pay Gap in the UK: 2022.* London: ONS.

Whitehouse, G., Zetlin, D. and Earnshaw, J. (2001) 'Prosecuting pay equity: Evolving strategies in Britain and Australia', *Gender, Work & Organization*, 8 (4): 365–86.

Wigand, C. (2021) *Pay Transparency: Commission Proposes Measures to Ensure Equal Pay for Equal Work.* Brussels: Publications Office of the European Union. Available at: https://ec.europa.eu/commission/presscorner/detail/en/ip_21_881 (Accessed: 20 November 2023).

Wilson, F. (2014) 'May the best man win', *Equality, Diversity and Inclusion*, 33 (4): 361–71.

Wintour, P. (2015) 'Lib Dems push through mandatory reporting of gender pay gaps', *The Guardian*, 6 March.

Wisniewska, A., Ehrenberg-Shannon, B. and Gordon, S. (2018) 'Gender pay gap: How women are short-changed in the UK', *Financial Times*, 25 September.

Women and Equalities Committee (2018) *Fathers and the Workplace.* London: The Stationery Office. Available at: https://publications.parliam ent.uk/pa/cm201719/cmselect/cmwomeq/358/358.pdf (Accessed: 20 November 2023).

Women and Equalities Committee (2019) *Enforcing the Equality Act: The Law and the Role of the Equality and Human Rights Commission. Tenth Report of Session 2017–19.* London: The Stationery Office. Available at: https://publications.parliament.uk/pa/cm201719/cmselect/cmwomeq/1470/1470.pdf (Accessed: 20 November 2023).

Wong, J.C. (2020) 'Coronavirus divides tech workers into the "worthy" and "unworthy" sick', *The Guardian*, 12 March.

Working Families (2018) *Top Employers for Working Families: Benchmark Report 2018*. London: Working Families. Available at: https://www.workingfamilies.org.uk/wp-content/uploads/2018/09/2018-Top-Employers-for-Working-Families-Benchmark-Report.pdf (Accessed: 20 November 2023).

Wright, A. (2011) 'Modernising away gender pay inequality? Some evidence from the local government sector on using job evaluation', *Employee Relations*, 33 (2): 159–78.

Wrohlich, K. (2017) 'Gender pay gap varies greatly by occupation', *DIW Economic Bulletin*, 7 (43): 429–35.

Yauch, C.A. and Steudel, H.J. (2016) 'Complementary use of qualitative and quantitative cultural assessment methods', *Organizational Research Methods*, 6 (4): 465–81.

Index